Gateway

B1

Student's Book

David Spencer

MACMILLAN

Contents

Listening	Writing	Speaking	Exam success/Study skills
Family relationships Family dinners – radio programme Meeting at a party – exchanging personal information	Making notes An informal email Paragraph topics	Asking for personal information Pair interviews Pronunciation: Intonation in questions Role-play: at a party	Reading: Multiple-choice activities Speaking: Information role-plays Grammar: Using reference material Writing: Keeping a mistakes checklist
Crime news – radio SIS quiz Shoplifting Talking about last weekend	Making notes An informal letter	Giving opinions Pair interviews Reporting a past event Role-play: last weekend	Listening: True/false activities Writing: Knowing about evaluation Vocabulary: Using a dictionary Reading: Prediction
Dubbing actors Information for a summer school	Mini-dialogues Definitions A language biography Paragraphing	Describing places Asking for information Role-play: information about a summer course	Use of English: Multiple-choice cloze activities Speaking: Evaluation Knowing what type of learner you are Listening: Keeping calm
Health problems Accidents – an interview	Notes and messages Abbreviations Exchanging messages	Asking about experiences in a photo Describing a scene Using fillers	Reading: Matching activities Writing: Content and style Vocabulary: Keeping vocabulary records Speaking: Words you don't know
Describing TV programmes Robin Hood and Maid Marian – radio interview Finding out the news Making suggestions: what to watch	Descriptions and opinions An email – favourite TV programmes	Pair interviews Comparing ideas Talking about inventions Role-play: planning activities and negotiating	Listening: Identifying the speaker activities Speaking: Negotiating Reading: Reading for general information Grammar: Use and form

Listening	Writing	Speaking	Exam success/Study skills
Environmental problems A school meeting Making arrangements	Making notes A summary A short story A formal letter	Pair discussion Talking about your environment Making arrangements Pronunciation: Intonation – showing enthusiasm	Use of English: Sentence transformation activities Writing: Writing in exam conditions Listening: First listening, second listening Writing: Organising ideas into paragraphs
Describing jobs A summer job in the USA Requesting information about working conditions	Describing personal qualities Making notes A letter of application and CV	Discussing personal qualities and jobs Describing and guessing jobs Asking for and giving advice Role-play: Information about a summer job	Reading: True/false activities Listening: Multiple-choice activities Vocabulary: Efficient vocabulary revision Speaking: Making mistakes
Feelings The story of Romeo and Juliet A conversation about a party Discover your secret self! (questionnaire)	Making notes A personal description	Speaking Re-telling a story Finding out about childhood experiences Evaluating a questionnaire Reporting a past event	Speaking: Reporting past events Writing: Answering the question Reading: Reading for specific information Listening: Listening outside the classroom
Fiction and non-fiction James Patterson – radio programme Conversation in a bookshop Books and films survey	Reporting information Making notes Reporting results of a questionnaire	Discussing reading habits Reporting personal statements Interviewing a famous person Making offers: Shopping	Reading: Missing sentence activities Listening: Completing notes Reading: Reading for pleasure Writing: Brainstorming
Sir Tim Berners-Lee: radio programme Wikipedia: radio programme Photo description	Trivia questions Text messages and abbreviations	Discussing computer use Presentation about your country Group Quiz Talking about photos: Speculation	Use of English: Cloze activities Speaking: A conversation based on a photo Reading: Guessing from context Speaking: Practice makes perfect

1 Family matters

Grammar ▸ Present simple and present continuous ▸ Articles
Vocabulary ▸ Ages and stages of life ▸ The family ▸ Noun suffixes *-ment, -ion, -ence*
Speaking ▸ Asking for personal information
Writing ▸ An informal email

▸ Vocabulary

Ages and stages of life

1 **Work with a partner. Match the photos with these words. What ages go with each stage of life?**

baby child middle-aged adult
senior citizen teenager young adult

e baby, 0-3 approximately

2 **Put the stages of life in order. Begin with *birth*.**

adolescence birth childhood
death middle age old age

3 **1.01 Listen, check and repeat.**

a

b

e

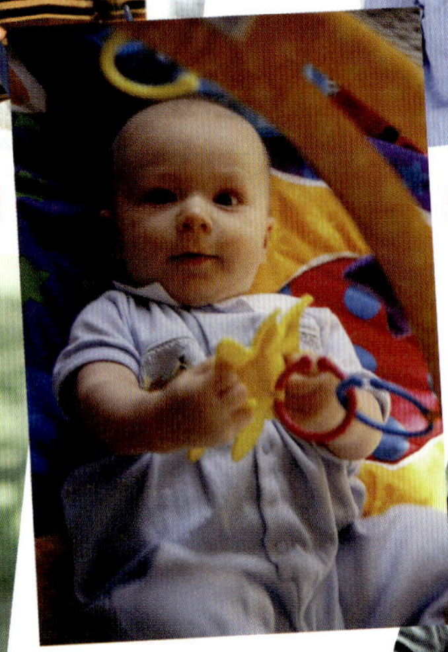

c

d

f

The family

4 **Divide these words into three lists: Male/Female/Male or Female.**

aunt brother-in-law cousin
daughter grandfather grandson
husband nephew niece
stepfather uncle wife

Male	Female	Male or Female
husband	*daughter*	*cousin*

5 **Match the words in 4 with these descriptions.**

1 the man that a woman is married to
husband
2 the brother of one of your parents
3 your mother's new husband in a second or later marriage
4 a daughter of your brother or sister
5 the son of one of your children
6 the brother of your husband or wife

6 **SPEAKING** **Work with a partner. Take it in turns to define the other words in 4. Can your partner say the family member?**

It's the son of your brother or sister.

Nephew.

7 **Complete the sentences with these words.**

born divorced one-parent only child partner single

1 If you are ...., you aren't married.
2 An .... doesn't have brothers or sisters.
3 You can use the word .... to describe either a husband or wife or the person that someone lives with.
4 If you are married and then end the marriage, you are ....
5 .... families are families where only the father or the mother lives at home and looks after the children.
6 Approximately 670,000 babies are .... every year in Britain.

8 **LISTENING** **1.02 Listen to three people talking about themselves and their families. Choose the correct alternative for each person.**

1 Joshua is a child/a teenager. He has a big/small family.
2 Olivia is a child/a teenager. She has got a big/small family. She lives with her father/grandfather. She spends a lot of time with her aunt/cousin.
3 Jessica is a senior citizen. She's got four/twelve children. She is married/divorced.

9a **SPEAKING** **Make notes about your family. Use the words from this page.**

I live with mum and dad, one sister, often visit grandparents

9b **Tell other people about your family using your notes.**

I live with my mum, dad and sister. My mum's name is ...

1 Look at the photos. What can you see in them? What do you think the text is about? Guess.

2 Read the text and choose a good title.

1 *New technology in the USA* 2 *Protection 24 hours a day – is it a good idea?* 3 *Unhappy families*

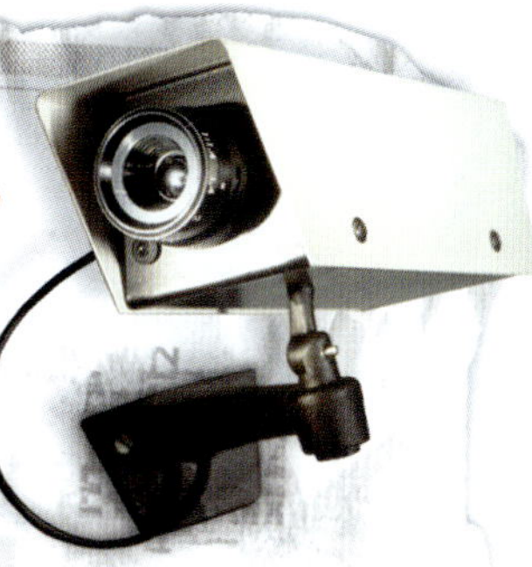

WHAT ARE YOUR PARENTS DOING NOW?

Maybe they're watching you, listening to you or finding out where you are. How? It's all thanks to new high-tech equipment from specialist companies in the USA.

A company called BladeRunner has a jacket with a GPS system inside. It costs $500, and for $20 a month your parents can always see where you are (or where your jacket is!). But that's nothing. Do your parents want to know what you're eating? No problem. MyNutriKids tells them what you're having for lunch at school. Do your parents want to know your exam results? GradeSpeed is a service which gives them that information. Do they want to know what online conversations you're having? IMSafer tells them. You usually arrive on time for extra-curricular sports classes. But if one day you don't arrive on time, there's a service which informs your parents. And there's another service which sends them a message if you go outside a specific area.

So, are your parents protecting you or are they spying on you? Babies and small children need constant care and protection. But is it really important for parents to know where their teenage kids are every minute of the day? Adolescents need to take their own decisions and make their own mistakes. Mistakes are an important part of growing up, of passing from childhood to independence. We think it's important for parents to give their children the opportunity to do this.

EXAM SUCCESS

Here is a multiple-choice reading activity. In this type of exercise you have three or four options. You choose the option that is best according to the information in the text. If you aren't sure of the correct answer, what can you do?

EXAM SUCCESS ▸ page 150

3 Read the text again and choose the best answers.

1 The BladeRunner jacket
a costs $500.
b only works if you pay regularly.
c has a mobile phone inside.

2 GradeSpeed
a helps students to work fast in exams.
b helps students to have good results in exams.
c gives parents information about exam results.

3 One of the services
a tells parents if their children do not arrive at a place on time.
b stops children from entering a new zone.
c tells children if they are going into a dangerous place.

4 A lot of the new technology
a is dangerous for children.
b gives parents information about their children.
c is difficult to use.

5 In the article, it says that for young people it is
a bad to make mistakes.
b important to listen to parents.
c important to have the chance to make mistakes.

4 Match the underlined words in the text with their definitions.

1 something you do at school, but not part of your normal studies *extra-curricular*
2 things that you do wrong, that are incorrect ....
3 connected to the Internet ....
4 chance, possibility ....
5 permanent attention and help ....
6 written or spoken information that you send to somebody ....
7 tells ....

5 SPEAKING **What about *you*?**

1 Do your parents usually know what you are doing?
2 Imagine. Your parents give you a GPS jacket. Would you wear it? Why/Why not?

I think my parents usually know where I am.

Me too. My parents always call me when I'm not at home.

GRAMMAR GUIDE

Present simple and present continuous

1a Look at these sentences. Which sentences are in the present simple and which are in the present continuous?

1 You usually arrive on time for sports classes.
2 They're watching you now.
3 We think it's important.
4 Adolescents should take their own decisions.

1b Match the sentences in 1a with the explanation of their uses in a–d.

a For actions that are happening now or temporary actions.
b For regular or routine actions.
c For things that are always or generally true.
d With certain verbs like *love, like, hate, think, believe, know, understand, want, need.*

1c Complete the sentences with the correct form of *study*.

Present simple
Affirmative: He *studies* history.
Negative: He .... physics.
Question: .... he .... English?

Present continuous
Affirmative: She .... English now.
Negative: She .... maths now.
Question: .... she .... French?

GRAMMAR REFERENCE ▸ page 16

STUDY SKILLS

When you have a problem with grammar, where can you find help?

STUDY SKILLS ▸ page 146

2 Look at the picture. Describe what the people are doing. Use the present continuous form of these verbs.

call chat drink laugh listen ride run sit study walk wear

A boy is listening to music.

3 Complete the dialogue about the picture using the present simple or present continuous form of the verbs given.

MUM: Can you see Mike?
DAD: Yes, I can.
MUM: What **(a)** .... he .... (do) now?
DAD: Right now he's **(b)** .... (ride) a bike.
MUM: Impossible. He never **(c)** .... (take) his bike to school on Fridays. **(d)** .... he .... (wear) a helmet at the moment?
DAD: No, he **(e)** ....
MUM: He normally **(f)** .... (wear) a helmet when he **(g)** .... (ride) his bike.
DAD: Let me call him to find out what **(h)** .... (happen) . . . Mike? What **(i)** .... you .... (do)?
MIKE: Oh, hi, Dad. Well, you know I usually **(j)** .... (play) football on Fridays. But because this Friday is Pete's birthday we decided to come to the park. Pete **(k)** .... (have) his bike here.
DAD: Why **(l)** .... you .... (not wear) a helmet?
MIKE: How **(m)** .... you .... (know) that? Dad! **(n)** .... you .... (spy) on me again?!

4 Find these words and phrases in the dialogue in 3. Which go with the present simple and which go with the present continuous?

1 at the moment
2 never
3 normally
4 now
5 on Fridays
6 right now
7 this Friday
8 usually

at the moment = present continuous

5 Complete the sentences with the present simple or present continuous form of these verbs.

lie look after need not understand shout work

1 I can't come out at the moment because I .... my baby sister.
2 Why .... you ....? My grandfather can hear you.
3 My cousin always .... in a restaurant on Saturday afternoons.
4 Can you say that again? I ....
5 Can I help you, Dad? .... you .... anything?
6 My sister .... down right now because she doesn't feel well.

6 Write questions for these answers.

1 *What do you do on Fridays*? I play basketball on Fridays.
2 ....? My mum is working at the moment.
3 ....? My uncle and aunt live in Liverpool.
4 ....? No, my cousin isn't studying at university.
5 ....? My grandparents go for a walk in the mornings.
6 ....? My family and I usually go to the cinema at the weekend.

7 SPEAKING Use the questions in 6 to interview your partner. When you finish, think of similar questions to ask.

What do you do on Fridays?

I go out with my friends.

Noun suffixes *-ment*, *-ion*, *-ence*

1 Look at these words from the text on page 7.

equip**ment** independ**ence** protect**ion**

The parts of the word in **bold** are suffixes. Suffixes change the type of word, e.g. from an adjective to a noun.

2 Complete the words in the table and then use your dictionary to check the words.

-ment

Verb	Noun
1 *equip*	equipment
move	2 ....
improve	3 ....
4	retirement

-ion

Verb	Noun
5	protection
inform	6 ....
invent	7 ....
8	discussion

-ence

Adjective	Noun
9	independence
10	adolescence
different	11 ....
12	confidence

3 Complete the sentences with nouns from 2.

1 .... is the period between childhood and being an adult.
2 He and his brother are very similar. There isn't a big .... between them.
3 The computer is a brilliant ....
4 She doesn't live with her family. She likes having complete ....
5 You can find a lot of .... about many different topics on the Internet.
6 A hat can give you .... from the sun.

Click onto... Teenagers and parents

International cultural knowledge

British teenagers and their parents

1 Strict parents are parents who have very clear rules for their children to follow and obey. Work with a partner. Do you think these statements are true (T) or false (F)? Guess.

1 British parents are very strict. T/F
2 British parents don't like being strict. T/F
3 An experiment on TV shows that British teenagers hate strict parents. T/F

2 Read the text. Check your answers from 1.

3 Read the text again and answer the questions in your own words.

1 What is 'The world's strictest parents'?
It's a television programme about British adolescents and discipline.
2 Who is Andrea Wiseman?
3 What negative things do British teenagers do, in Wiseman's opinion?
4 What negative things do British parents do, in Wiseman's opinion?
5 What are the negative effects on teenagers when parents act in this way?
6 What happens to the British teenagers in 'The world's strictest parents'?

Strict parents

'What's the problem with British teenagers?'

Many British newspapers and TV programmes are asking this question at the moment. A lot of people are saying that there are problems with teenagers at school, on the streets and in their homes. Why? What, or who, is responsible for these problems?

A recent BBC television series explores these questions. It's called 'The world's strictest parents'. Is that because British parents are very strict? Just the opposite, it seems.

The director of the programme, Andrea Wiseman, explains why they are making it. She thinks that in the United Kingdom teenagers pay no attention to adults. They don't want to do well at school. They think they can do what they like and they are only interested in new fashions and Hollywood celebrities.

Why are British teenagers like this? Wiseman says it's because their parents give their children everything they can. But they give their children no limits, no rules, no discipline because they want their children to be 'free'. They don't tell their children to work hard because they don't want their kids to have any stress.

The problem with this is that parents give their sons and daughters no cultural values. When a teenager does something bad and their parents say something, the teenagers immediately say 'My parents are really strict' or 'My parents aren't fair'.

So what happens in the TV programme? Some problematic British teenagers go and live with parents in different parts of the world. They live with families that believe in traditional discipline and cultural values. In Ghana, Jamaica, Botswana and the southern US state of Alabama, the teenagers have the experience of living with parents who want and expect good behaviour and hard work. The results are interesting. In the end, the British teenagers seem to prefer having strict parents!

▸ WORD BOOSTER

Match the words and definitions.

1 explores	a the way that someone does things, for example, at school
2 celebrities	b famous people
3 discipline	c treated in a good and equal way
4 values	d the way that we make people obey rules
5 fair	e ideas that are important in our lives
6 behaviour	f looks at, investigates

4 What about *you*?

1 Would you like to watch this programme on TV? Why/Why not?
2 How strict do you think parents are in your country?

I'd like to watch it.

Why?

Because I'd like to see the British teenagers living in these different countries.

Popular culture

'Girls just want to have fun' by Cyndi Lauper

5 Look at the picture. What is happening?

6 1.03 Listen to the song and match the picture to a verse.

7 Now read the words to the song and match a sentence to each verse. There are four sentences but only three verses.

1 The girl's father is angry because people call his daughter at unusual times. *verse* ....
2 The girl's brother is angry because they have different opinions about things. *verse* ....
3 The girl's mother is angry because her daughter stays out late. *verse* ....
4 The girl doesn't want a boyfriend to control her. *verse* ....

8 What about *you*?

1 What do you think of the song's words and music?
2 How does the song make you feel?

I think the words are really good.

Me too. What about the music?

Verse 1
I come home in the morning light,
My mother says "When you gonna live your life right?"
Oh, mama dear,
We're not the fortunate ones,
And girls, they want to have fun
Oh, girls just want to have fun

Verse 2
The phone rings in the middle of the night,
My father yells "What you gonna do with your life?"
Oh, daddy dear,
You know you're still number one,
But girls, they want to have fun
Oh, girls just want to have fun

Chorus
That's all they really want
Some fun
When the working day is done,
Oh, girls, they want to have fun,
Oh, girls just want to have fun

Verse 3
Some boys take a beautiful girl,
And hide her away from the rest of the world
I want to be the one to walk in the sun
Oh, girls, they want to have fun,
Oh, girls just want to have fun

Chorus

i INSIDE INFORMATION

- This song first appeared in 1984. It won the first ever MTV Best Female Video award.
- The song appears in many films, adverts and TV series, including an episode of *The Simpsons*.
- The song is one of the first songs about girl power. Cyndi Lauper was an inspiration for artists like Madonna.

1a SPEAKING **Work with a partner. Describe the photos. Who can you see? Where are they? What are they doing? How are the people feeling, and why? If you are not sure of something, use *I think* and/or *I imagine*.**

1b Ask and answer these questions.

1 What time do you usually have dinner?
2 Where do you usually have dinner?
3 Who do you usually have dinner with?
4 What do you usually do when you have dinner – talk, watch TV, listen to music ... ?

2 LISTENING 1.04 **Listen to a radio programme about family dinners. Match the people and their situations.**

A eats with the family just once a week
B eats with the family but they don't talk
C makes dinner for the family every day
D never arrives home in time for dinner
E eats and talks with the family every day
F usually eats with the family but isn't eating with them today
G always eats alone because mum and dad work
H has to order pizza because nobody has time to cook

Mike	1
Chris	2
Sally	3
Alice	4
Jennifer	5
Daniel	6

3 SPEAKING **What about *you*?**

Do you think it's important to eat with your family? Why/Why not?

I think it's important to eat together.

Why?

Because you can talk about what you did that day or talk about your problems.

Grammar in context

GRAMMAR GUIDE

Articles

1 Look at these sentences and then complete rules 1–5 with *a/an*, *the* or *no article*.

a I think family dinners are a great thing.
b Family dinners are **an** important time for us.
c **The** dinner I'm eating today isn't good.
d **The** government talks a lot about family dinners.
e I'm **a** computer technician.

1 We use ....*no article*.......... when we talk about things in general.
2 We use .... to talk about a specific person or thing or a person or thing mentioned before.
3 We use .... to talk about a singular, countable person or thing for the first time, or to say that the person or thing is one of a number of things or people.
4 We use .... to talk about someone or something that is unique.
5 We use .... to say what somebody's profession is.

GRAMMAR REFERENCE ▶ page 16

2a PRONUNCIATION 1.05 **Listen to how we pronounce *the* in List A and in List B. What is the difference in pronunciation? Why is this?**

List A:	List B:
the problem	the end
the dinner	the important thing
the government	the evening
the weekend	the afternoon

2b Listen again and repeat.

3 Complete the sentences with *the* if necessary.

1 Today on .... programme we're talking about .... family dinners.
2 I'm going to .... fridge to see if there's anything to eat.
3 I think .... communication is essential.
4 In my house .... breakfast isn't an important meal.
5 Adults don't always arrive home on time because of .... work.
6 I don't like .... food at school.
7 In .... films they often show .... families eating together.

4 Read the text and choose the correct alternative.

(a) *An/The* interesting study in the USA shows **(b)** *the/0* importance of family dinners. The results show that **(c)** *0/the* teenagers who eat with their families five or six times a week usually get **(d)** *0/the* top marks at school. There is probably **(e)** *a/the* simple explanation for this. Rakeish Bedesi is **(f)** *0/the* president of ApplyingtoSchool.com. This is **(g)** *a/the* service helping students who want to go to **(h)** *0/the* university. He says he sees **(i)** *a/the* big difference between families that discuss things and families that don't. When you eat together and talk about **(j)** *0/the* different opinions and options, students can plan for the future. Do you want to be **(k)** *0/a* great inventor one day? Talk about it over dinner!

5 Look at these questions. Add *a*, *an*, *the* or *0* if the question does not need an article.

1 Do you think ....*0*.... family dinners are important?
2 Are .... family dinners .... important part of life in your country?
3 Do you think .... children and .... parents talk a lot in your country?
4 Do you talk about .... important things when you have .... dinner?
5 Do you think .... food you eat makes a difference to your school marks?
6 Do you like .... food at your school?
7 Do you listen to .... music at dinnertime?

6 SPEAKING Interview your partner using the correct questions in 5.

Do you think family dinners are important?

Yes, I do. I think they are an important part of family life.

1 **Complete this personal information file with information about you and your brothers, sisters or best friend.**

Brothers/Sisters/Best friend:	What you usually do on Saturdays:
Age:	What you usually do on Sundays:
What they do:	Your likes/dislikes:
How often you see them:	

2 **Look at these four people and their personal information files. Tell your partner which people are similar to you. Explain why.**

Oliver is similar to me because he's got one brother and he does sport on Sundays.

Liam
- one brother, one sister
- brother at university, sister works
- goes out with friends on Saturdays
- plays tennis on Sundays

Oliver
- one brother
- brother at university
- goes out with friends on Saturdays
- does sport on Sundays

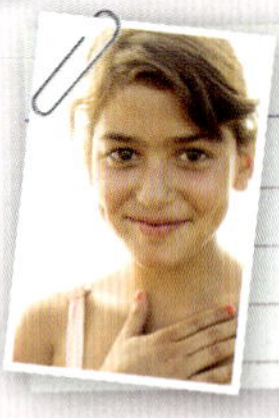

Emma
- one brother
- brother studies at school
- watches films on Saturdays
- doesn't like sport

Philippa
- one sister
- sister lives in the USA
- plays tennis on Saturdays
- plays computer games on Sundays

3 LISTENING 1.06 **Listen to two teenagers talking at a party. Look at the personal information files in 2. Which two people are talking?**

4 **Work with a partner. Complete the dialogue with the correct questions. Look at the Speaking Bank for help.**

(a) ....?

Yes, I've got one brother.

Me too. **(b)** ....?

He's 22.

(c) ....?

No, he doesn't. He's at university in Manchester.

(d) ....?

About once a month, when he comes home for the weekend.

That's good! I see my brother every day because he's only fourteen. **(e)** ....?

I usually go out with my friends on Saturdays and we sometimes play football on Sundays. **(f)** ....?

My brother and I often go to the cinema on Saturdays. But I never play football because I don't like sport.

Speaking Bank

Useful questions to ask for personal information

- Have you got any brothers or sisters?
- What do you do at the weekend/in the evenings/ on Wednesdays?
- What about you?
- Do you like ... ?
- What do you think of ... ?
- How often do you ... ?

5a PRONUNCIATION 1.07 **Listen again and check your answers.**
Which questions in the dialogue go with Diagram A?
Which go with Diagram B?

Diagram A **Diagram B**

5b **Listen and repeat the questions.**

5c **Complete the rules.**

1 In *Wh-* questions (e.g. *What's your name?*) the intonation usually goes up/down at the end of the question.

2 In *Yes/No* questions (e.g. *Is your name Anna?*) the intonation usually goes up/down at the end of the question.

6 SPEAKING **Practise the completed dialogue in 4 with your partner. Pay special attention to the correct intonation in questions.**

Practice makes perfect

7a SPEAKING **Work with a partner. Do this role-play using the dialogue in 4 and the Speaking Bank to help you.**

You meet an English boy/girl at a party.
- Find out if he/she has brothers or sisters.
- Tell him/her about your family.
- Find out what he/she does at the weekend.
- Tell him/her what you do in your free time.

7b **Change partners and repeat.**

EXAM SUCCESS

In information role-plays, how can you keep the conversation going? EXAM SUCCESS ▸ page 150

1 **Look at this advert from a teenager called Alanna. What does Alanna want? Would you be interested in contacting her? Why/Why not?**

e-pal.com

Name Alanna
My country Ireland
My age 14-18

Category	Language – English
Main aim	Find an international e-pal
I speak	English and a little Spanish
My interests	Music, books, travel
Message	Hi! I'm from Dublin. I've got two brothers, two sisters and a pet dog called Buttons! I love travelling and discovering new countries, new music and new books. If you want to practise your English and make new friends, write to me.

Reply

2 **Read this reply to Alanna's advert. Do you think this person is a good e-pal for Alanna? Why/Why not?**

Message - Hi Alanna!

From: Silvia <silvialombardi@mailnet.com> To: Alanna <teacakes@realmail.com>
Subject: Hi Alanna!

Hi Alanna!

1 I'm Silvia. I'm from Florence in Italy. Let me tell you about myself.

2 I'm from quite a big family. I've got two brothers and a sister. My sister and I are almost the same age and we go everywhere together. My father works in a bank and my mother is a teacher. My mum teaches at my school. That's often a good thing, but sometimes it can be really bad ;-).

3 I love listening to all types of music, but especially pop and rock. My favourite group is an Italian group called *Negramaro*. Do you know them? Right now I'm listening to their latest CD.

4 English is my favourite subject at school. This year I'm doing extra classes and I also read books in English. At the moment I'm reading a Sherlock Holmes book.

5 Anyway, that's all for now. Write back soon if you'd like to be my e-pal.

Best wishes
Silvia :-)

3 **Look again at the email in 2 and complete the information in the Writing Bank.**

Writing Bank

Useful words and expressions in informal emails

- To begin an informal email we usually use the word *Hi*.
- We use contractions like *I'm* or ....
- We can use emoticons like *:-)* or ....
- We can use the word .... to change the subject.
- To finish an informal email letter we can use:
  That's .... for now.
  Write .... soon.
  Best ....

STUDY SKILLS

When you finish writing, what do you need to check?

STUDY SKILLS ▸ page 146

4 **Match the paragraphs in Silvia's email with their content.**

Paragraph 1	favourite subject at school
Paragraph 2	main hobby
Paragraph 3	basic personal information
Paragraph 4	asking for a reply
Paragraph 5	family

Practice makes perfect

5 **Look at the task and write the email. Use Silvia's email and the Writing Bank to help you.**

Write an email with information about yourself to a new e-pal. Tell your e-pal:

- basic personal information
- information about your family
- information about your main hobby
- information about your favourite subject at school.

Language reference and revision

Grammar reference

Present simple

Form

Affirmative	I/You/We/They **work.** He/She/It **works.**
Negative	I/You/We/They **don't (do not) work.** He/She/It **doesn't (does not) work.**
Question	**Do** I/you/we/they **work?** **Does** he/she/it **work?**
Short answers	Yes, I/you/we/they **do.** No, I/you/we/they **don't.** Yes, he/she/it **does.** No, he/she/it **doesn't.**

Time expressions we often use with the present simple:
always, usually, often, sometimes, rarely, never, once/twice/three times a day/week/month/year, on Mondays/Tuesdays

Spelling

See page 149 for rules about spelling the third person singular form.

Use

We use the present simple to talk about:

1 regular habits and routines.
We have our English class on Thursdays.

2 permanent situations.
They live in a big city.

3 general and scientific facts.
Water boils at 100°C.

See notes below about state and action verbs.

Present continuous

Form

Affirmative	subject + **am/are/is** + verb+*ing* *We're waiting.*
Negative	subject + **am not/aren't/isn't** + verb+*ing* *She isn't listening.*
Question	**Am/Are/Is** + subject + verb+*ing*? *Are they watching?*
Short answers	Yes, subject + **am/are/is**. No, subject + **am not/aren't/isn't**. *Yes, I am. No, they aren't.*

Time expressions we often use with the present continuous:
now, right now, at the moment, today, this week

Spelling

See page 149 for rules about spelling the *-ing* form.

Use

We use the present continuous to talk about:

1 actions in progress at the moment of speaking.
I can't answer the phone. I'm having a shower.

2 temporary actions and situations.
John's living in New York for a few months.

NOTE: Some verbs are not usually used in the present continuous because they describe states not actions:
have (=possess) need love hate want prefer believe know understand think (=have an opinion) mean hear see seem

Articles

A/An

We use **a/an** with singular, countable nouns. We use it when we mention something for the first time, or to say that the person or thing is one of a number of things or people.
I've got a dog. It's a labrador.

We use **a/an** to say what somebody's profession is.
He's an engineer.

The

We use **the** with countable (singular and plural) and uncountable nouns. We use it to refer to something or somebody previously mentioned.
I've got a dog. The dog is really big.

We also use **the** to talk about specific things or people.
The people I saw yesterday were friendly.
The cheese is in the fridge.
The dogs in that park don't look very dangerous.

We also use **the** to talk about something unique, something that there is only one of.
the sun, the government (in a particular country), the world

No article

We do not use an article with plural countable nouns or uncountable nouns when we are talking about people or things in general.
People are friendly here.
I like cheese.
Tigers are dangerous.

Vocabulary

1 Ages and stages of life

adolescence baby birth child childhood death middle age middle-aged adult old age senior citizen teenager young adult

2 The family

aunt born brother brother/sister/father/mother-in-law cousin daughter divorced grandfather/mother grandson/daughter husband nephew niece one-parent family only child partner single sister son stepfather/mother uncle wife

3 Noun suffixes *-ment, -ion, -ence*

equipment improvement movement retirement discussion information invention protection adolescence confidence difference independence

4 Other words and phrases ▸ page 136–7

Grammar revision

Present simple and present continuous

1 Write the third person singular form and the *-ing* form of the verbs below.

Verb	Third person singular	*-ing* form
1 have		
2 lie		
3 write		
4 try		
5 get		
6 miss		
7 do		
8 cut		

WORKBOOK ▸ page 4

/ 8 points

2 Choose the correct word to complete the sentences.

1 He's .... a new pair of jeans today.
a wears b carries c wearing d carrying

2 When .... your sister have English lessons?
a is b do c does d has

3 I'm not sure if he .... French or German right now.
a studies b studys c study d 's studying

4 I'm sorry, I .... what you're telling me.
a 'm not understanding b not understand
c not understanding d don't understand

5 Where's your cousin? He normally .... on time.
a come b is arriving c arrives d is coming

6 Ah! Now I .... what you mean.
a see b 'm seeing c 'm knowing d 'm not understanding

7 Stop talking to her because she .... to you.
a don't listen b isn't listening
c 's listening d never listens

8 Why .... she doing anything?
a hasn't b isn't c doesn't d don't

WORKBOOK ▸ page 4

/ 8 points

Articles

3 Choose the correct alternative.

1 It's *a/the/0* beautiful day and *a/the/0* sun is shining.

2 *A/The/0* young girl walks into a restaurant. *A/The/0* girl sits down and orders a pizza.

3 My cousin loves *a/the/0* books. He's *a/the/0* writer.

4 Pete's uncle is *a/the/0* doctor. He says *a/the/0* cigarettes are bad for your health.

WORKBOOK ▸ page 7

/ 8 points

Vocabulary revision

Ages and stages of life – The family

1 Complete the text with the appropriate words.

'My name's Harry. I live with my mum. She's middle-(a) .... I think she's 50 this year. My dad doesn't live with us because my parents are (b) .... I'm an (c) .... child. I haven't got brothers or sisters but I spend a lot of time with my (d) .... , George. He's the son of my Uncle Jack. He's young. I remember when he was born. In fact, I was there at the hospital on the day of his (e) .... My Aunt Angela, Uncle Jack's (f) .... , is really nice too. My mum says she wants to get married again, but I don't really want to have a (g) .... father. I prefer my mum not to get married and to stay (h) ....'

WORKBOOK ▸ page 2

/ 8 points

Noun suffixes -ment, -ion, -ence

2 Complete the sentences with the correct form of these words.

adolescent different improve independent
inform invent move protect

1 She usually gets 50% or 60% in her exams but in this exam she has 90%. That's a big ....

2 Can you ....? I can't see the blackboard if you sit there.

3 I love my MP3 player! What a great .... !

4 This program .... your computer from viruses.

5 There are two or three .... between the present simple and the present continuous.

6 She wants to be a secondary school teacher because she likes working with ....

7 A dictionary gives you .... about new words.

8 He doesn't want to get married at the moment. He wants to be .... and free.

WORKBOOK ▸ page 5

/ 8 points

Total / 40 points

2 Criminal records

Grammar ‣ Past simple ‣ Past continuous
Vocabulary ‣ Crimes ‣ Criminals
‣ Phrasal verbs connected with investigating and finding
Speaking ‣ Reporting a past event
Writing ‣ An informal letter

‣ Vocabulary

Crimes

1 **Work with a partner and match the pictures with these words.**

burglary mugging murder piracy
robbery shoplifting theft vandalism

d burglary

2 1.08/9 **Listen and repeat.**

a

b

c

d

e

f

g

h

3 **Complete the sentences with the correct form of these verbs. You can use one word three times.**

burgle ~~kill~~ mug pirate rob steal vandalise

1 A murder is when somebody ...*kills*... another person.
2 A burglary is when somebody .... a house and .... things from it.
3 A robbery is when somebody .... a bank or a person.
4 Vandalism is when somebody .... public property and damages it.
5 Shoplifting is when somebody .... things from a shop.
6 Piracy is when somebody .... software such as CDs and DVDs by copying them illegally.
7 Mugging is when somebody .... another person and takes their money using violence.
8 A theft is when somebody .... something.

4 **What is the difference between *rob* and *steal*? Use your dictionary to check your answer.**

‣ STUDY SKILLS

Why is it good to guess information about words before you look them up in a dictionary? STUDY SKILLS ‣ page 146

5 LISTENING 1.10 **Listen to four radio news items. What are the crimes?**

1 .... 3 ....
2 .... 4 ....

Criminals

6 **Try to complete the table without using a dictionary. Then use your dictionary to check and complete the table.**

Crime	Criminal
burglary	1 *burglar*
murder	2
robbery	3
shoplifting	4
theft	5
vandalism	6
piracy	7
mugging	8

7a SPEAKING **All of these crimes are serious. Put them in order of how serious you think they are, from 8 (very serious) to 1 (not so serious).**

7b **Work with a partner. Compare your ideas.**

I think murder is very serious. I give it an 8.

I agree. What do you think about mugging?

Reading

1 Look at these pictures. They illustrate newspaper stories about crimes or criminals. Can you match the titles of the stories with the pictures? There is one title you do not need.

1. **Now you see it, now you don't**
2. And this photo is me stealing your car
3. **The perfect police officer**
4. Burglar in a box
5. **Let me back in!**

a

c

b

d

2 Work with a partner. From the titles and pictures, what do you think happens in each story? Guess.

What about the story with the car?

I think that somebody steals the car when the boy is taking a photo of it.

3 Read the stories and match the pictures, titles and texts.

Story A	Title	Picture ....
Story B	Title	Picture ....
Story C	Title	Picture ....
Story D	Title	Picture ....

STUDY SKILLS

Why is it useful to look at pictures and the title of texts before you read them? STUDY SKILLS ▸ page 146

A

Prison guards in Vienna got a big surprise yesterday. They discovered a young man just outside the prison. They thought that he was escaping. But they found out that the young man, Detlef Federsohn, was trying to get back in! Federsohn was in prison for two years for theft. When he left prison and lived on the outside, he decided that he preferred life inside. 'Life is great in prison,' said Federsohn. 'They give you your meals, wash your clothes and let you watch television. I can't do that with my mum.'

B

A gang of robbers wanted to rob the famous magician David Copperfield last week. They learnt an important lesson: never mug a magician. Four young people attacked Copperfield after a show in Florida, last week. Copperfield had money, his passport, and his mobile phone in his pockets. But when the robbers were looking for something to steal, he showed his pockets to the thieves and the objects weren't there! The thieves didn't wait to look for them. The police arrested the men when they were running away ... after a call from Copperfield on his disappearing phone.

C

A British car thief made a basic mistake. Lee Hoskins was stealing an Opel Astra when he came across a camera inside the car. So what did he do? He and his girlfriend took photos of each other next to the car. Soon afterwards, they crashed the car. They quickly ran away from the scene of the crime but they left the camera inside the car. The police soon worked out who the thief was! 'Some criminals can be really stupid,' said a police officer looking into the case.

D

A Colombian criminal had an original idea for a burglary. He got inside a box and a friend sent him by post to the house of a rich businessman. But the businessman was surprised and suspicious when the large parcel turned up at his house. He didn't think it was normal to receive this big parcel and so he called the police. When the thief finally came out of the box, he saw ten police officers standing there waiting for him.

4 Read the stories again and answer the questions.

1. Why were the prison guards in Vienna surprised by Detlef Federsohn?
2. Why didn't Detlef Federsohn want to live with his mum?
3. Who attacked David Copperfield?
4. Why didn't they steal anything from Copperfield?
5. What photos did Lee Hoskins take?
6. How did the police catch Lee Hoskins?
7. How did the Colombian burglar get into the rich man's house?
8. Why wasn't the burglar's plan successful?

5 Match the underlined words in the stories with their definitions.

1. stopped and took to the police station *arrested*
2. people who look after a place or person ....
3. a box or package that you send by post ....
4. breakfast, lunch, dinner ....
5. how you feel when you think something is not normal and could be bad or dangerous ....
6. crime, incident ....
7. using the postal service ....
8. let somebody see something ....

6 SPEAKING What about *you*?

Which story do you prefer and why?

I like the story about the magician.

Why?

Because he's very clever. The criminals didn't steal anything from him.

GRAMMAR GUIDE

Past simple

1a Look at these sentences. Which sentences are in the present simple and which are in the past simple?

a Four young people attacked him.
b What did he do?
c They give you your meals.
d He was outside the prison.
e He had money in his pockets.
f My mother doesn't do that.
g He didn't think about it.
h The objects weren't there.

1b When do we use the past simple?

1c In 1a find a sentence with …

1 a form of *be* in the past simple affirmative *d*
2 a form of *be* in the past simple negative ....
3 a regular verb in the past simple affirmative ....
4 an irregular verb in the past simple affirmative ....
5 a past simple question ....
6 a verb in the past simple negative ....

1d Complete the sentences with the correct past simple forms of *be*, *walk* and *go*.

Affirmative: He *was/walked/went* there yesterday.
Negative: He .... there yesterday.
Question: .... he .... there yesterday?

GRAMMAR REFERENCE ▶ page 28

2a PRONUNCIATION Look at the three lists. How do we pronounce the *-ed* ending in each list?

List A:	finished	watched	liked	passed
List B:	wanted	needed	painted	started
List C:	stayed	arrived	discovered	planned

2b 1.11 Listen, check and repeat.

2c In which list is the *-ed* ending pronounced /ɪd/? Which letters come just before *-ed* in the words in this list?

3 Work with a partner. Write an A to Z of irregular past simple forms. How many can you think of in five minutes?

A – ate, B – bought, C – …

4 Complete the text with the past simple form of the verbs.

One night a girl and her boyfriend **(a)** *were* (be) in the middle of a long phone conversation about their future. Suddenly the boyfriend **(b)** .... (stop) talking. The girl **(c)** .... (become) very worried. She **(d)** .... (begin) to shout but he **(e)** .... (not reply). She **(f)** .... (think) that her boyfriend **(g)** .... (be) in some kind of danger. At first, the girl **(h)** .... (not know) what to do. But then she **(i)** .... (make) a decision and **(j)** .... (call) the police. Officers **(k)** .... (run) to her boyfriend's house in Nuremburg, Germany. They **(l)** .... (expect) to find a murderer or a burglar, but they **(m)** .... (not find) any criminals. They just **(n)** .... (find) the boyfriend sleeping next to the phone!

5 Complete these questions about the text in 4 with the past simple form of the verbs.

1 What *were* (be) the boy and girl in the middle of?
2 What .... the boy .... (do)?
3 Why .... the girl .... (start) shouting?
4 What .... she .... (think)?
5 What .... she .... (decide) to do?
6 What action .... the police .... (take)?
7 .... they .... (find) any criminals?

6 SPEAKING Work with a partner. Take it in turns to ask and answer the questions in 5.

7a SPEAKING Work in pairs. Student A: look at the information below. Student B: turn to page 159. Prepare questions to ask your partner to find the missing information.

1 When was Bonnie Parker born?

7b Interview your partner.

Student A

Bonnie and Clyde were a pair of notorious criminals. Bonnie Parker was born in **(a)** .... in Rowena, Texas. She was very intelligent.

Clyde's full name was **(b)** .... He was born in 1909 in Ellis County, Texas.

Bonnie **(c)** .... in 1930. They committed many crimes in the next four years. They robbed **(d)** .... banks, although generally they preferred small shops and petrol stations. They often stole cars too. Once Clyde sent a letter to Henry Ford, to thank him. He told him that **(e)** ....!

But Clyde also had a violent side. He probably killed ten or eleven people.

In January 1934 **(f)** .... helped some friends to escape from a Texas prison. But the Texas police decided that it was time to stop Bonnie and Clyde. **(g)** .... killed the pair of criminals when they were in their car.

Bonnie and Clyde were so famous that many people went to see the car and tried to steal their clothes!

Phrasal verbs connected with investigating and finding

1 Find the phrasal verbs in the stories on page 19 and match them to the definitions below.

come across find out look for ~~look into~~ turn up work out

1 investigate *look into*
2 find by accident ....
3 solve a problem by considering the facts ....
4 try to find ....
5 discover ....
6 arrive or appear unexpectedly ....

2 Rewrite these sentences using the correct form of the phrasal verbs in 1.

1 Detectives are trying to find the murderer.
Detectives *are looking for the murderer*.

2 The CIA began to investigate the case.
The CIA ....

3 They found the knife by accident in the garden.
They ....

4 The knife appeared unexpectedly in the garden.
The knife ....

5 Sherlock Holmes used logic to solve crimes.
Sherlock Holmes ....

6 After their investigation, they soon discovered where the thief was.
After their investigation, they ....
....

3 How many sentences can you make with the words in the table? Your sentences must include the phrasal verbs in 1.

I looked for the key.

I	looked found came worked	out for across	the key. the answer. the identity of the criminal.

Click onto... The police and the SIS

Cross-curricular – History
The origins of the British Police

1 You are going to read some facts about the British Police. Before you read, why do you think these words or numbers appear in the text? Guess.

1 1827	5 panda cars
2 Bobbies	6 999
3 green	7 1 metre 78
4 1915	8 Scotland Yard

I think 1827 is when the British Police began.

2 Read the text and check your answers.

The origins of the British Police

- The British Police force was the first modern police force in the world. It began in 1827.
- People sometimes call police officers 'Bobbies'. This is because the person who started the police force was Sir Robert (Bobby) Peel.
- Sir Robert Peel didn't want the police to wear green. Green was the colour of the army uniform and the army wasn't very popular at the time. So Peel decided to make police uniforms blue. This was the colour of the navy. The navy was popular.
- The first police woman started work in 1915. Women became a regular part of the police force at this time because many men were away fighting in the First World War.
- The emergency number to call the police in Britain is 999. They chose this number because on old telephones it was very difficult to ring the number by accident.

- People called the first police cars 'panda cars' because they had panels of different colours, sometimes black and white, or often blue and white.
- In the past, to be a police officer you needed to be 1 metre 78 or more. Now it isn't important how tall or short you are.
- The first police headquarters were in a place called Great Scotland Yard. In 1890 they moved to a different place. People called this New Scotland Yard. Then, in 1967, the police built a new, modern headquarters which is also called New Scotland Yard! It is just 450 metres from the Houses of Parliament in London.

WORD BOOSTER

Match the words and definitions.

1	army	a	special clothes that you wear for work or school
2	uniform	b	a large group of soldiers who fight on land
3	popular	c	central offices
4	navy	d	a large group of soldiers who fight at sea
5	by accident	e	something that many people like
6	headquarters	f	not wanting to, by mistake

International cultural knowledge
The British Secret Intelligence Service

3 Work with a partner and do the Secret Intelligence Service quiz.

4 1.12 Listen. Did you choose the correct answers in the quiz?

5 What about *you*?

1 Do you think real secret agents have exciting lives? Why/Why not?
2 Would you like to be a secret agent or a police officer? Why/Why not?

I think they probably have exciting lives because they travel a lot.

I don't agree.

Are you the James Bond of the future?

Do you have the intelligence to work for the Secret Intelligence Service (SIS)? Prove it by choosing the correct answers. If you don't know, guess!

1 The popular name for the SIS is *MI5/MI6*.
2 The SIS generally works *in Britain/outside Britain*.
3 The director of the SIS is *M/C*.
4 In real life, the SIS *has/doesn't have* a director of technology, like the character Q in the James Bond films.
5 The headquarters of the SIS in London has *a secret nuclear bunker/a secret tunnel under the River Thames*.

Literature

Casino Royale by Ian Fleming

INSIDE INFORMATION

- The author of the James Bond novels was English. His name was Ian Fleming. During the Second World War, Fleming worked with spies in the Intelligence department of the British Navy.
- *Casino Royale* was the first James Bond novel. It appeared in 1953. They made a film of *Casino Royale* in 2006, with Daniel Craig as Bond.
- In *Casino Royale* Bond's mission is to destroy Le Chiffre, an important Russian agent. Le Chiffre loses all his money when he plays cards with Bond. But Le Chiffre and his men kidnap Vesper, the woman who is working with Bond. Mathis is another local agent working with Bond. The text here describes what happens when Bond follows Le Chiffre and Vesper in his car.

The Crash

Soon Bond was speeding along the coast road. There was no wind, and the night was clear.

Bond drove faster and faster. He was angry. Why had M sent Vesper – a woman – on this job? He knew that Le Chiffre's men would give him the girl if he gave them the cheque. Well, he wouldn't do it! This job was more important than Vesper. All right, he would try and catch the Citroën. But if he didn't catch them, he would go back to his hotel. He would say nothing to Mathis about the Citroën. He would not pay Le Chiffre's men the forty million francs. Tomorrow he would show Mathis the note. He would ask Mathis what had happened to Vesper.

Bond's Bentley was travelling at 160 kilometres an hour. The Citroën was only a kilometre or two ahead. Bond took a gun from under the driver's seat. He put it on the seat beside him.

There were three men and the girl in the Citroën. Le Chiffre was driving. The man who had carried the walking-stick gun was beside him. There was a thick handle next to the man's left hand. The handle came from the floor of the car.

The tall, thin gunman was sitting in the back seat. Vesper was next to him. She had a sack over her head. It was tied around her neck with a piece of rope.

Le Chiffre watched Bond's car in his driving mirror. The Bentley was only a kilometre behind. When he went round a corner, Le Chiffre slowed to fifty kilometres an hour. He could see a crossroads ahead.

'Get ready,' he said to the man beside him.

The man put his fingers round the handle. At that moment, the Bentley's headlights came round the corner.

'Now!' said Le Chiffre.

He stopped the car and all three men jumped out. They ran back to the crossroads. Each man carried a gun.

The Bentley was speeding towards them.

6 1.13 **Read and listen to the text. What do you think is going to happen just after this scene?**

7 **Read the text again. Decide if the sentences are true (T) or false (F).**

1 The weather was good that night. T/F
2 Bond decided to give Le Chiffre the cheque. T/F
3 Bond was driving the Bentley and Le Chiffre was driving the Citroën. T/F
4 There were five people in the Citroën. T/F
5 Vesper was sitting in the back seat of the car. T/F
6 Le Chiffre drove very fast to escape from Bond. T/F
7 Le Chiffre and his men are planning a surprise attack on Bond. T/F

8 **Correct the false sentences in 7.**

WORD BOOSTER

Match the words and pictures.

1 cheque
2 sack
3 driving mirror
4 crossroads
5 headlights

a

b

c

d

e

PROJECT

9a **Work in groups. Do you know anything about the fictional British detective Sherlock Holmes? Make notes on these topics:**

- personality and appearance
- the author who created Sherlock Holmes
- famous stories and films
- British life at the time

9b **Each person in the group should choose one of the topics, find out more information and look for illustrations.**

9c **In your group, decide how to present your information to the rest of the class. Prepare it and present it.**

1 **SPEAKING** **Work with a partner and discuss these questions.**

1 What can you see in the photo?
2 What type of objects do people steal from shops?

▶ EXAM SUCCESS

You are going to do a 'true/false/not mentioned' listening activity. What do you think is the first thing to do in this type of activity? EXAM SUCCESS ▶ page 150

2 **LISTENING** **1.14** **You are going to hear two teenagers talking about a shoplifting incident. Listen and decide if each statement is true (T), false (F) or if the information is not mentioned (NM).**

1	The boy stole a pair of sunglasses when he was five.	T/F/NM
2	The boy was staying with his uncle at the time.	T/F/NM
3	The boy's mum was looking for a pair of sunglasses too.	T/F/NM
4	The sunglasses were red.	T/F/NM
5	An old man saw the boy when he was stealing the sunglasses.	T/F/NM
6	A policeman arrested the boy while he was leaving the supermarket.	T/F/NM
7	The boy doesn't like wearing sunglasses now.	T/F/NM

3 **Compare your answers with your partner.**

4 **Listen again and check your answers. What did the boy decide to do after this crime?**

GRAMMAR GUIDE

Past continuous

1a **Look at sentences 1–4 and match them to the explanation of their uses in a–d.**

1 My mum was looking for something. ...c...
2 While I was waiting for my mum I saw some sunglasses. ....
3 I just put the sunglasses in my pocket. ....
4 She took me back to the supermarket and I gave the sunglasses back. ....

a A completed action in the past.
b Two completed actions in the past that happened one after the other.
c An activity in progress in the past.
d An activity in progress in the past interrupted by a sudden action.

1b **Complete the rule.**
We make the past continuous with the past simple of .... + verb *-ing*.

GRAMMAR REFERENCE ▶ page 28

2 **SPEAKING** **This supermarket needs a new security officer. Have you got good powers of observation and memory? Look at the scene for two minutes. Then work with a partner. Take it in turns. One of you closes the book and the other asks questions.**

3 **Work individually. Write complete sentences to answer the questions about the story.**

One afternoon a young girl was sitting in a café drinking tea.

1 What else was she doing? *She was talking on her mobile phone.*

Suddenly a man ran into the café and shouted her name.

2 What was the girl's name? ....

3 What was the man wearing? ....

4 What was the man carrying? ....

The young girl didn't appear to be very happy to see the man. She immediately started to look inside her bag.

5 What was she looking for? ....

6 What did she take out of her bag? ....

The man ran quickly towards the girl.

7 Then what did he do? ....

8 What did the girl do and why? ....

9 How did the story end? ....

4 **Read your complete story to your partner. Are your stories similar or different? Which story do you prefer?**

One afternoon a young girl was sitting in a café drinking tea. She was talking on her mobile phone. Her name was ...

5 **Complete the dialogue by putting the verbs in the correct form of the past continuous or past simple.**

POLICE OFFICER: So, can you tell us, sir? What **(a)** *were* you *doing* (do) at 10pm last night?

ROBIN BANKS: Let's see. I think I **(b)** .... (help) my mum with the shopping at 10pm.

POLICE OFFICER: Really? When we **(c)** .... (ring) your mum last night at 10pm she **(d)** .... (not do) the shopping. She **(e)** .... (watch) TV at home.

ROBIN BANKS: Ah, now I remember. I **(f)** .... (run) at that time.

POLICE OFFICER: **(g)** .... anybody **(h)** .... (see) you while you **(i)** .... (run)?

ROBIN BANKS: Erm. Yes, my friend Jack Door saw me.

POLICE OFFICER: Jack Door? Impossible. Didn't you know? He's in prison.

ROBIN BANKS: Oops! Anyway, why are you asking me all these questions?

POLICE OFFICER: Well, Mr Banks, our cameras **(j)** .... (catch) you running last night. You **(k)** .... (run) out of the National Bank and you **(l)** .... (carry) a bag with ten thousand pounds in it.

6a **SPEAKING** **What you were doing at these times? Think of three things that are true and three that are false. You need to make your partner think that your false stories are true.**

1 at 8am last Saturday
2 at 10pm last Saturday
3 at 9am on Sunday
4 at 7pm yesterday
5 at midnight last night
6 at 7.30am this morning

6b **Interview your partner. Which information do you think is false? Look at this example.**

What were you doing at 8am last Saturday?

I was revising English.

Why were you revising English at 8am?

Because I had an exam last week and I didn't have any other time to study.

Why not?

Because at ten o'clock I went away with my friends for the weekend.

I think it's false!

1 SPEAKING **Work with a partner. Say what you can see in each picture.**

PLACES

a

b

c

OBJECTS

d

e

f

CRIMES

g

h

i

2 LISTENING **1.15 Listen to two teenagers talking about last weekend. Which pictures from 1 appear in the story?**

3 **Work in pairs. Student A: complete the gaps in Sophie's dialogue. Student B: complete the gaps in Jake's dialogue.**

Sophie: Hi there. How are you? Did you have a good **(a)** ....?

Jake: No, not really.

Sophie: Why not? What was the **(b)** ....?

Jake: Well, I went out with my friends on Saturday night and something terrible **(1)** ....

Sophie: **(c)** ....?

Jake: We were in the town centre. We went to that new **(2)** ...., *Gino's*. We had a great time but when we were leaving a boy and a girl suddenly came up to me and asked me the time. I told them and then we left. A few minutes later, when we were going home on the bus, I wanted to call my parents. I looked for my **(3)** .... everywhere but I couldn't find it.

Sophie: **(d)** .... what did you do next?

Jake: We went back to look for it but it wasn't there. I think the boy and girl **(4)** .... it when they were asking me the time.

Sophie: Oh no! So what happened **(e)** ....?

Jake: After that, I called the **(5)** .... to block the number. But now I haven't got a **(6)** ....

Sophie: That's **(f)** ....!

4 **Listen again and check your answers.**

5 SPEAKING **Work in pairs. Practise reading the dialogue aloud.**

6 **Look at the words and expressions in the Speaking Bank. Tick the ones which appear in the dialogue.**

Speaking Bank

Useful words and expressions of sequence and time

- At first
- First of all
- Then
- Next ✓
- After that
- In the end
- Finally
- Suddenly
- A few minutes/hours/days later
- The next day

Practice makes perfect

7a SPEAKING **Choose a place, object and crime from 1. Make notes to invent what happened to you last weekend.**

7b **Work with a partner. Student A: Ask Sophie's questions from 3. Student B: Answer the questions. Use the Speaking Bank and your notes to help you. Now change roles.**

1 **Read the letter and look at the picture story. What differences can you find between the letter and the pictures?**

There are two friends in the letter, but only one in the picture story.

6 Smithdown Road,
Oldham,
OL3 8RG.

10th January 2011

Hi Ellie,

Thanks for your letter. I thought about you yesterday. Do you remember when you lost your bag? Well, yesterday I was walking home from school with two of my friends when we found a handbag in the street. It looked new.

At first we didn't know what to do. Our first idea was to take it to the police but my friend Luke thought we should open the bag to find out who it belonged to.

So I opened it. Inside there was a mobile phone and money, but no identification. I thought I recognised the mobile phone but I wasn't sure.

Suddenly my mum appeared at the end of the road. She was looking for something. When she saw me she ran up to me and said, 'What are you doing with my bag?' I couldn't believe it – it was my mum's new bag!!

Write back soon and tell me all your news!

Love,

Josh

X

2 **Look again at the letter in 1 and complete the information in the Writing Bank.**

Writing Bank

Useful expressions and conventions in informal letters

- In informal letters, we write *our address* and .... in the top right corner.
- Then we write Dear or .... and the name of the person.
- We often begin with Thanks for your .... or I'm writing to tell you about …
- To end an informal letter we can use Write back soon and ....

3 **Imagine that you found something unusual last week. Make notes to answer the questions.**

1 When did you find it?
2 Where were you?
3 Who were you with?
4 What did you find?
5 Why was it unusual?
6 What did you do with the object?
7 What happened in the end?

Practice makes perfect

4 **Look at the task and write the letter. Use your notes from 3 and the Speaking and Writing Banks to help you.**

Last week you found something unusual. Write a letter to a friend telling them about what you found. Tell them:

- what you found and where
- why the object was unusual
- what you did next and what happened in the end.

EXAM SUCCESS

What are the criteria for getting a good mark in your English writing exams? EXAM SUCCESS ▸ page 150

Language reference and revision

Grammar reference

Past simple of be

Form

Affirmative	I/He/She/It **was** there. You/We/They **were** there.
Negative	I/He/She/It **wasn't (was not)** there. You/We/They **weren't (were not)** there.
Question	**Was** I/he/she/it there? **Were** you/we/they there?
Short answers	Yes, I/he/she/it **was**. No, I/he/she/it **wasn't**. Yes, you/we/they **were**. No, you/we/they **weren't**.

Past simple of regular and irregular verbs

Form

Affirmative	I/You/He/She/It/We/They **walked** home. I/You/He/She/It/We/They **went** home.
Negative	I/You/He/She/It/We/They **didn't (did not) walk** home. I/You/He/She/It/We/They **didn't (did not) go** home.
Question	**Did** I/you/he/she/it/we/they **walk** home? **Did** I/you/he/she/it/we/they **go** home?
Short answers	Yes, I/you/he/she/it/we/they **did**. No, I/you/he/she/it/we/they **didn't**.

Spelling

See page 149 for rules about spelling the third person singular form.

Use

We use the past simple to:

1 describe finished actions or situations in the past.
I went to San Francisco in 2005.

2 to say that one thing happened after another.
When the letter arrived, he opened it and read it.

Past continuous

Form

Affirmative	I/He/She/It **was** watching. You/We/They **were** watching.
Negative	I/He/She/It **wasn't (was not)** watching. You/We/They **weren't (were not)** watching.
Question	**Was** I/he/she/it watching? **Were** you/we/they watching?
Short answers	Yes, I/he/she/it **was**. No, I/he/she/it **wasn't**. Yes, you/we/they **were**. No, you/we/they **weren't**.

Use

We use the past continuous to:

1 talk about activities in progress at a moment in the past.
At six o'clock I was watching a film.

2 describe scenes in a story or description.
The sun was shining and the birds were singing.

3 talk about an activity in progress when another, shorter activity happened or interrupted it. It tells us that an action was in progress, but not that the activity was finished.
I was crossing the road when I saw the accident.

We often use **while** and **as** with the past continuous.
While/As I was crossing the road I saw an accident.

Remember that some verbs are not usually used in the continuous (see page 16).
I wanted to see the concert.
~~*I was wanting to see the concert.*~~

Vocabulary

1 Crimes

nouns: burglary mugging murder piracy robbery shoplifting theft vandalism

verbs: burgle kill mug pirate rob steal vandalise

2 Criminals

burglar mugger murderer pirate robber shoplifter thief vandal

3 Phrasal verbs connected with investigating and finding

come across find out look for look into turn up work out

4 Other words and phrases ▸ page 137–8

Grammar revision

Past simple

1 Change these sentences from present simple to past simple.

1 Richard and I are students at this school.
....

2 What's the problem?
....

3 We leave school at 5 o'clock.
....

4 She catches the bus at that stop.
....

5 What time do you finish work?
....

6 She doesn't teach English.
....

7 Running makes me tired.
....

8 They've got a problem.
....

WORKBOOK ▶ page 12 — / 8 points

Past continuous

2 Complete the sentences with the past continuous form of these verbs.

cry listen read ride sit sleep wait write

1 At nine o'clock last night I .... a detective novel.
2 Which CD .... you .... to?
3 He .... a letter, it was an email.
4 .... the baby .... at 2am?
5 I .... my bike this morning.
6 They .... for the bus, it was a taxi.
7 Which chair .... you .... in?
8 My grandmother .... because she was very sad.

WORKBOOK ▶ page 15 — / 8 points

Past continuous and past simple

3 Choose the correct alternative.

1 While I *travelled/was travelling* to work, my phone suddenly *rang/was ringing*.
2 The boy *stole/was stealing* the apple while nobody *looked/was looking*.
3 Craig *drove/was driving* home when he *remembered/was remembering* it was his mum's birthday.
4 Sam *broke/was breaking* the window and then he *ran/was running* away.

WORKBOOK ▶ page 15 — / 8 points

Vocabulary revision

Crimes

1 Complete the sentences with these words. There are more words than sentences.

burglary burgle kill mug mugger murderer piracy pirate rob shoplifter shoplifting steal theft thief vandal

1 When you .... someone, you attack them to steal from them.
2 When you .... from a person or a place, you take money or objects illegally.
3 .... is the crime of entering a house or building illegally to take things.
4 When you .... someone, you take their life.
5 A .... is when you take something illegally.

WORKBOOK ▶ page 10 — / 5 points

Criminals

2 Complete the sentences with words from 1.

1 A .... is someone who makes and sells illegal copies of software, for example.
2 A .... is someone who steals from a shop.
3 A .... is someone who damages and destroys things for no reason.
4 A .... is someone who takes another person's life.
5 A .... is somebody who steals things in general.

WORKBOOK ▶ page 10 — / 5 points

Phrasal verbs connected with investigating and finding

3 Complete the sentences with these prepositions.

across for into out out up

1 I was looking **(a)** .... my keys yesterday but I couldn't find them anywhere. I hope they turn **(b)** .... soon. If you come **(c)** .... them, could you tell me?
2 They can't find the murderer, so a new detective is going to look **(d)** .... the case. If they use logic, they can probably work **(e)** .... who the criminal is. It's urgent to find **(f)** .... who did it.

WORKBOOK ▶ page 13 — / 6 points

Total / 40 points

Gateway to exams *Units 1–2*

Reading

Tip for Reading Exams

In multiple-choice reading activities, remember …

If you aren't 100% sure of the correct answer, begin by taking away any answers which you know aren't correct.

EXAM SUCCESS ▸ page 150

1 Look at the photo. The teenager is wearing a 'hoodie', a jacket or sweatshirt with a hood which can cover your head or face. Do you like hoodies? How often do you wear one?

2 Read the text and write a title for it.

____

Hoodies – yes or no? That is the question in many shopping centres in the UK. Hoodies are very popular with today's teenagers, but people often make a direct connection between hoodies and crime.

Bluewater shopping centre in Kent recently decided to stop teenagers wearing hooded tops from entering shops. Teenagers can't wear any clothes that cover their faces or heads. The main reason for this is that security cameras cannot identify teenage criminals who are wearing hoodies.

But not all shopping centres are doing the same thing. A representative from a big shopping centre in Manchester said: 'We don't think it's necessary to stop all teenagers who are wearing these clothes. We prefer to look at each case on a personal level. Some people just wear hoodies because that's the fashion.'

People on the streets have different opinions. Jo Sparr, a senior citizen from Manchester, said: 'I don't like them. You can't see the person's face. It's really bad when you see a big group of teenagers together all wearing hoodies. I want hoodies to be illegal, not only in shopping centres but also in city centres.' Middle-aged Rob Dyson said: 'They're only clothes. It doesn't make any difference to me what these kids wear. Just wearing a hoodie doesn't make you a criminal.'

So what do the police say about all of this? Manchester Police looked into the question and found that 1.2% of robberies were by people wearing hoodies. But at Bluewater shopping centre they are happy. Now that teenagers can't wear hoodies, there isn't much shoplifting in the centre.

So, hoodies – yes or no? It depends on who you speak to.

3 Read the text again and choose the best answers.

1 The Bluewater shopping centre had problems because

- **A** hoodies are popular.
- **B** people who wear hoodies are criminals.
- **C** it is difficult to know exactly who somebody is when they wear a hoodie.

2 The shopping centre in Manchester

- **A** thinks all teenagers are the same.
- **B** stops some people if they do something bad.
- **C** likes hoodies because they're in fashion.

3 People on the streets

- **A** agree that hoodies are bad.
- **B** want to stop big groups of teenagers wearing hoodies.
- **C** have different ideas about hoodies.

4 Police statistics show that

- **A** people wearing hoodies are often criminals.
- **B** most people who steal don't wear hoodies.
- **C** the number of crimes by people wearing hoodies is going down.

5 The text says that

- **A** hoodies are a bad thing.
- **B** it isn't clear that hoodies are a bad thing.
- **C** shops don't like hoodies.

Listening

Tip for Listening Exams

In true-false activities, remember …

Before you listen, read the questions. They can give you ideas about the topic of the text and the vocabulary you are going to hear. EXAM SUCCESS ▸ page 150

4 1.16 You are going to listen to two people talking about an unusual incident that was on the news. Listen and decide if the statements are true (T) or false (F).

1 The unusual incident was with an American university professor. T/F
2 The professor wanted to cross the road to go to a conference. T/F
3 'Jay-walking' is the American word for what the professor did. T/F
4 The professor knew that he was breaking the law. T/F
5 The professor went to prison for eight days. T/F

Speaking

Tip for Speaking Exams

In information role-plays, remember …

Use basic question words like *Who? What? When? Where? How? Why?* to help keep the conversation going.
EXAM SUCCESS ▸ pages 150

5 Look at this situation and make a list of questions that you can ask.

There is a new student from England in your school.

- Ask them to tell you about a member of their family who is special to them.
- Find out information about this person and why they are special.
- Tell them about a member of your family who is special to you.

Which member of your family is special to you? How often do you see this person?

6 Make notes with your answers to the questions in 1.

my sister *every day*

7 Work with a partner and act out the role-play in 1. Use your questions and notes if necessary.

Writing

Tip for Writing Exams

In writing exams, remember …

It's important to know what the examiners want to see in your answer. Find out how many marks there are and what you need to do to get a good mark.
EXAM SUCCESS ▸ page 150

8 Write an informal email to an e-pal. Describe a good friend at school. Follow this paragraph plan and remember to use typical words and expressions.

Paragraph 1: Basic personal information about your friend (name, age, where from)

Paragraph 2: Hobbies

Paragraph 3: Favourite subject at school

Paragraph 4: Ask for a reply

'Can Do' Progress Check

CEF

1 How well can you do these things in English now? Give yourself a mark from 1 to 4.

1 = I can do it very well.
2 = I can do it quite well.
3 = I have some problems.
4 = I can't do it.

a I can talk about routines and what's happening now using the present simple and present continuous. ☐
b I can ask for and give basic personal information. ☐
c I can make nouns using the suffixes *-ment*, *-ion*, *-ence*. ☐
d I can understand conversations about families and family life. ☐
e I can write a basic informal email about myself or somebody I know well. ☐
f I can report past events using the past simple and past continuous. ☐
g I can explain sequences of events in the past using expressions of sequence and time. ☐
h I can understand written and spoken texts about crimes and the police. ☐
i I can talk about different crimes and investigations. ☐
j I can write a basic informal letter about a past event. ☐

2 Decide what you need to do to improve.

1 Look again at my book/notes.
2 Do more practice exercises. ⇨ WORKBOOK pages 2–19
3 Other: ______________________________

3 Lost in translation

Grammar	‣ Countable and uncountable nouns ‣ Relative pronouns ‣ *Some, any, much, many, a lot of, a few, a little*
Vocabulary	‣ Countries, nationalities and languages ‣ Learning a language ‣ Negative prefixes *un-, in-, im-, ir-, il-*
Speaking	‣ Asking for information
Writing	‣ A language biography

‣ Vocabulary

Countries, nationalities and languages

1 **Work with a partner and complete the table.**

Country	Nationality	Language(s)
1 Brazil	Brazilian	Portuguese
2 Austria	*Austrian*	
3	Welsh	
4 Japan		
5		Dutch
6	Egyptian	
7	Argentinian	
8		Polish
9	Swiss	Romansh, …
10 Russia		

2 1.17 **Listen and check your answers.**

3a PRONUNCIATION **Mark the main stress in each word in 1.**

Brazil Brazilian Portuguese

3b 1.18 **Listen again, check and repeat with the correct stress.**

4a SPEAKING **Which of the countries in 1 would you like to visit? Why? Make notes.**

Wales – like rugby, go camping …
Japan – love the fashion and shopping

4b **Work in small groups. Use your notes to talk about the countries you would like to visit and explain why.**

I'd like to visit Wales because I enjoy watching rugby. I want to visit Cardiff and go camping.

Learning a language

5 **Look at these words. They are all verbs. What nouns can you make from them?**

memorise practise revise ~~study~~ translate

study – student

6 **Look at these words. Decide if we use *do* or *make* with each word. Can you think of other verbs we can use with the words?**

English an essay an exam
an exercise homework a mistake

do English, study English, learn English

7 SPEAKING **Interview your partner with these questions about learning English. Are your answers similar?**

1 How do you study English outside school?
2 How do you revise vocabulary before an exam?
3 How often do you translate from and into English?
4 How do you feel about writing in English?
5 How often do you do English homework?
6 When do you take English exams?
7 How do you feel when you make mistakes in English?
8 Do you prefer practising speaking, writing, reading, and listening or doing grammar and vocabulary exercises?

How do you study English outside school?

I do my homework and I sometimes read books in English. I watch DVDs in the original version too.

‣ STUDY SKILLS

Why is it useful to reflect on how you learn English?

STUDY SKILLS ‣ page 146

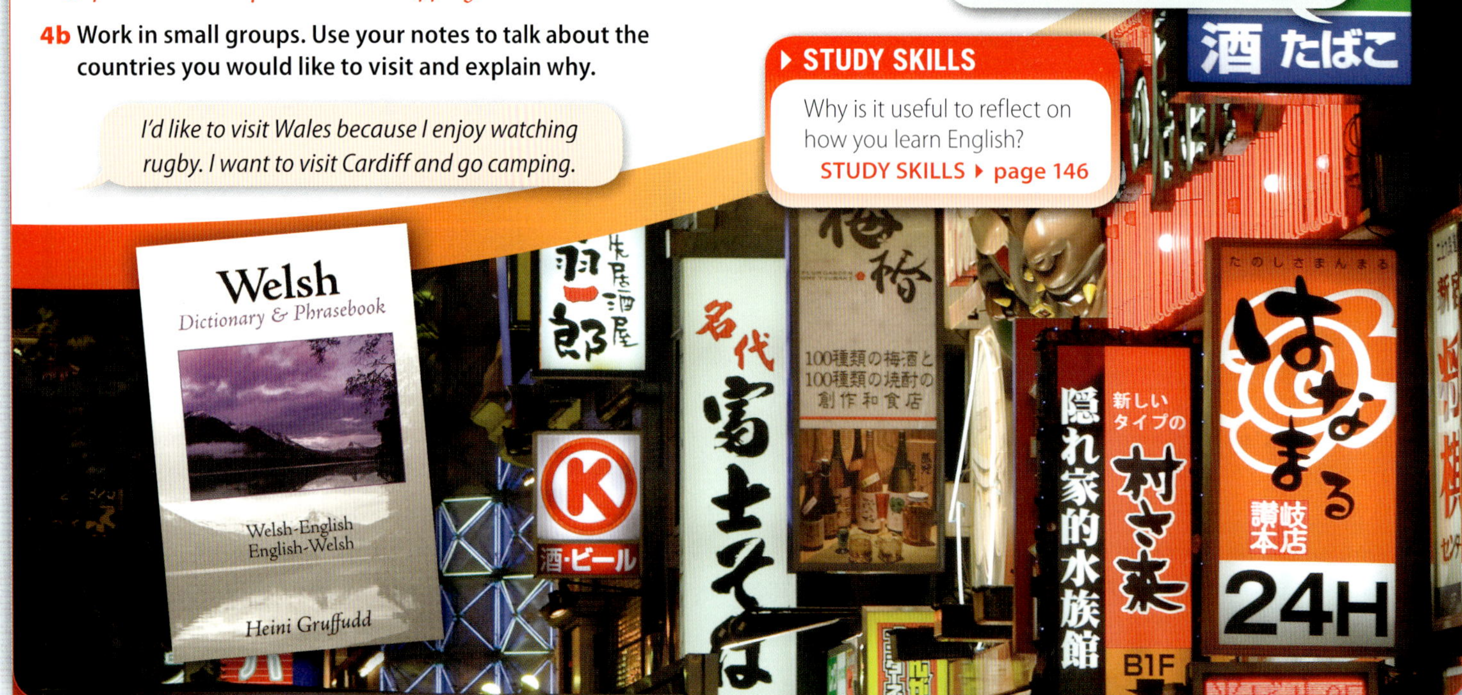

1 **Work with a partner. Look at these book covers? Could you read these books? Why/Why not?**

Translating the world's best seller

1 There are more than 400 million Harry Potter books in the world. But approximately 100 million copies do not contain any lines from the author's original text. That's because they are translations. At the moment, there are versions in over sixty languages, including Welsh, Latin and Ancient Greek.

2 Jean-François Menard, the French translator of the Harry Potter books, translated the 700-page fourth book in just 63 days. The translators didn't have much time because they could only begin when the English version appeared in the shops. This was because the author wanted the story to be a total secret. In a few countries where the general public's level of English is very high (for example in Scandinavia), it was very important to translate the book quickly. If not, people in those countries could just buy the original English version, not the translation.

3 In other countries such as China, there were unofficial, pirate translations. People sold them on the streets illegally. The author didn't receive any money from these books and often the translations were not very good. A pirate version in Venezuela in 2003 contained many mistakes. The translator occasionally put a few of his own informal messages into the text, for example 'Here comes something I can't translate, sorry', or 'I didn't understand what that meant.'

4 It's true that the translation of J. K. Rowling's books had some special difficulties. One big problem was with invented words and names. There are a lot of these words in the series – approximately 400! Spanish readers find most of these words exactly the same as in English. So, *quidditch** and *muggles*** are unchanged in the Spanish versions. But in Brazil the translator invented her own Portuguese words to express the ideas and sounds of the original words. So we have *quadribol* to translate *quidditch*, and *trouxas* instead of muggles.

* *Quidditch* is the invented sport that Harry Potter plays.
** *Muggles* are humans who haven't got magical powers.

2 **You are going to read a text about translating the Harry Potter books. Read the first sentence of each paragraph and match them with these topics.**

a Paragraph .... why the translators needed to work fast
b Paragraph .... the number of translated Harry Potter books
c Paragraph .... some problematic translations
d Paragraph .... why translating Harry Potter wasn't easy

3 **Read the text again. Are these statements true (T), false (F) or is the information not mentioned (NM)?**

1 More than half of all Harry Potter books are translations. T/F/NM
2 There is a Japanese version of the Harry Potter books. T/F/NM
3 The Harry Potter translators didn't have the books before the general public. T/F/NM
4 Scandinavian translators need to work fast because not many people can read the English version. T/F/NM
5 Some people translated the books without official permission. T/F/NM
6 The official translation in Venezuela contained some stupid comments. T/F/NM
7 People had to do a test to become official translators of the Harry Potter books. T/F/NM
8 All the translators used the same technique to translate Rowling's invented words. T/F/NM

4 **Correct the false sentences in 3.**

5 **Match the underlined words in the text with their definitions.**

1 forms of something that are different from the original *versions*
2 from time to time ....
3 have ....
4 in the place of ....
5 more than ....
6 not different, the same as before ....
7 person who translates ....
8 problems ....

6 **SPEAKING What about *you*?**

1 Do you have any Harry Potter books or DVDs? What do you think of them?
2 Do you prefer reading books or watching films in the original version or in your own language? Why?

I've got the first three Harry Potter books and the first DVD. I love Harry Potter!

GRAMMAR GUIDE

Some, any, much, many, a lot of, a few, a little

1a Find these words in the text on page 33. Are they countable or uncountable?

1 book 2 day 3 time 4 shop 5 money 6 mistake

1b Look at these sentences. The words in bold all express quantity. Then answer questions a–e about the words.

1 The Harry Potter books presented **some** special difficulties.
2 They needed **some** time to do the job well.
3 They do not contain **any** lines from the original text.
4 Did the author receive **any** money from these books?
5 There were not **many** mistakes in the official translations.
6 There was not **much** time.
7 There are **a lot of** invented words.
8 They didn't have **a lot of** time.
9 He added **a few** informal messages into the text.
10 They had **a little** time to check their work, but not much.

a Which words do we use with uncountable nouns?
some, any, much, a lot of, a little
b Which words do we use with plural countable nouns?
c Which words often appear in negative sentences and questions?
d Which words do we use to talk about large quantities?
e Which words do we use to talk about small quantities?

GRAMMAR REFERENCE ▸ page 42

2a Complete the dialogue with *some* or *any*.

JAMIE: Alex, I'm going shopping this afternoon. What do we need to get? Have we got **(a)** .... **bananas**?
ALEX: Yeah, we've got **(b)** .... **bananas** but we haven't got **(c)** .... **tomatoes** or **potatoes**.
JAMIE: What about **sugar**? Have we got **(d)** .... **sugar**?
ALEX: No, we haven't got **(e)** .... **sugar**, but we have got **(f)** .... **chocolate**. And we need to get **(g)** .... **biscuits** too.
JAMIE: OK. Listen. I think I'll get **(h)** .... **hamburgers** for dinner tonight.
ALEX: Good idea. In that case, get **(i)** .... **tomato ketchup** too. We haven't got **(j)** .... at the moment. And get **(k)** .... **yoghurt** for dessert!

2b All the words in bold are types of food, but they all have something else in common. Can you guess what it is?

3 Choose the correct alternative.

Nobody knows exactly how **(a)** much/many words there are in total in the English language but there are **(b)** a lot/a lot of. One reason why there are so **(c)** many/much is that English takes words from **(d)** much/many other languages. Look at the words for food in exercise 2a for example. There may be **(e)** a few/a little words there that come from your language. **(f)** Some/Any of the words come from South America – potato, tomato and chocolate. There aren't **(g)** any/many words from Chinese in the English language, but ketchup is one of them. Originally, ketchup was the name for a type of fish sauce in China. Teenagers in Britain don't eat **(h)** many/much fish sauce but they do eat **(i)** lots/lots of hamburgers. There is **(j)** some/any confusion about the origin of the word hamburger but **(k)** a lot of/much people think that it comes from German. Because Britain and France are neighbours it is normal that there are **(l)** a few/a lot of French words in English – hundreds in fact. Biscuit is just one example. On the other hand, **(m)** a lot of/many fruit travels a long way to get to Britain. That explains why the word banana comes from an African language. There are also **(n)** a few/a little words from Turkish, like yoghurt. And, finally, if you ask for **(o)** a few/a little sugar in your coffee, you're using two Arabic words. Just by being in an English kitchen you can travel to **(p)** much/many countries!

4 **Work with a partner. Complete these sentences about your language. Use these words and phrases for ideas. You may complete each sentence with two or three different ideas.**

English/French/German/Russian words prepositions phrasal verbs irregular past forms prefixes present tenses words beginning with z words with more than 12 letters

1 There are some *French words and some German words*.
2 There are a lot of ________.
3 There aren't any ________.
4 There aren't many ________.
5 There are a few ________.

5a SPEAKING **Work individually. Look at the photos and choose a country. Make notes about things that there are or aren't in this country. Use these ideas.**

animals bicycles food fruit modern/old buildings monuments mountains offices people snow tourism trees water

5b SPEAKING **Work in pairs. You need to discover your partner's country by asking questions with *any, much, many, a lot of, a few, a little*. Your partner can only answer 'Yes' or 'No'.**

Is there any snow there?

Yes, there is.

Is there a lot of snow?

No, there isn't.

Do many people live there?

No, only a few people live there.

Negative prefixes *un-, in-, im-, ir-, il-*

1 **Look at these words. What do they have in common? What is the opposite of each word?**

illegal impossible incorrect informal invisible irregular unhappy unusual

2 **Choose the correct alternative.**

1 Many common English verbs, such as *go, do* and *make*, have a regular/an irregular past form.
2 Authors aren't usually happy/unhappy about pirate versions of their books.
3 'A books' is correct/incorrect English.
4 You couldn't see the words. They were visible/invisible.
5 'Dear Sir or Madam' is a formal/informal expression.
6 It is legal/illegal to sell pirate copies of books or CDs in shops.
7 It is possible/impossible to translate a long book in two days.

3a PRONUNCIATION 1.19 **Listen to these two dialogues. How is the pronunciation of the word *irregular* different in the two dialogues? Why is this?**

3b **Practise saying the words in 1. Say the words with normal stress and then say them with stress on the negative prefix.**

3c **Listen, check and repeat.**

4a SPEAKING **Work with a partner. Write mini-dialogues similar to the second dialogue in 3a.**

It's possible to go up Mount Everest in a day.

No, it isn't. It's impossible!

4b **Practise saying the dialogues. Stress the negative prefix.**

Click onto... Very different languages

International cultural knowledge

English as an international language

1 Work with a partner and discuss these questions.

1 What do you think the countries marked on the map have in common?
2 In the text you are going to read, they call English 'the world's language'. Why do you think they call it this?

2 Read the text. Do any of your ideas from exercise 1, question 2 appear?

INSIDE INFORMATION

- Bill Bryson is an American writer who is very popular in Britain.
- His books include travel books (*Notes from a Small Island* is about Britain), biographies (*Shakespeare: The World as Stage*) and science (*A Short History of Nearly Everything*).

How many people speak English in the world? This is a difficult question because so many people speak it in so many different countries and situations. David Graddol is a British linguist who wrote a study about English called *English Next*. Graddol says that there are approximately 450 million native English speakers around the world, in about 70 countries. Just to compare that with other languages, some people calculate that there are 885 million native speakers of Mandarin Chinese. But in the case of Mandarin Chinese people do not generally speak it outside China. This means that, at the moment, it is not really a world language in the same way as English. As David Graddol tells us, there are probably a billion people learning English as their second language. China alone produces over 20 million English speakers a year! Now the English language does not just belong to the English – as Bill Bryson shows in the text below, it belongs to the whole world.

The world's language

'Already Germans talk about *ein Image Problem* and *das Cash-Flow*, Italians program their computers with *il software*, French motorists going away for a weekend break pause for fewer *fuelling stops*, Poles watch *telewizja*, Spaniards have a *flirt*, Austrians eat *Big Mäcs*, and the Japanese go on a *pikkunikku*. For better or worse, English has become the most global of languages, the lingua franca of business, science, education, politics, and pop music. For the airlines of 157 countries (out of 168 in the world), it is the agreed international language of discourse. In India there are more than 3,000 newspapers in English. ... When Volkswagen set up a factory in Shanghai it found that there were too few Germans who spoke Chinese and too few Chinese who spoke German, so now Volkswagen's German engineers and Chinese managers communicate in a language that is alien to both of them, English. Belgium has two languages, French and Flemish, yet on a recent visit to the country's main airport in Brussels, I counted more than fifty posters and signs and not one of them was in French or Flemish. They were all in English.'

3 Now write the line numbers where you can find this information about English.

1 Many people are native speakers of English.
2 Many people are learning English as a second language.
3 Other languages often use English words.
4 Many companies and businesses use English.

4 Read the text again. Why do these words or numbers appear in the text?

1 pikkunikku	4 Volkswagen	7 450 million
2 weekend break	5 Brussels airport	8 three thousand
3 157	6 seventy	

1 Japanese people use this word but it's really the English word 'picnic'.

5 What about *you*?

1 Did any of the information about English surprise you? Why?
2 How important do you think it is in your country to learn English? Why?

I didn't know that they use English words in Japanese.

Me neither.

WORD BOOSTER

Match the words and definitions.

1 native speaker	a spoken or written language
2 belongs to	b somebody who speaks a language from birth
3 airline	c began, created
4 discourse	d British Airways, Lufthansa, Iberia, etc.
5 set up	e is part of something
6 factory	f unusual, from a different culture
7 alien	g building where people make or produce things

Cross-curricular – Language
A language with no numbers

6 **Look at the photo of the Pirahã tribe. What language do you think they speak? Do you think they have many words or not? What words do you think are important for them?**

7 **1.20 Look at these notes about the Pirahãs. Listen to a radio programme about them and fill in the missing information.**

The Pirahã tribe

Live in 1 .... 2 .... people speak the Pirahã language. Have 3 .... or 4 .... different sounds. Difference between men and women because men use 5 .... sounds. Count using the words one, 6 .... and 7 .... only. Counting is 8 .... for them. The Pirahã 9 .... stories. The Pirahã only have 10 .... for family members. Pirahã language is simple because 11 ....

Popular culture
Learning to speak Klingon

LEARNING TO SPEAK KLINGON

The Klingons are an alien race. They first appeared in the science fiction TV series Star Trek. The Klingons love violence and war. And they have their own language.

The inventor of the Klingon language was Mark Okrand. Okrand has a PhD in linguistics. He began working on Star Trek in 1982. A friend of a friend told him that they were looking for a linguist to write a short dialogue in Vulcan (the language of the famous character Mr Spock). Okrand wrote the dialogue and enjoyed it. Two years later they asked him to write a few words for some scenes in Klingon. This time he didn't just write words, he invented a complete grammar. This grammar has some familiar and some unfamiliar elements. One unusual thing is the word order.

Over 300,000 people bought The Klingon Dictionary, written by Okrand. But there are probably only 2,000 people in the world who can speak Klingon. Many of these people only know a word or two. But some invent poems and stories or write translations, including translations of Shakespeare.

But it's one thing to write Klingon, and it's another thing to speak it. There are only 20 or 30 people who can have a conversation in Klingon. There is an annual Klingon conference and it is one of the few places where people can have these conversations. I went to one of their conferences in 2007.

On the first afternoon of the conference, I saw a small group of people around a table. They were talking in Klingon, slowly, and using dictionaries a lot, but they were communicating. I sat and listened. I was happy when, at last, I understood my first spoken Klingon sentence: Ha'DibaHvISopbe' ('Animal I it eat not'= I'm a vegetarian).

Later at the conference, I met two people who were chatting in Klingon. They were Captain Krankor and his girlfriend Agnieszka. When he is wearing his Klingon costume, Krankor only speaks Klingon. He travels with a guitar and sings Klingon translations of The Beatles and The Rolling Stones!

Arika Okrent

8 **You are going to read about a language called Klingon. Before you read, work with a partner. What would you like to know about this language? Write four questions.**

How many people can speak Klingon?
Where can you learn it?

9 **Read the text. Does it answer any of your questions? What are the answers?**

10 **Read the text again and write questions for these answers.**

1 ....? In 1982.
2 ....? Over 300,000 people.
3 ....? About 2,000.
4 ....? Only twenty or thirty.
5 ....? At an annual conference.
6 ....? Ha'DibaHvISopbe'
7 ....? He only speaks Klingon.

1 When did Mark Okrand begin working on Star Trek?

11 **Who are these people?**

1 He was the inventor of the Klingon language.
2 His famous literary works exist in Klingon.
3 He speaks Klingon when he wears special clothes.
4 There are Klingon versions of their songs.
5 He speaks Vulcan.

WORD BOOSTER

Match the words and definitions.

1	alien	a	talking in a friendly way
2	violence	b	from another planet
3	familiar	c	use of physical force to attack others
4	annual	d	once a year
5	chatting	e	describes something that people know well

INSIDE INFORMATION

- The first *Star Trek* series appeared in 1966. The series was popular in many countries for many years.
- There are over ten *Star Trek* films. In 2009, the story of *Star Trek* began again with the eleventh film.
- *Star Trek* fans are mad about the films and series. They have a special name, *Trekkies* or *Trekkers*, and they have regular conventions.

Listening

1 **Work with a partner. Who are the people in these photos? What do you know about them or their films?**

a b c d

2 LISTENING 1.21 **Listen to four speakers. Match each speaker to an actor in 1. What is the connection between them?**

Speaker 1 .... Speaker 3 ....
Speaker 2 .... Speaker 4 ....

STUDY SKILLS

Is it necessary to understand every word when you listen to a text in English? Why/Why not? STUDY SKILLS page 146

3 **Listen again and match the speakers and the correct information. Two speakers have more than one answer.**

A worked on a video game.
B has a lot of competition to get work.
C wanted to act when she was small.
D doesn't imitate the actors that she dubs.
E is physically similar to the actor he dubs.
F worked very fast.
G doesn't want people to see her.
H doesn't usually speak fast.

Speaker	
1	
2	
3	
4	

Grammar in context

GRAMMAR GUIDE

Relative pronouns

1a **Look at these sentences.**

1 France is a place **where** they dub a lot of films.
2 I'm the person **who** does Angelina Jolie's films.
3 *Mission Impossible* is the film **which** made me famous in China.
4 I become the character (**that**) she plays.
5 That was the moment **when** I decided to become an actor.
6 That was the first film **that** became popular.
7 He's the actor **whose** films I like the most.

Which words in bold refer to:

a people? ...*who*... and ....
b things? .... and ....
c possessions? ....
d places? ....
e times? ....

1b **Look at sentences 4 and 6. Why is it possible to omit *that* in sentence 4, but not in sentence 6?**

GRAMMAR REFERENCE ▸ page 42

2 **Look at the relative pronouns in these sentences. In which sentences can you omit the relative pronoun?**

1 That's the film **that** I saw last week.
2 English is a language **which** millions of people speak.
3 Arnold Schwarzenegger is an actor **who** later became a politician.
4 The credits are a list of people **who** worked on a film or TV programme.
5 I'm sure she's the actress **that** appeared in *Fantastic Four*.
6 The first thing **that** I did was to switch on the TV.
7 That was the series **which** made him famous.
8 He never forgot the people **who** helped him at the start of his career.

> **EXAM SUCCESS**
>
> You are going to do a multiple-choice cloze activity. You have a text with gaps. You must fill in each gap with one of three or four words given. Why is it a good idea to read the complete text first, without thinking about the gaps? EXAM SUCCESS ▸ page 150

3 Read the text and fill in the gaps.

Poland is one country **(1)** ....*where*........ dubbing films is not popular. In Poland, actors don't copy the original, English-speaking actors. Instead there is just one speaker **(2)** .... simply reads all the original English dialogue in Polish. While you are listening to the speaker, you can also hear the original English version in the background. This is something **(3)** .... is very popular in Poland. It doesn't seem unusual to watch popular films and series and hear a middle-aged man reading the dialogue of a group of teenage girls. People have their favourite speakers **(4)** .... they like the quality of their voices. One popular speaker, **(5)** .... CV includes some big Hollywood films, says he has his own rule: 'Interpretation, yes; expression, no.' There is one thing **(6)** .... creates problems for speakers. Polish words are generally long, in comparison to English. And they have a **(7)** .... of consonants. Sometimes translators simplify and cut the dialogue because speakers need to read slowly. In 2001, a television channel used six different voices on a famous American comedy series. They wanted to see if dubbing could be popular. This experiment **(8)** .... work. They had a lot of phone calls from people who were very unhappy **(9)** .... they did this!

	A	B	C	D
1	which	where	whose	–
2	–	who	whose	does
3	who	can	what	which
4	but	which	because	why
5	whose	his	who	that
6	this	who	when	that
7	lot	lots	many	little
8	don't	wasn't	can't	didn't
9	who	where	when	which

4 Match the sentence halves using appropriate relative pronouns.

Mumbai, or Bombay, is the place where they make Bollywood films.

1 ~~Mumbai, or Bombay, is the place ...~~
2 Brad Pitt is the actor ...
3 Christmas and summer are times ...
4 J. R. R. Tolkien was the writer ...
5 *In Old California* (1910) was the first film ...
6 Spiderman and Batman are superheroes ...
7 Krzysztof Kieślowski was a Polish director ...

a a lot of new films appear in cinemas.
b made the film *Mr and Mrs Smith* with Angelina Jolie.
c became famous for his films *Red*, *White* and *Blue*.
d ~~they make Bollywood films.~~
e books became a series of very popular films.
f adventures became very successful films.
g was made in Hollywood.

5a SPEAKING Choose six words from the Vocabulary sections in Units 1–3. Write definitions of the words using *who, that, which, where, when, whose*.

5b Read your definitions to your partner. Can your partner identify the words?

It's a person who attacks you to take money or objects from you.

A mugger.

It's the stage of life when you're a child.

Childhood.

6 Complete these sentences with true information about you.

1 .... is a place where I'm usually happy.
2 .... is an object which is really important to me.
3 .... was a year when something special happened to me.
4 .... is a person who is special to me.
5 .... is a place where I want to go one day.
6 .... is a language that I want to learn.
7 .... is a film that I love.

7 SPEAKING Work with a partner. Compare your sentences in 6 and discuss your answers.

Home is a place where I'm usually happy.

Me too. But I wrote 'the swimming pool'. I go swimming every weekend. I love it.

1 SPEAKING **Work with a partner. Ask and answer the questions.**

1 Do you usually study English in the holidays?
2 Did you study English last summer?
3 If so, where did you study and what did you do?

2a SPEAKING **Look at this advert for a school that organises summer courses for students of English. Think about these questions and make a note of your answers.**

1 Do you think it's a good place to learn English in the summer? Why/Why not?
2 You want to do a summer course to practise English. What factors are important in deciding where to study?

Cardiff English Centre

Learn English in Wales!

Based in the heart of Cardiff, the Cardiff English Centre has been welcoming students to Wales for over 20 years. As a small school we are able to give students the personal care and attention they need to make the most of their stay and have fun while learning English. Why not contact us to find out more?

Daffodil House, 47 Town Road, Cardiff, Wales, CF1 OBE
Email: info@cardiffenglishcentre.com

2b **Work with a partner. Compare your answers.**

3 LISTENING 1.22 **Listen to a student asking for information about the Cardiff English Centre. Does he ask about any of the factors you thought of in 2?**

4 **Listen again and choose the correct alternative.**

Course begins: 10th June / 10th July / 12th July
Course lasts: one week / 10 days / two weeks
Accommodation: organised / not organised
Price: £815 / £860 / £950
Other activities include: excursions, discos, sailing

5 **Look at the useful expressions in the Speaking Bank. Read the dialogue in 6 and tick the expressions which appear in it.**

Speaking Bank

Useful expressions for checking understanding

- Sorry, did you say ... ?
- Could you repeat that?
- Pardon?
- I'm not sure I understood.

6 **Complete the dialogue with the correct information in 4.**

RECEPTIONIST: Good morning. This is the **(a)** .... English Centre. How can I help you?
STUDENT: Good morning. I'd like some information about your summer courses, please.
RECEPTIONIST: Yes, of course. We have a course for students between 14 and 17. It begins on **(b)** ....
STUDENT: Sorry, did you say **(c)** .... ?
RECEPTIONIST: Yes, that's right. The course lasts **(d)** ....
STUDENT: Do you organise accommodation?
RECEPTIONIST: **(e)** ...., we **(f)** ....
STUDENT: How much is the course?
RECEPTIONIST: The price of a **(g)** .... course is **(h)** ....
STUDENT: Could you repeat that?
RECEPTIONIST: Yes, I said the price is **(i)** ....
STUDENT: Does the price include other activities?
RECEPTIONIST: Yes, it does.
STUDENT: What other activities are there?
RECEPTIONIST: There are **(j)** ...., there are **(k)** ...., and there are sports activities, including **(l)** ....
STUDENT: Oh, that sounds interesting. Can you send me a registration form?
RECEPTIONIST: Yes, of course. Can you give me your name and address?
STUDENT: Yes, it's ...

7 SPEAKING **Practise the dialogue in 6 with your partner.**

Practice makes perfect

8a SPEAKING **Work with a partner. Do this role-play using the questions from 6 and the Speaking Bank to help you.**

You want to find out the following information about summer courses at a language school:
- the starting date of the course
- the length of the course
- if accommodation is organised or not
- the price
- other activities on the course

Student A: You are the receptionist at the Sydney English Centre. Look at page 159.

Student B: You want information about the Sydney English Centre.

8b **Now change roles.**

Student B: You are the receptionist at the San Francisco English Centre. Look at page 159.

Student A: You want information about the San Francisco English Centre.

EXAM SUCCESS

What do you need to do to get a good mark in a speaking exam? EXAM SUCCESS ▸ page 150

Developing writing *A language biography*

1 **A language biography is a text where you describe your experiences of learning a different language. Read this language biography written by a student of English. What similarities are there between her experiences and yours?**

We both started learning English at primary school.

My name is Alexandra Maslova and I'm 16 years old. I'm Russian and my mother-tongue is Russian. Apart from Russian, I can speak English. I started learning English when I was at primary school. I was seven years old. Primary school was where we listened to, and sang, a lot of songs in English. We also played games and read some stories. We didn't study a lot of grammar in primary school but we learnt a lot of vocabulary and we practised speaking. At the moment I'm studying English at secondary school. We study a lot of grammar and vocabulary, but we don't speak much. We study vocabulary by writing a list with new words and revising it. From time to time we do vocabulary tests. We don't do many translations in lessons, but we do lots of grammar exercises. Outside school I don't really speak much English. For homework, we often read special English readers which our teacher gives us. When we finish them, we usually write summaries. I listen to a lot of English because I love English and American music and I also watch DVDs in English. When I was thirteen I went to London for a holiday. When I was there I met some great people. I'd like to go somewhere else in the UK, to Oxford for example. I like learning English by doing activities and games in pairs. I make a few mistakes when I speak English, but I write the corrections down and revise them from time to time.

2 **The text in 1 is not divided into paragraphs. Read it again and mark where each new paragraph should begin. Use the plan below to help you. When you finish, read the information in the Writing Bank.**

Paragraph 1: basic personal information

Paragraph 2: language-learning experiences at primary school

Paragraph 3: language-learning experiences at secondary school

Paragraph 4: language-learning experiences outside school, including trips

Paragraph 5: how you prefer to learn a language

3 **Make notes for the paragraphs in 2 with information about yourself and your experiences of learning English.**

Writing Bank

Paragraphs

We use paragraphs to group similar ideas and information together and express them more clearly. When you write a text in English, brainstorm your ideas and then group those ideas into logical paragraphs.

4 Practice makes perfect

Write your own language biography using your notes in 3. Organise your information into five clear paragraphs.

Language reference and revision

Grammar reference

Countable and uncountable nouns

Book, **mistake**, **shop**, **euro** are all examples of countable nouns. We can count *books*, *mistakes*, *shops*, *euros* and so there is a singular and plural form. Some things, for example liquids, we cannot count and so we do not usually use a plural form. These are uncountable nouns. Other examples are **milk**, **money**, **bread**. Many words can be both countable and uncountable. It depends on the context.

Coffee is bad for you. (uncountable = in general)
Bring me two coffees. (countable = two cups of coffee)

I haven't got much time. (uncountable = in general)
I went there three times. (countable = on three occasions)

With uncountable nouns we can often make them countable by adding **a piece of** before the word.

advice, furniture, information, news (uncountable)

a piece of advice, a piece of furniture, a piece of information, a piece of news (countable)

Some, any, much, many, a lot (of), a few, a little

Use

We use **some** with uncountable nouns and with plural countable nouns, in affirmative sentences.
I've got some books. *We've got some free time.*

We use **any** with uncountable nouns and with plural countable nouns, in negative sentences and questions.
I haven't got any money. *Are there any books?*

We use **much, many, a lot (of)** to talk about big quantities. We often use **much** in negative sentences and questions, with uncountable nouns.
I haven't got much time. *Have you got much water?*

We often use **many** in negative sentences, with plural countable nouns.
I haven't got many books. *Have you got many books?*

We use **a lot of** in affirmative and negative sentences and in questions, with countable and uncountable nouns.
I've got/I haven't got a lot of time/books.
Have you got a lot of time/books?

We use **of** when **a lot** comes before a noun. But when there is no noun after **a lot** we do not use **of**.
Have you got any water? Yes, I've got a lot.

A lot of and **lots of** are the same.
I've got a lot of time. = I've got lots of time.

We use **a few** and **a little** to talk about small quantities.
We use **a few** with plural countable nouns.
There are only a few problems.

We use **a little** with uncountable nouns.
We've only got a little time.

Relative pronouns

Use

We use relative pronouns to give information about the person, thing, place or time in the first half of the sentence.

J. R. R. Tolkien is the person who/that wrote The Lord of the Rings.
That's the book which/that he translated.
That's the actor whose film I saw yesterday.
Liverpool is the place where I was born.
Sunday is the day when I go for a run with my friends.

We use **who** and **that** for people, **which** and **that** for things, **whose** for possessions, **where** for places, and **when** for times.

We can omit **who**, **which**, or **that** when a noun or pronoun comes immediately after. **Who**, **which**, or **that** are the object of the second half of the sentence.

That's the film that I saw. = That's the film I saw.
She's the actress that my brother likes. = She's the actress my brother likes.

but

That's the film that was popular.
She's the actress that made the film.

Vocabulary

1 Countries, nationalities, languages

Countries: Argentina Austria Brazil Egypt Japan The Netherlands Poland Russia Switzerland Wales

Nationalities: Argentinian Austrian Brazilian Dutch Egyptian Japanese Polish Russian Swiss Welsh

Languages: Dutch English French German Italian Japanese Polish Romansh Russian Spanish Welsh

2 Learning a language

do/study English
do/write an essay
do/take an exam do an exercise
do homework make a mistake
memorise memorisation
practice (n.) practise (v.) revise
revision student study
translate translation

3 Negative prefixes

unhappy **un**official **un**usual
incorrect **in**formal **in**visible
impossible **il**legal **ir**regular

4 Other words and phrases

page 138–9

▶ Grammar revision

Some, any, much, many, a lot (of), a few, a little

1 Complete the sentences with *some, any, much, many, a lot (of), a few,* or *a little*.

1 I haven't got many English magazines, only ....
2 We haven't got .... information about this country – nothing at all.
3 It didn't rain last summer so there was only .... water in the river.
4 I haven't got .... money, just five euros.
5 A: Were there .... people at the concert?
B: Yes, thousands.
6 We haven't got .... time before the train leaves, only five minutes.
7 He gave me .... good advice.
8 There were only .... people at her party, four or five I think.

WORKBOOK ▶ page 22

/8 points

Relative pronouns

2 Join the two sentences to make one sentence. Use *who, which, that, whose, where,* or *when*.

The Coen brothers are film directors. Their films often win prizes. *The Coen brothers are film directors whose films often win prizes.*

1 Jerzy Dudek is a football player. He speaks Polish and English.
....
2 Woolton, in Liverpool, is a beautiful place. My grandparents live there.
....
3 Last year was a special year. Many important things happened that year.
....
4 That's the teacher. Her classes are brilliant.
....
5 This is a great book. They want to make it into a film.
....
6 Pirahã is an interesting language. Only 200 people speak it.
....
7 Sergei Lukyanenko is a Russian author. He writes fantasy novels.
....
8 We go to the cinema on Wednesdays. There's a special price on Wednesdays.
....

WORKBOOK ▶ page 25

/8 points

▶ Vocabulary revision

Learning a language

1 Complete the sentences with these words. You need to use one word twice.

do exercise make practice practise revision translation

1 Yesterday we wrote a .... of an English poem into Polish.
2 Before the exam, he did some .... by having a quick look at his notes.
3 Anybody can .... a mistake.
4 Yesterday's exam was just a .... , it wasn't the real one.
5 Did you .... the exercises yesterday?
6 This is the fourth .... on this page.
7 You have to .... regularly to speak English well.
8 At our school we .... English and German.

WORKBOOK ▶ page 20

/8 points

Countries, nationalities and languages

2 Complete the sentences with the correct country, nationality or language.

1 Dutch people are from ....
2 In Argentina they speak ....
3 People in Wales speak English and ....
4 Swiss people are from ....
5 Austrians speak ....
6 .... people are from Poland.
7 People from Egypt speak ....
8 People from Egypt are ....

WORKBOOK ▶ page 20

/8 points

Negative prefixes

3 Complete the words.

1 sad = un_ _ _ _ _
2 wrong, with a mistake = in_ _ _ _ _ _ _
3 not following the usual rules, e.g. *go – went* = ir _ _ _ _ _ _ _
4 criminal = il _ _ _ _ _
5 you cannot do it = im _ _ _ _ _ _ _ _
6 relaxed and friendly, casual = in _ _ _ _ _ _
7 you cannot see it = in _ _ _ _ _ _ _
8 strange = un _ _ _ _ _

WORKBOOK ▶ page 23

/8 points

Total /40 points

4 Fit and well

Grammar
- Present perfect with *ever, never, for, since, just, yet, already*
- Present perfect and past simple

Vocabulary
- Parts of the body
- Health problems and illnesses
- Compound nouns connected with health and medicine

Speaking
- Describing a scene

Writing
- Notes and messages

Vocabulary

Parts of the body

1 **Work with a partner and put these words in the correct place in the photo.**

arm back chest ear elbow finger
foot hand head knee leg neck
nose stomach throat toe tooth

2 1.23/4 **Listen, check and repeat.**

Health problems and illnesses

3 **Work with a partner. Complete each phrase with three parts of the body.**

1 I've got a broken .... / .... / ....
2 Have you got a/an .... / .... / .... ache?
3 My .... / .... / .... hurts.

4 **Complete the texts with the correct form of these words. Use a dictionary if necessary.**

cough flu pain sore temperature virus

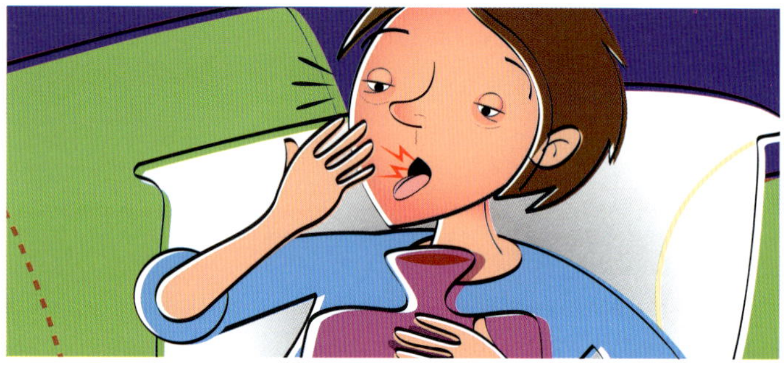

Karen isn't very well at the moment. She's got a very bad cold, or perhaps it's **(a)** .... She **(b)** .... all the time and so now she has a **(c)** .... throat.

Pete has a very high **(d)** .... , 39.5°C. He's got **(e)** .... in his arms and legs. Perhaps it's a **(f)** .... because a lot of people are ill at school at the moment.

5 LISTENING 1.25 **Listen to four people. What health problem does each one have?**

Speaker 1 .... Speaker 3 ....
Speaker 2 .... Speaker 4 ....

6 SPEAKING **Work in small groups. Each person mimes an illness. The rest of the group guesses what it is.**

STUDY SKILLS

To learn vocabulary, it is essential to keep a record of new words. Do you do this? How do you organise the words?

STUDY SKILLS ▸ page 147

1 Work with a partner. Ask and answer these questions.

1. How often do you catch a cold? What do you take to stop a cold?
2. What do you think is good advice for somebody with a stomach virus?
3. Do you know any unusual ways to stop a cold?
4. Do you sometimes feel sick when you travel by car, plane or ship?

2 Read these newspaper articles. Match each question in 1 with one of the three articles.

1 ...c... 3 ....

2 .... 4 ....

GOOD HEALTH Tuesday, July 24, 2010

HEALTH WATCH *This week's news*

a

SEASICK ON DRY LAND

Have you ever been on a boat or a ship? If you have, you probably know about seasickness, that terrible feeling caused by going up and down non-stop on the sea. But imagine feeling seasick when you're not at sea. Mrs Jane Houghton has been seasick for the last four years. She was at sea for three days. When she got off the boat, she started to feel seasick and she has never recovered. One unusual thing about her illness is that she only feels OK when she is moving in a car, boat or aeroplane. It's difficult for Mrs Houghton to work because when she sits at her computer she feels terrible. Mrs Houghton has created a website with information about her illness. She wants people to know about it. Perhaps one day doctors will find a cure.

b

STAY AT HOME

A large number of people have a stomach virus called the norovirus at the moment. This virus can cause stomach ache, high temperatures and pains in your arms and legs. Doctors have told patients to stay at home for two days after the illness has gone. Professor Steve Field says: 'We recommend that patients stay at home, take paracetamol and drink lots of water. It is also important that they wash their hands regularly.' The Health Protection Agency has said that this year there are twice as many people with the virus as last year. There are between 600,000 and one million cases of norovirus in the UK each year.

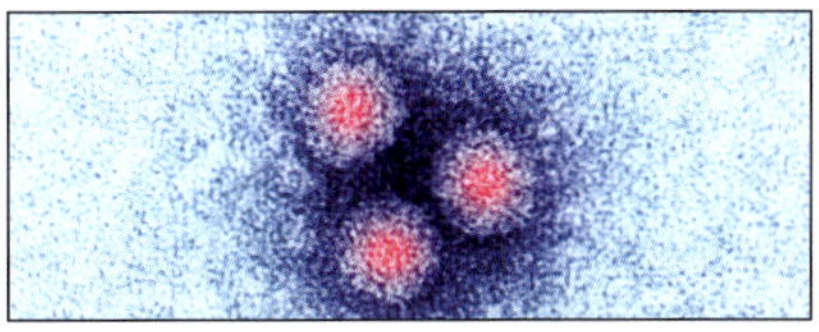

c

Letter of the week

ANSWERED BY DR LUCY SMITH

Dear Lucy,

I've had a bad cold for over a week. I'm taking medicine but it doesn't do anything. My mum says that chicken soup can help me. Is she mad?

Sarah Johnson

Dr Lucy Smith answers: 'Your mother's cure for a cold is what we call an "old wives' remedy". A lot of people think that it's a mad idea with no scientific basis. But a new study has shown that many of these "old wives' remedies" do work. And scientists have found out that chicken soup is a great cure for a cold. All kinds of hot soup can help to get rid of a sore throat. And hot soup also helps to kill viruses quickly. So relax, your mum isn't mad!'

EXAM SUCCESS

You are going to do a matching activity for this reading text. In this type of activity, you say which text or part of a text contains a specific piece of information. What do you think is a good way to do this type of exercise?

EXAM SUCCESS ▸ page 151

3 Which article ...

1. talks about an old, traditional cure for an illness? ....
2. recommends taking a type of drug? ....
3. mentions one person with problems at work? ....
4. mentions a recent discovery in the world of medicine? ....
5. talks about the usual number of people who suffer a specific illness? ....
6. talks about an unusual illness? ....
7. gives information to help one person? ....
8. mentions personal hygiene? ....

4 Match the underlined words in the text with their definitions.

1. something that stops a pain or illness ....
2. take away/stop something bad ....
3. felt normal or good again after an illness ....
4. stupid, silly ....
5. frequently ....
6. two times more, double the quantity ....
7. left, got back to the land ....

5 SPEAKING What about *you*?

How serious do you think the different health problems are? Why?

I think the first problem is really very serious because she can never sit and relax.

GRAMMAR GUIDE

Present perfect with ever and never

1a Look at these sentences and match them to the explanation of their uses in a–c.

1 Have you ever been on a boat or a ship?
2 I've had a bad cold for a week.
3 She has created a website with information.

a an experience or experiences which happened at an unspecified moment in the past
b a past action which has a result in the present
c a situation that started in the past and continues to the present

1b Complete the rule.

We make the present perfect with the present simple of **have** + the .... of the main verb.

1c Complete the sentences with the present perfect forms of *see* and *visit*.

Affirmative: He .... the doctor.
Negative: He .... the doctor.
Question: .... he .... the doctor?

1d Look at these sentences and choose the correct alternative.

1 Have you *ever/never* caught a cold?
2 I've *ever/never* been seriously ill.

1e Choose the correct alternative.

1 *Ever/never* means at any time in your life.
2 *Ever/never* means at no time in your life.
3 **Ever** and **never** go just *after/before* the past participle.

GRAMMAR REFERENCE ▸ page 54

2 Complete the sentences with the present perfect.

1 I *have decided* (decide) to study medicine at university.
2 My friend .... (meet) a famous doctor.
3 We .... (do) a project about the history of medicine at school.
4 My mum .... (not buy) any headache tablets.
5 I .... (not see) the doctor this year.
6 .... Dad .... (go) to the hospital?

3 Complete the sentences adding *ever* or *never* in the correct place.

1 Have you had hot soup to stop a cold?
2 I've felt sick in a car.
3 She's taken antibiotics.
4 Has your dad seen an accident?
5 Sam and I have written a story about doctors.
6 Have you been in a plane?

4 Write questions to ask your partner.

catch a cold? → *Have you ever caught a cold?*

1 stay in bed because of flu?
....
2 have a very high temperature?
....
3 sleep in a hospital?
....
4 be on a ship?
....
5 take medicine that tastes really bad?
....
6 visit a friend in hospital?
....
7 break your arm?
....
8 watch a hospital drama?
....

5a SPEAKING Work with a partner. Ask and answer the questions in 4.

5b When you finish, tell a different student about your partner.

Adam has never stayed in bed because of flu, but he has broken his arm.

GRAMMAR GUIDE

Present perfect with *for* and *since*

6a Look at these sentences.

1 She has been seasick **for** the last four years.
2 I've had a bad cold **since** last Friday.

We use **for** and **since** with the present perfect to talk about things that started in the past and continue in the present. When do we use **for** and when do we use **since**?

6b Look at this question and answer.

How long have you known Andy?
For ten months.

Do we use **How long** to ask about frequency or duration?

GRAMMAR REFERENCE ▸ page 54

7 Put these time expressions in the correct column.

6 o'clock 7th February 2002 an hour Friday ten seconds the age of five the day I met you three days ~~twenty minutes~~

for	since
twenty minutes	

8 Complete the sentences with information about you. Use the correct form of the present perfect and a time expression.

I *have been* (be) at this school since *I was twelve*.

1 I .... (know) my English teacher for ....
2 I .... (have) short/long hair for ....
3 I .... (live) in this area since ....
4 I .... (have) this watch for ....
5 I .... (wear) jeans since ....
6 I .... (be) able to swim since ....
7 I .... (live) in my home for ....

9a SPEAKING **Guess your partner's answers in 8 and write them down.**

9b Ask your partner questions to find out if you were right.

How long have you been at this school?

I've been here for just one year.

Compound nouns connected with health and medicine

1 We make compound nouns by joining two nouns or an adjective and a noun. Join words from column A and column B to make compound nouns, then match them with the correct definitions. Use your dictionary if necessary.

A	B
1 pain	aid
2 heart	room
3 health	centre
4 waiting	killer
5 food	attack
6 first	poisoning

	Definition
☐ a	a place where people wait, for example, to see a doctor
1 b	a medicine that reduces pain
☐ c	basic medical help that you give to someone when they have an accident
☐ d	a building where people can go to see a doctor or nurse
☐ e	when somebody has a lot of pain in their chest and their heart stops working
☐ f	an illness you get from eating food which is in bad condition

2 1.26 **Listen and check your answers.**

3a PRONUNCIATION 1.27 **Listen again to the pronunciation of the compound nouns in 1. Where is the stress in words 1–5? Is it on the first word or the second word? And in 6?**

3b Practise saying the words with the correct stress.

4 Complete the sentences with the compound nouns in 1.

1 When I'm ill I go to the .... near my house.
2 Please take a seat in the .... The doctor will see you in ten minutes.
3 Salmonella is a type of ....
4 My neighbour has died of a .... He never did any exercise and he had a very bad diet.
5 I want to learn .... so that I know what to do if there's an emergency.
6 A: My back really hurts.
B: Why don't you take a .... ?

Click onto... Famous doctors

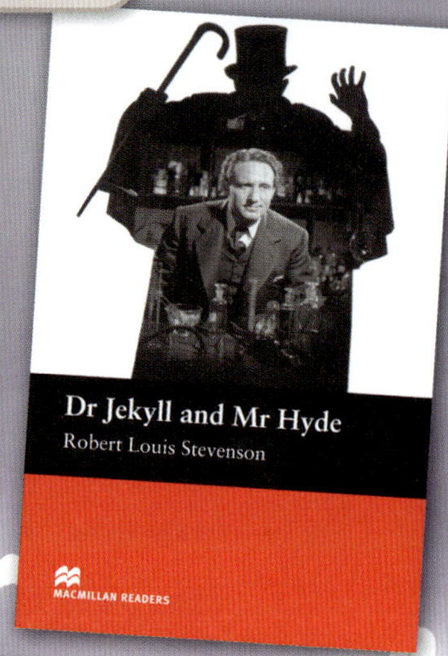

Literature

Dr Jekyll and Mr Hyde and *Frankenstein*

1 Work with a partner and discuss these questions.

1 Have you ever read these books or seen films based on them?
2 Who was Frankenstein? What did he do?
3 Who was Dr Jekyll? What did he do?

2 Here are the endings of the two books. Which is the ending of *Frankenstein*? Which is the ending of *Dr Jekyll and Mr Hyde*? Underline words or information that help you to decide.

A

You know that I have spent many months in my laboratory. I'm sure you want to know about my work. What have I studied? What have I learnt? I have studied many drugs and chemicals, seeing their effect on the body and mind.

There is both good and evil in all of us. The mind has both a dark and a light side. I have tried to use chemicals to separate these two parts. I wanted to separate the dark, evil part of my mind from the good, light part. And I have succeeded.

I tried many drugs and almost killed myself. At last I made the right one but I wasn't sure. I had to try it. Late one night in my laboratory I drank the bright green liquid. I waited for a moment, then the drug began to work on my body. There was a terrible pain in my chest and after that I fell and lay on the floor for some time.

When at last I stood up, I felt different. There was no pain. I felt young and strong again. There is a mirror in the laboratory. I went to the mirror and saw that my face was different. This different man is a monster, the bad part of me. I cannot control him any longer. He takes over my body and uses it, thinking only of cruelty and murder. Only one drug can control him, a drug which I bought from Mr Maw the chemist's. But there was something unusual about Mr Maw's chemical and now he has no more. This is the last letter I am writing as a normal human being. Soon the monster inside me will come again and take over my body and my mind. I have locked myself in my laboratory. There is only one solution – poison. By killing myself I will also kill the monster.

Goodbye.

B

I have followed the Monster through forests and across deserts. At last we have reached this place of ice and snow. The cold is terrible, but the Monster feels nothing. He does not feel cold or heat. Now the journey has ended. The Monster is ready to stand and fight. He is big and strong, but I have my gun. I will be able to kill him before he kills me.

'Do not kill me yet,' the Monster cried. 'Listen to what I have to say.'

'What can you say to me?' I replied. 'You have destroyed everything I loved. You are a thing of evil, a wicked creature.'

'You made me,' the Monster replied. 'I did not wish to be evil. I wanted to be your friend. But you made me ugly and you ran away from me. I asked you to create a friend for me but you destroyed her. I had no family to love, so I destroyed yours. It is your fault.'

As I listened to the Monster's words, my mind was filled with horror.

'What you say is true,' I cried. 'I was the murderer of those I loved!'

'Now that you have said these words, my life of misery and unhappiness is complete,' said the Monster sadly. 'You are the guilty one, not me. Now I shall go far away from this place to my death.'

And with one last look at me, the Monster turned and went.

I have decided to die in this terrible place. The story of my life has ended. Here I will stay until my body is hard and cold. Goodbye, and may God forgive me.

INSIDE INFORMATION

- *Dr Jekyll and Mr Hyde* was written by Robert Louis Stevenson in 1886. Stevenson also wrote the popular novel *Treasure Island*.
- Robert Louis Stevenson was born in Scotland. He was often ill but he enjoyed travelling and adventure. He visited places such as Hawaii and Honolulu and he died in Samoa.
- *Frankenstein* was written by the British author Mary Shelley. She was 19 when she wrote it. It was published in 1818.
- *Frankenstein* is the name of a doctor who wants to create life. Shelley had the idea for her story when a group of writers spent a rainy night reading ghost stories. That night they decided to have a competition to write their own horror stories.

WORD BOOSTER

Match the words and definitions.

1	evil, wicked	a	take control of
2	take over	b	substance that can kill you
3	reach	c	close something with a key
4	poison	d	very bad, with bad intentions
5	lock	e	arrive at
6	destroy	f	break, ruin
7	misery	g	'You are the one who did this bad thing.'
8	'It is your fault.'/ 'You are the guilty one.'	h	state of being very unhappy

3 Read the extracts again and answer the questions.

Frankenstein

1 What effect does the weather have on Frankenstein? And on the Monster? Why?
2 Why is the Monster angry with Frankenstein?
3 What happens to the Monster at the end of the story?
4 What happens to Frankenstein at the end of the story?

Dr Jekyll and Mr Hyde

5 What was the purpose of Dr Jekyll's experiment?
6 What happened when Dr Jekyll drank the bright green liquid?
7 Why can't Dr Jekyll control Mr Hyde now?
8 How does Dr Jekyll beat Mr Hyde at the end of the novel?

4 Complete these sentences about the stories in an appropriate way.

1 Both stories are about ....
2 In both stories, science ....
3 One similarity/difference between the stories is that ....
4 The narrator in each story is ....
5 When the narrator tells the story in the first person (I), it usually makes the story ....

5 What about *you*?

1 Which of the two stories do you prefer? Why?
2 Imagine they are making new films of these two books. Choose good actors to play the parts of Dr Jekyll/Mr Hyde, Frankenstein, and Frankenstein's monster. Explain your choices.

I prefer Frankenstein because I think the monster is a really interesting character.

He's frightening, but really he's a good person.

Popular culture

'How to save a life' by The Fray

6 1.28 Listen to the song and put the verses in the correct order.

7 What about *you*?

What do you think of the song?

I love the music.

Me too, and I like the singer's voice. It's a really emotional song.

☐

Step one, you say we need to talk
He walks, you say 'Sit down, it's just a talk'
He smiles politely back at you
You stare politely right on through

☐ CHORUS

Where did I go wrong? I lost a friend
Somewhere along in the bitterness
And I would have stayed up with you all night
Had I known how to save a life

☐

As he begins to raise his voice
You lower yours and grant him one last choice
Drive until you lose the road
Or break with the ones you've followed

☐

Some sort of window to your right
As he goes left and you stay right
Between the lines of fear and blame
You begin to wonder why you came

☐

Lay down a list of what is wrong
The things you've told him all along
And pray to God he hears you
And pray to God he hears you

☐

Let him know that you know best
'Cause, after all, you do know best
Try to slip past his defence
Without granting innocence

☐

He will do one of two things
He will admit to everything
Or he'll say he's just not the same
And you'll begin to wonder why you came

WORD BOOSTER

Match the words and definitions.

1 stare	a pass quickly
2 blame	b ask yourself
3 wonder	c let somebody have something
4 bitterness	d speak loudly, shout
5 slip past	e speak quietly
6 grant	f responsibility for doing something bad
7 raise your voice	g feeling of anger and unhappiness because of a bad experience
8 lower your voice	h look at something or someone for a long time

INSIDE INFORMATION

- *The Fray* are from the USA. This song was number one for a long time in many different countries.
- The song appeared in the TV hospital drama *Grey's Anatomy* and was used to promote the series. It became the unofficial theme tune.
- The song is about the singer's experiences working at a centre for adolescents with problems.

Listening

1 **Look at the pictures. They are all of the same person. Work with a partner. What can you see in each picture?**

a

b

c

d

2 LISTENING 1.29 **Listen to an interview with the person in the pictures. Put the pictures in the order that you hear the person mention them.**

3 **Listen again. Are the sentences true (T) or false (F)? Correct the false sentences.**

1 People have a special name for Steve because of his accidents. T/F
2 Steve has had 15 accidents in total. T/F
3 Steve hasn't had an accident for a long time. T/F
4 Steve was working when he had his last accident. T/F
5 On Friday 13th one year Steve had two accidents. T/F
6 Steve and his family are worried about his accidents. T/F

4 SPEAKING **What about *you*?**
What do you think of Steve's story? Why?

I think it's sad because he has lots of accidents.

Grammar in context

GRAMMAR GUIDE

Present perfect with just, yet, already

1a **Look at these sentences and complete rules 1–3 with *just, yet* or *already*.**

a I **'ve** just **had** an accident.
b He**'s** already **had** a lot of serious accidents.
c I **haven't hurt** myself badly yet.
d **Has** he **broken** his leg yet?

1 We use the present perfect with .... to talk about very recent events.
2 We use .... to talk about something that has not happened, but we think it is going to happen soon.
3 We use .... to talk about something that has happened, possibly before we expected.

1b **Choose the correct alternative.**

1 We use **yet** in *affirmative/negative* sentences and questions.
2 **Yet** usually goes at the end of the sentence, but **already** and **just** usually go *after/before* the past participle.

GRAMMAR REFERENCE ▶ page 54

2 **What do you think has just happened in these pictures? Write sentences.**

1

He's just hurt himself.
He's just had an accident.
He's just fallen.

2

....
....

3

....
....

4

....

....

5

....

....

3a SPEAKING **Write six sentences about yourself, two with *already*, two with *yet*, and two with *just*.**

I've already done my history homework.

3b **Change your sentences into questions to ask your partner.**

Have you already done your history homework?

3c **Interview your partner with your questions.**

GRAMMAR GUIDE

Present perfect and past simple

4 Look at this part of a dialogue and then answer questions 1–4.

PRESENTER: Have you ever had two accidents at the same time?

STEVE: Yes, I have.

PRESENTER: What happened?

STEVE: It was when I was a boy. I fell off a horse and a car hit me.

1 Is the presenter's first question in the past simple or the present perfect?

2 Does the question ask about general experience or a specific moment in the past?

3 Is the presenter's second question in the past simple or the present perfect?

4 Does the question ask about general experience or a specific moment in the past?

5 Complete the dialogue by putting the verbs in the present perfect or past simple.

ALAN: **(a)** .... you ever .... (break) your leg?

DAVE: Yes, I **(b)** .... Two years ago I **(c)** .... (go) skiing and I **(d)** .... (break) my left leg.

ALAN: I **(e)** .... never .... (break) my leg but I **(f)** .... (have) some bad accidents in the past. For example, I **(g)** .... (crash) my bike at least five times.

DAVE: **(h)** .... you .... (fall) off your bike last week?

ALAN: No, I **(i)** .... Last week I **(j)** .... (ride) a horse and I **(k)** .... (fall) off!

6 SPEAKING **Ask your partner if they have ever done these things. Ask follow-up questions in the past simple to find out details of their experiences.**

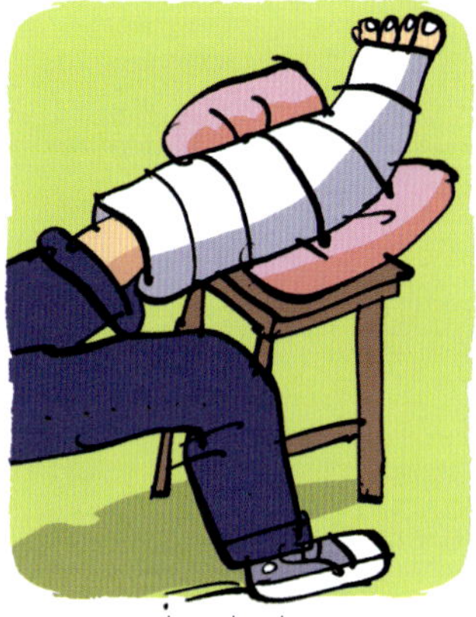

break a leg

eat insects

meet a famous person

visit Britain

Have you ever broken your leg?

Yes, I have.

Where were you when you broke it?

1 SPEAKING **Work with a partner. Look at these photos. What is the connection between them?**

a

b

c

2a LISTENING **1.30 Listen to a girl describing one of the photos. Which photo is she describing?**

2b Which of these questions does the girl answer? Tick the questions that she answers.

1. Where are the people?
2. What type of people are they?
3. What are the people doing?
4. What are they wearing?
5. What things or objects are in the picture?
6. What has just happened before the scene?
7. When is the scene taking place (morning, night, summer, winter, etc.)?
8. Have you ever been in a situation like the one in the picture? When? What happened?
9. What do you think about the picture?

3 SPEAKING **Compare answers with your partner. Do you remember what information the girl gives? Together, practise describing the same photo.**

4 Fillers are words or sounds, which give you time to think without stopping the conversation. Listen to the girl again. Tick the fillers she uses in the Speaking Bank.

Speaking Bank

Useful expressions for filling the conversation

- Errr … ✓
- Well …
- The thing is …
- I'm not (really/totally/completely) sure but …
- Maybe …
- You know …
- I think …
- I imagine …
- It looks like …
- I imagine that …

STUDY SKILLS

What do you do if you don't know the English word for something when you are describing a picture or having a conversation in English?

STUDY SKILLS ▸ page 147

Practice makes perfect

5 SPEAKING **Work with a partner. Each describe a photo, using the questions from 2b and the Speaking Bank to help you.**

Choose one of the photos on this page. Describe the photo. Have you ever been in a situation like the one in the picture? When? What happened? What do you think about the picture?

1 **Read these three notes and messages. Write one sentence to explain the situation in each one.**

a

Mum,
My friend, Phil, fell and hurt his knee playing basketball at school. The sports teacher took him to St. Andrew's Hospital. I've gone to see him. Can you come and meet me there after work?

Kate.

PS Bring him some magazines – 'Basketball Giants' or something. Phil's really bored!

b

I wanted to ask you if I could borrow your laptop but you weren't here. I need it to write up a project at school. I've taken it to school but I promise I'll look after it. You don't mind do you? After all, that's what brothers are for! I'll bring it back asap!
Sue

c

Jenny,

Get Well Soon!

I was really sorry to hear that you're ill. I only found out yesterday when Martha told me. I know you don't want any visits at the moment, so I'm sending this note and some chocolates. I hope you can eat them! Don't worry about maths, physics, French, etc. I've taken notes for you and I'll give them to you when I see you.

Get well soon!!

Sam

2 **Look at the notes and messages in 1 again and complete the information in the Writing Bank.**

Writing Bank

Useful expressions in notes and messages

- In notes and messages it is normal to begin simply with the name of the person we are writing to.
- We usually write short, direct sentences in messages. For example, we often use imperatives like ...., rather than Could you bring him some magazines?
- We often use abbreviations like PS or .... to keep messages short.
- We use expressions like I was really .... when we are writing about bad news, or Congratulations! when you are happy for somebody.
- We use the expression .... when we want somebody to recover from an illness or accident quickly.

3 **Match the abbreviations and their meanings.**

1 PS	a as soon as possible
2 e.g.	b for example (Latin: *exempli gratia*)
3 NB	c please pay special attention (Latin: *Nota Bene*)
4 asap	d here is some additional information to my letter or note (Latin: *Post Scriptum*)
5 i.e.	e and other things of the same type (Latin: *etcetera*)
6 etc	f that is, this is exactly what I mean (Latin: *id est*)

Practice makes perfect

4a **Look at the task and write the message. Use the expressions from the Writing Bank and the abbreviations from 3.**

You've just gone to visit your friend at his home because he hasn't been at school for two days. He's just gone out to the chemist's. You don't have your mobile phone so you leave him a message. Include this information:

- find out how he is
- find out what he has done in the last two days
- tell him what you've done at school
- tell him some news about one or two of your friends.

4b **Give your message to your partner. Write a reply to your partner's message.**

EXAM SUCCESS

Look at the instructions for the writing task in 4. Can you write in any way you like? Is the style (formal or informal) important?

EXAM SUCCESS ▸ page 151

Language reference and revision

Grammar reference

Present perfect

Form

Affirmative	subject + **have**/**has** + **past participle** *She has broken her leg.*
Negative	subject + **haven't**/**hasn't** + **past participle** *We haven't been in hospital.*
Question	**have**/**has** + subject + **past participle** *Have you visited somebody in hospital?*
Short answers	Yes + subject + **have**/**has**. No + subject + **haven't**/**hasn't**. *Yes, I have.* *No, they haven't.*

Use

We use the present perfect to talk about:

1 an experience in someone's lifetime, without saying the exact time when the event occurred. When it happened is not important.
I've been to hospital.

2 recent events which have a result in the present.
She's found her keys. (= She has her keys now.)

3 actions or situations that began in the past but continue in the present.
Helen's been a doctor for ten years.
(= Helen started to work as a doctor ten years ago and she is still a doctor now.)

Ever, never, for, since, just, already, yet

We can use **ever** in questions with the present perfect. It means 'at any time in your life'.
Have you ever studied medicine?
Ever comes just before the past participle.

We can use **never** in negative sentences in the present perfect. It means 'at no time in your life'.
I've never had a serious accident.
Never comes just after the first verb.

For and **since** are used when the present perfect is describing actions or situations that began in the past and continue in the present. We use **for** with periods of time and **since** with moments in time. With this use of the present perfect we use the question 'How long ... ?'
How long have you been a nurse?
I've been a nurse for three months/since January.
For and **since** go just before the time expression.

We use **just** with the present perfect to emphasise the fact that something happened very recently.
I have just finished my homework.
(= I finished my homework only a few moments ago.)
Just goes after the first verb.

We use **already** to talk about something that has happened earlier than we expected.
Don't do the shopping. I've already done it.
Already usually goes just after the first verb, or at the end of the sentence for emphasis.

We use **yet** to ask if something we expect has happened, or to say that it hasn't. It is used in questions or negative sentences.
Have you done your homework yet?
I haven't finished all the questions yet.
Yet usually goes at the end of a sentence or clause.

Present perfect and past simple

The present perfect describes actions in the past but without saying the specific moment when they happened.
I've been to England.

If we say the specific moment in the past when something happened we *must* use the past simple.
I went to England last year.

Vocabulary

1 Parts of the body

arm back chest ear
elbow finger foot hand
head knee leg neck nose
stomach throat toe tooth

2 Health problems and illnesses

broken cold cough
earache flu headache hurt
pain sore stomach ache
temperature toothache virus

3 Compound nouns connected with health and medicine

first aid food poisoning
health centre heart attack
painkiller waiting room

4 Other words and phrases ▶ page 139–140

Grammar revision

Present perfect with ever, never, for, since

1 Choose the correct alternative.

1 Mark and I have *took/taken* a lot of photos.
2 *Has/Have* you and Hannah started the project?
3 They've been friends *for/since* they were kids.
4 Have you *ever/never* felt sick in a car?
5 My friend and I have *ever/never* been to Scotland.
6 We haven't had an English test *for/since* ages.
7 How *long/much time* have you known Samantha?

WORKBOOK ▸ page 30

/ 7 points

Present perfect and past simple

2 Are these sentences correct? Correct them if necessary.

1 Danny has been to Romania last year.
2 Have you seen the Eiffel Tower when you were in Paris?
3 A: Did your sister ever ride a horse?
B: Yes, she loves horse-riding.
4 I've seen this film twice.
5 My brother's 18. He went to the USA three times.
6 Did you speak to the teacher yesterday?

WORKBOOK ▸ page 33

/ 6 points

Present perfect with already, yet, just

3 Lily's mum is in hospital and Lily has to do the jobs around the house. Look at her list of jobs and write sentences in the present perfect with *already*, *yet* and *just* for the things she has and hasn't done. Remember! We use *just* for things done a short time ago.

1 ....
2 ....
3 ....
4 ....
5 ....
6 ....

WORKBOOK ▸ page 33

/ 6 points

Vocabulary revision

Parts of the body

1 Label the parts of the body.

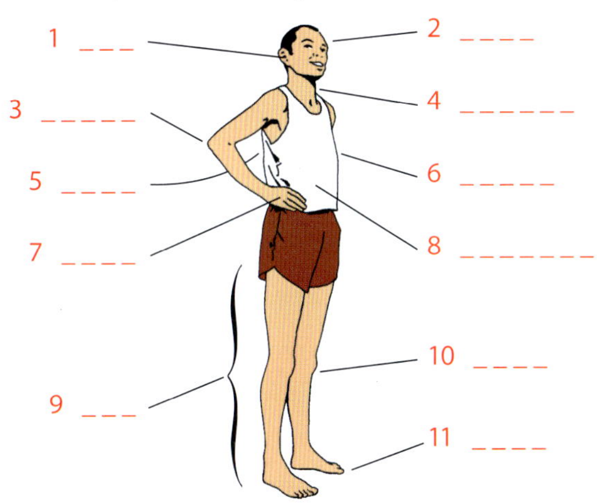

WORKBOOK ▸ page 28

/ 11 points

Illnesses

2 Look at the pictures and identify the health problems.

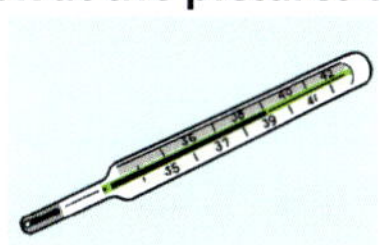

1 She's got a _ _ _ _ _ _ _ _ _ _ _.

3 He's _ _ _ _ _ _ _ _.

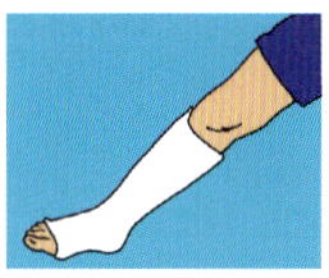

2 She's got a _ _ _ _ _ _ leg.

4 A lot of people are ill because of a _ _ _ _ _.

WORKBOOK ▸ page 28

/ 4 points

Compound nouns connected with health and medicine

3 Complete the compound nouns with the correct words.

1 Sit in the .... room. The nurse will call you when it's your turn.
2 My sister had an accident but there was someone there who knew first ....
3 She ate something bad and now she's got food ....
4 Take this pain .... three times a day if your back hurts.
5 My neighbour is a doctor at the .... centre down the road.
6 Quick! Get a doctor. I think this man is having a heart ....

WORKBOOK ▸ page 31

/ 6 points

Total / 40 points

Gateway to exams Units 3–4

Reading

Tip for Reading Exams

In matching activities, remember …

Read all the text once quickly to get a general understanding. Then read the information that you need to find. Look for the section of the text where you think this information appears and look at it again in more detail. **EXAM SUCCESS ▸ page 151**

1 Look at the title of the text you are going to read.

Being bilingual is good for your brain

Work with a partner and answer these questions.

1 Why do you think that being bilingual is probably good for the brain?

2 How do you think scientists discovered this?

2 Read the text. What answers does it give to the questions in 1?

A recent study says that speaking two languages can help old people to stay mentally active. Dr Ellen Bialystok and her team of scientists at York University in Canada planned some special tests. Then they asked 104 people between the ages of 30 and 88 to do them. From the tests, the scientists found out that people who can speak two languages are very good at thinking fast.

The scientists did different experiments and came to the conclusion that being bilingual can help old people to think quickly. Investigation has shown that playing musical instruments, dancing or reading can also help to keep you mentally active. Simple activities like doing crosswords or playing board games like chess or monopoly can also have a positive effect.

Dr Bialystok thinks that speaking different languages is very good for you and your brain. Half of the people who did the tests came from Canada and only spoke English. The other half came from India and could speak English and a language called Tamil. The scientists tested vocabulary skills and maths ability. They also checked how fast the people did the activities. The ones who could speak two languages did the exercises quickly and well. The people who spoke only one language weren't so good.

The British Alzheimer's Society was very interested in the discoveries. 'It is possible that if we learn a second language when we are young, it can help us even when we are old,' said Professor Clive Ballard. Ballard is the Alzheimer's Society's Director of Investigation. 'Education in general can certainly help the brain to stay active.'

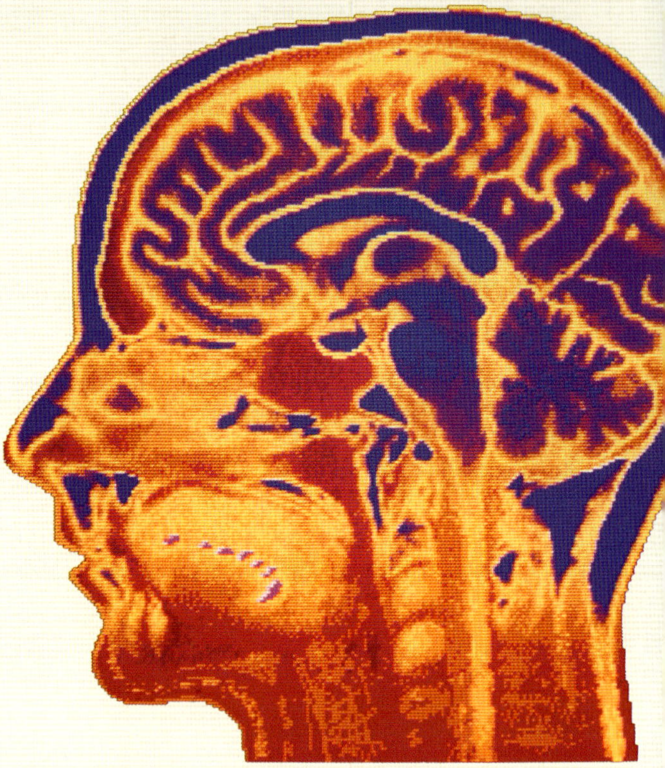

3 Read the text again and match the people in 1–6 with the information in a–f.

1 The British Alzheimer's Society

2 Professor Clive Ballard

3 104 people from Canada and India between the ages of 30 and 88

4 Dr Ellen Bialystok and her team

5 The Canadians, who only spoke English,

6 The Indians who did the tests

a had the idea for this investigation into bilingualism.

b did the tests that the scientists invented.

c were the people who spoke English and Tamil.

d didn't do the tests as quickly.

e wanted to know about the results.

f thinks that all education is good for the brain.

4 What about *you*?

1 Are you bilingual? Do you know anybody who is?

2 What are the advantages of being bilingual?

Use of English

Tip for Use of English Exams

In multiple-choice cloze activities, remember ...

Read the complete text first without thinking about the gaps. This helps you to get a general understanding of the text.

EXAM SUCCESS ▸ page 150

5 Complete the text by choosing the correct option: A, B, C or D, to fill each gap.

In China they have used acupuncture for thousands and thousands of years. But now a school in England **(1)** ...... just started to use it with their students. Stanchester Community School is the school **(2)** ...... they have begun this project. At this school they have a teacher who has spent time living in China, studying acupuncture with Chinese experts. This teacher has **(3)** ...... acupuncture to a small group of students at the school **(4)** ...... 2005. These students suffer different problems. A very common problem that the students have is stress, usually stress caused by exams or homework. People **(5)** ...... suffer from stress often have headaches, backache, or stomach ache. The students all say that they enjoy the treatment and they say that it has **(6)** ...... helped them a lot. It makes them feel good and relaxed. In fact, many of the students also say that now they have started to sleep really well. Let's hope that the students haven't started to sleep in class **(7)** ......!

	A	B	C	D
1	**A** has	**B** is	**C** have	**D** was
2	**A** that	**B** who	**C** where	**D** which
3	**A** give	**B** gave	**C** gives	**D** given
4	**A** since	**B** for	**C** at	**D** on
5	**A** -	**B** who	**C** when	**D** what
6	**A** yet	**B** ever	**C** never	**D** already
7	**A** just	**B** yet	**C** already	**D** never

Speaking

Tip for Speaking Exams

In speaking exams, remember ...

It's important to know what the examiners want to hear. Find out how many marks there are and what you need to do to get a good mark.

EXAM SUCCESS ▸ page 150

6 Work with a partner. Look at pages 40 and 123. Each choose a different photo. Take it in turns to talk about your photos using the questions below.

1 Where are the people and what are they doing?
2 What type of people are they?
3 What are they wearing?
4 What else is in the picture?
5 How do you prefer to learn a language?

Writing

Tip for Writing Exams

In writing exams, remember ...

Include all the information in the instructions or you will lose marks. And don't forget to write in the correct style (formal or informal).

EXAM SUCCESS ▸ page 151

7 You are staying with an English teenager called Joe. You haven't got a mobile phone. This afternoon you are at home alone but you need to go out to the chemist's to buy some medicine and then take it to a friend. Leave Joe a message. Include this information.

- Explain where you have gone and why.
- Inform them who is ill.
- Give the address of the person who is ill and their telephone number.
- Ask Joe to ring you when he gets home.

'Can Do' Progress Check

CEF

1 How well can you do these things in English now? Give yourself a mark from 1 to 4.

1 = I can do it very well.
2 = I can do it quite well.
3 = I have some problems.
4 = I can't do it.

a I can talk about different quantities. ☐
b I can understand written and spoken texts about different languages. ☐
c I can make negative adjectives by using prefixes. ☐
d I can ask for information about language courses and check that I have understood. ☐
e I can write a text about my experiences of learning a language. ☐
f I can report general and recent experiences in the past using the present perfect. ☐
g I can talk about activities which continue up to now using the present perfect with *for* and *since*. ☐
h I can discuss health problems and illnesses. ☐
i I can describe scenes in photos and pictures using fillers. ☐
j I can write basic notes and messages. ☐

2 Now decide what you need to do to improve.

1 Look again at my book/notes.
2 Do more practice exercises. ⇨ WORKBOOK page 20–37
3 Other: ....

5 TV world

Grammar ‣ Comparatives and superlatives ‣ *Less ... than* and *(not) as ... as* ‣ *Too* and *(not) enough*
Vocabulary ‣ TV programmes ‣ Adjectives describing TV programmes ‣ Adjectives ending in *-ing* and *-ed*
Speaking ‣ Negotiating
Writing ‣ Descriptions and opinions

Vocabulary

a

b

c

d

TV programmes

1 **Work with a partner and match the photos with these words.**

advert cartoon chat show
comedy documentary drama
film game show reality show
soap sports programme the news

2 1.31/2 **Listen and repeat.**

3 **Think of examples of programmes for the other words in 1.**

drama – House, CSI

4 PRONUNCIATION **Where does the stress come in each noun or compound noun in 1?**

cómedy chát show

5 SPEAKING **Look at the words in *italics* in the questions. Check that you understand them. Then use the questions to interview your partner.**

1 What is your favourite type of TV *programme*?
2 What is your favourite *series*?
3 What *channel* is it on?
4 Who usually *turns* the TV *on* in your house?
5 What time do you usually *switch* the TV *off*?
6 Who is in charge of the *remote control* in your house?

Adjectives describing TV programmes

6 **Look at these adjectives. Do they have a positive (+) meaning or a negative (–) meaning?**

awful boring cool funny informative
interesting moving popular scary

7 **Match the adjectives in 6 with the definitions.**

1 when something gives a lot of information *informative*
2 when something makes you laugh ....
3 when something makes you feel frightened ....
4 when something is very bad ....
5 when something makes you want to know more ....
6 when something isn't interesting ....
7 when many people like something ....
8 when something is very good ....
9 when something makes you feel very emotional ....

8 LISTENING 1.33 **Listen to five people talking about TV programmes. What type of TV programme are they talking about?**

1 .... 4 ....
2 .... 5 ....
3 ....

9a SPEAKING **Think of things or people for each adjective in 6 and make a note of them.**

funny – Jim Carrey, The Simpsons

9b **Work with a partner and compare your ideas.**

I think Jim Carrey is really funny.

Oh no! I think he's awful.

1 **You are going to read a blog. The title is *Turn Off TV Week*. What do you think *Turn Off TV Week* is?**

2 **You have four minutes to read the blog and decide if each person thinks *Turn Off TV Week* is a good idea or a bad idea. Do not stop reading if there are words you don't understand.**

1 Bob Martin good/bad
2 JaneW good/bad
3 JoPike good/bad

Turn Off TV Week

Blog

by BOB MARTIN on FEBRUARY 25, 2011

The annual Turn Off TV Week starts today. The idea is to live without TV for a whole week. The people who organise it say that television is a bad thing. Personally, I'm not sure that they're right. First of all, the organisers say that the kids of today are lazier and in worse physical condition than kids of the past because they spend all their time in front of the TV. But a recent study of 10,000 US children aged 10 to 15 found no connection between TV and physical fitness. Children who don't watch TV don't always do more physical activity. And even the world's biggest TV addict can find an hour in the day to do exercise. In my case, soaps always make me want to turn off the TV and go down to the gym!

I agree that there are lots of terrible programmes on TV. But I don't agree with saying 'No TV'. I just think we need some more intelligent programmes. TV can be informative, funny and moving. And, yes, it can be awful too. The most important thing is to think about what we watch and be more selective. Another thing that is not black and white is the idea that TV only stops us from communicating with others. An American professor found that parents in homes with no TV have an hour of conversation with their children every day. In other homes, there was only 38 minutes of conversation ... a week! That's bad. But TV can also bring people together and help to start conversations. Is there a better way to begin a conversation than by chatting about the latest episode of your favourite series?

Turn off my TV? OK. But I also plan to continue turning it on when there's something good on.

[2 COMMENTS]

Post a comment

JaneW – 25 Feb 2011, 10:11 AM

I agree. You can't say that all TV is bad. It's as stupid as saying that all books are good, or that all pop music is bad. Maybe a lot of TV is bad. But the idea is to look for the good programmes. I always read the TV guide and decide what I'm interested in watching. I watch my favourite programmes and I also try some new programmes too. I watch them and then I switch the TV off.

JoPike – 25 Feb 2011, 11:01 AM

OK, I agree there are some good programmes on TV. But we all know that the most popular programmes are awful. Unreal reality shows, boring football matches, stupid soaps. That's why Turn Off TV Week exists, and that's why I like it. It tells people that there are more important things in life than knowing what's happening on Big Brother.

3 **Read the blog again and write down evidence from each person's text to justify your answers in 2.**

STUDY SKILLS

Why can it be useful to set yourself a time limit the first time you read a text? **STUDY SKILLS ▸ page 147**

4 **Choose the best answers.**

1 A recent study in the USA shows that
a TV makes children fat.
b watching less TV generally makes children fitter and more active.
c watching less TV doesn't really make children more active.

2 Bob Martin thinks
a a lot of TV is bad, especially soaps.
b a lot of TV is bad, but not soaps.
c all TV is awful.

3 Bob thinks that TV
a has a negative effect on conversation.
b only stops conversation.
c can have a positive effect on conversation.

4 JaneW
a likes all types of programmes.
b only watches programmes that she knows and likes.
c knows when to switch the TV on and off.

5 JoPike
a hates all TV.
b thinks sports programmes are OK.
c doesn't like the same TV programmes as the general public.

5 **Match the underlined words in the text with their definitions.**

1 one part or 'chapter' of a TV series *episode*
2 talking in a friendly way ....
3 describes a person who chooses carefully ....
4 not having something ....
5 describes a person who knows 100% that something is true ....
6 do something once to see if it is good ....
7 use (*v.*) ....
8 once a year (*adj.*) ....

6 **SPEAKING What about *you*?**

1 Do you think TV is a good or a bad thing? Why?
2 How much TV do you watch on weekdays and at the weekend?

I think a lot of TV programmes are really bad.

I don't agree. Some programmes are quite interesting.

GRAMMAR GUIDE

Comparatives and superlatives

1a Look at the comparative and superlative form of these adjectives.

Adjective	Comparative	Superlative
1 long	longer	the longest
2 big	bigger	the biggest
3 lazy	lazier	the laziest
4 important	more important	the most important
5 bad	worse	the worst

Now match the adjectives to the correct rule.

a adjectives with two syllables or more, use *more/most* + the adjective *4*

b one-syllable adjectives which end in one vowel + one consonant, double the last consonant and add *er* ....

c two-syllable adjectives ending in *y*, omit *y* and add *ier* ....

d one-syllable adjectives, add *er* ....

e irregular adjectives with no set rule ....

1b Use the rules in 1a to write the comparative and superlative form of these adjectives.

1 funny ....
2 good ....
3 boring ....
4 short ....
5 fat ....

1c Complete the sentences with the correct words.

1 The new series is more popular .... the old one.

2 She's the .... popular actress in the USA at the moment.

GRAMMAR REFERENCE ▶ page 68

2a PRONUNCIATION 1.34 **Look at these sentences and listen. Then answer the questions.**

a Films are longer than game shows.
b Books are more interesting than films.
c This programme was better than that one.
d Soaps are more popular than reading.

1 Which colour represents the stress in the sentences: red or blue?

2 Which types of word receive the stress? Nouns, main or auxiliary verbs, articles … ?

2b Listen again and repeat the sentences.

3 Complete these sentences with the comparative form of the adjectives and *than*.

1 I think soaps are *more boring than* documentaries. (boring)

2 Adverts are .... a lot of TV programmes. (good)

3 Reality shows are .... chat shows. (bad)

4 Watching films at the cinema is .... watching them on TV. (interesting)

5 Watching TV is .... reading. (easy)

6 Will Smith is .... John Travolta. (thin)

4 Look at these words. They are words which we frequently use with comparative adjectives to modify them.

a bit a lot far much slightly

Choose the correct alternative in these sentences. Use your dictionary if necessary.

1 Watching TV is *far/a bit* more popular as a hobby than writing poetry.

2 Elijah Wood (born in 1981) is *much/slightly* older than Kirstin Dunst (born in 1982).

3 For most people, watching football on TV is *a lot/a bit* more exciting than watching yoga.

4 The programme lasted 60 minutes. It was *far/a bit* longer than normal, because they usually last 55 minutes.

5 SPEAKING **Complete these sentences with a logical opinion. Then work with a partner to compare your sentences.**

1 *Scarlett Johansson is* a lot younger than *Meryl Streep*.

2 .... slightly more popular than ....

3 .... far funnier than ....

4 .... much more informative than ....

5 .... a bit scarier than ....

6 .... much more boring than ....

7 .... a lot longer than ....

6a SPEAKING **Look at Brad Pitt in these two photos. Make notes comparing his appearance. Use these words for ideas.**

attractive bad funny good long
old serious short strong young

6b Work with a partner. Take it in turns to compare the two photos.

He's a lot younger in the second picture.

Yes, and his hair is much longer!

7 Complete the questions with the superlative form of the adjectives.

1 Who is *the most famous* (famous) actor from your country?
2 What is .... (interesting) way to spend free time in your opinion?
3 What is .... (boring) day of the week for you?
4 Who is .... (funny) person in the class?
5 Who is .... (happy) person you know?
6 What is .... (good) part of your day?

8a SPEAKING **Interview different people in the class using the questions in 7.**

8b Tell the class some interesting answers that your classmates gave you.

Lucy thinks bungee jumping is the most interesting way to spend free time!

Adjectives ending in *-ing* and *-ed*

1 Write the *-ing* or *-ed* forms of these words. Use your dictionary if necessary.

-ing	-ed
1 boring	*bored*
2 interesting	....
3	frightened
4 surprising	....
5 confusing	....
6	tired
7	relaxed
8 embarrassing	....
9	moved
10 disappointing	....

2 Choose the correct alternative. Then complete the rule.

1 When a film is excited/exciting, we feel excited/exciting.
2 When a situation is frightened/frightening, we feel frightened/frightening.
3 When a book is bored/boring, we feel bored/boring.

To describe how somebody feels, we use the .... ending.

3 Complete the sentences with the *-ed* or *-ing* form of the words.

1 I was .... (surprise) to hear that they've cancelled the series.
2 It was so .... (embarrass) when the presenter forgot what to say.
3 That new game show is really .... (confuse). I don't know what they have to do.
4 That film made me feel really emotional. I was .... (move).
5 The directors of the new show were very .... (disappoint) because not many people watched it.
6 Some people think that classical music is .... (bore).
7 I think classical music is really .... (relax).

4a SPEAKING **Look at these words. Then make notes with your opinions.**

exams spiders sport theme parks
watching documentaries

exams – tiring, make me feel frightened

4b Compare your ideas with a partner.

I think exams are really tiring.

Yes, and sometimes they make me feel a bit frightened.

Click onto... TV heroes

Cross-curricular – History of Science
John Logie Baird and Philo Farnsworth

1 **Work with a partner. Guess the answers to these quiz questions.**

2 **Read the text and find the answers to the quiz questions.**

3 **Read the text again and match the years and events.**

1925	First regular transmissions in colour
1926	First programmes for BBC, with sound
1928	First black and white image sent
1929	World's first public demonstration of TV
1936	BBC changed from mechanical to electronic system
1967	First transmission from London to New York

TELEVISION QUIZ

1. What nationality was the first person to transmit a black and white TV image?
2. What year was this?
3. When did televisions become common in homes?
4. When did the first regular colour TV programmes begin?

Television is one of the greatest technological inventions of the 20th century. A Scottish man called John Logie Baird invented it. Inventors in the USA and Europe were working on electronic television systems but Baird used a mechanical system. In 1925, he was able to send the first black and white picture – of the head of a doll – from one end of his flat to the other. He then used a local office boy, not the doll, and this teenager was the first person ever to appear on TV.

In January 1926, Baird invited scientists to his flat and showed them his invention. He called it a 'televisor'. Later that year Baird started the world's first TV station and gave it the name 2TV. In 1927, he sent images 730 kilometres from London to Glasgow using telephone cables. A year later, his company sent the first transatlantic TV images from London to New York. Baird made the first television programmes for the BBC in 1929. These programmes had sound, not just pictures.

However, Baird's system was very limited and basic. A totally electronic system was more popular and practical. The inventor of this electronic system was an American, Philo Farnsworth. In 1936, the BBC started using Farnsworth's system because the picture was better than Baird's.

More and more people had televisions after the Second World War. Colour TV began in the USA in the 1940s but only a small number of people had colour televisions in their houses. They were very expensive. In Britain and the USA, the first regular colour TV programmes only began in 1967.

Now, in the 21st century, we have digital television. TV has changed a lot since the face of a boy appeared on TV in John Logie Baird's flat!

INSIDE INFORMATION

- The letters BBC stand for the British Broadcasting Corporation.
- Between TV and radio, the BBC is probably the largest news service in the world. Its programmes go out to over 274 million homes in 200 countries.
- There are no adverts on the BBC, except for adverts for the BBC's own programmes.

▸ WORD BOOSTER

Match the words and the pictures.

1 doll 2 cable 3 century

a

b

c
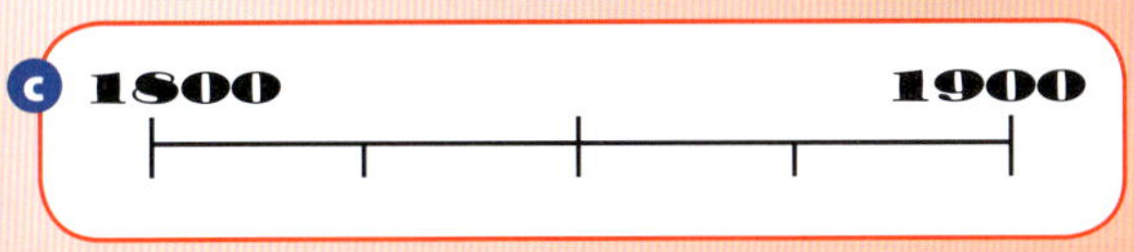

Match the words and the definitions.

1 flat a frequent
2 TV station b pictures
3 images c apartment, home
4 sound d company that makes TV programmes
5 regular e things you can hear

4 Are these statements true (T) or false (F)?

1 Baird invented an electronic TV system. T/F
2 The first TV images were of a boy. T/F
3 The first boy on TV wasn't a famous person. T/F
4 Baird was the first person to send TV images from England to the USA. T/F
5 The BBC decided to stop using Baird's system because it wasn't good enough. T/F
6 There weren't many TV programmes in colour in the 1950s. T/F

5 Correct the false statements in 4.

6 What about *you*?

Apart from TV, what do you think are the greatest inventions of the 20th century? Why?

I think the computer is probably the greatest invention of the 20th century.

Why?

Because you can do nearly anything with a computer.

Popular culture
Robin Hood and Maid Marian

7 Work with a partner. Make a list of things you know about Robin Hood and Maid Marian.

Robin Hood was in love with Maid Marian.

8 1.35 Robin Hood and Maid Marian have been heroes in British and American TV series and films since 1908. Listen to a radio interview about Robin and Marian. Do you hear any information you talked about in 7?

▸ WORD BOOSTER

Match the words and the definitions.

1 version a someone who shoots arrows
2 outlaw b rescue
3 save c criminal
4 brave d bad character in a book or film
5 archer e form of something that is different from the original
6 baddy f able to deal with danger or trouble without being scared

9 Listen again and answer the questions.

1 How many different TV and film versions have they made of Robin Hood?
2 Why does the film critic think that Robin Hood is so popular?
3 Why does the film critic talk about Mexico, Australia and China?
4 How has Maid Marian changed in recent years?
5 What does the film critic think about this change?
6 What is different about Robin Hood in this latest film version?

INSIDE INFORMATION

- Nobody knows if Robin Hood really existed or if he was only a fictional character. The name Robin Hood appears in official legal papers in England from 1228. But it seems that people used the name to talk about any criminal.
- Originally, people talked about Robin Hood as a criminal, not a hero.
- Some similar characters from around the world are: Vasily Bazhenny (Russia), Juraj Janosik (Slovakia), Ustym Karmaliuk (Ukraine) and Lampião (Brazil).

1 **Work with a partner. The photos show different ways of finding out the news. Which do you prefer and why?**

2 LISTENING 1.36 **Listen to a radio programme where people are calling to say how they like to find out the news. Match the speakers and their preference. There is one option you do not need.**

a The Internet	Amanda	1
b Radio	Jerry	2
c Weekly news magazine	Sarah	3
d Newspaper	Dan	4
e TV		

EXAM SUCCESS

In the next activity you need to identify the statements that a speaker makes. Do you think the speaker will say exactly the same words as in the statements you read?

EXAM SUCCESS ▸ page 151

3 **Listen again. Which speaker …**

1 finds out the news at breakfast time?
Amanda/Jerry/Sarah/Dan

2 thinks that pictures and images are an important part of the news?
Amanda/Jerry/Sarah/Dan

3 thinks the news on TV isn't very informative?
Amanda/Jerry/Sarah/Dan

4 thinks the most important thing is to find out the news quickly?
Amanda/Jerry/Sarah/Dan

5 is tired of working with computers?
Amanda/Jerry/Sarah/Dan

GRAMMAR GUIDE

Less … than, (not) as … as

1a Look at these sentences.

1 The news on TV is **as** good **as** the news on the radio.
2 Newspapers aren't **as** up-to-the-minute **as** the Net.
3 Newspapers are **less** up-to-the-minute **than** the Net.

1b Are these statements true (T) or false (F)?

1 We use **as … as** to say that two things, people or situations are similar. T/F
2 **Not as … as** and **less … than** have a similar meaning. T/F
3 **Not as … as** and **less … than** are the opposite of **more … than**. T/F

GRAMMAR REFERENCE ▸ page 68

2 **Rewrite these sentences but keep the same meaning. Use *as … as, not as … as, less … than*.**

1 American TV series are more violent than European series.
European series *aren't as violent as American TV series*.

2 Soaps are interesting, but game shows are equally interesting.
Game shows ……………………………………
…………………………………….

3 Computer games are more popular with today's teenagers than TV programmes.
TV programmes ……………………………………
…………………………………….

4 Football programmes on TV are exciting. Football programmes on the radio are equally exciting.
Football programmes on the radio ……………………………………
…………………………………….

5 Watching horror films at the cinema is scarier than watching them at home.
Watching horror films at home ……………………………………
…………………………………….

6 Books are more informative than TV documentaries.
TV documentaries ……………………………………
…………………………………….

3 SPEAKING **Work with a partner. Do you agree with the opinions in 2?**

What do you think about the first sentence?

I agree. I think American TV series are often very violent.

GRAMMAR GUIDE

Too and (not) enough

4a **Look at the sentences.**

1 On TV they're **too** interested in sensationalism.
2 The news on TV is**n't** serious **enough**.
3 It's good **enough** for me.
4 I spend **enough** time in front of the computer.

4b **Match the first and second halves of the rules.**

1 We use **too**
2 We use **not … enough**
3 We use **enough**

a to say a person, thing or situation is insufficient.
b to say a person, thing or situation is sufficient.
c to say a person, thing or situation is excessive.

4c **Look at the word order in the sentences 4a.**

1 Does **too** come before or after the adjective?
2 Does **enough** come before or after the adjective?
3 Does **enough** come before or after the noun?

GRAMMAR REFERENCE ▸ page 68

5 **Complete this text with these words.**

as enough food light modern
small surprising too

Nanook of the North

In 1922, Robert H. Flaherty made a silent documentary about the life of the Inuits in the Arctic. It was the very first documentary film and it caused a sensation. For the first time, people could see real life in a distant, exotic place. However, now some people say the film wasn't authentic **(a)** ___________ because Flaherty changed some things to make the film more exciting. For example, the Inuits already used guns to catch and kill animals. But, in the film, Flaherty wanted the Inuits to use traditional ways of hunting because guns looked too **(b)** __________. Scenes with guns weren't **(c)** ___________ enough for the American public. Another example was that Flaherty used big cameras to make the documentary. So when they went to film inside igloos, there was a problem. The igloos were too **(d)** __________, and they were **(e)** __________ dark. So the Inuits built a special igloo with just three walls, to give enough **(f)** _________ for filming. Maybe nowadays we can criticise Flaherty for not showing real life. But many of the directors of today's 'reality' shows admit that real life often isn't as interesting **(g)** ________ they would like and that they sometimes cheat to make their programmes more popular. *Nanook of the North* is still an incredible film and it captured images of a life that was already disappearing in 1922. The Inuits of Flaherty's film never had enough **(h)** __________ and Nanook died of hunger just two years after appearing in the film.

6 **Complete the sentences with the verb *to be* and *too* or *not … enough* plus the adjective.**

1 This film is for adults, and Corinne is only fifteen. She *isn't old enough* (old) to see it.
2 This game show .... (easy). Everybody always wins.
3 This cartoon .... (original). It's exactly the same as all the others.
4 Owen needs to improve. He .... (good) to be in the first team.
5 It .... (hot) in here. Can you open the window?
6 I can't watch this match because I'm so nervous. It .... (exciting)!
7 That horror film was awful. It .... (scary). I was so bored I fell asleep!

▸ STUDY SKILLS

When you do a grammar exercise there are two main types of things to think about. What are they?

STUDY SKILLS ▸ page 147

7a **SPEAKING** **Look at the questions. Make notes with ideas. Use these adjectives with *too* and *enough*.**

attractive clever fast fit good healthy
lazy long old serious short slow young

1 Could you be a newsreader on national TV at the moment?
2 Could you win a gold medal running 100 metres at the Olympic games next week?
3 Could you be a popular Hollywood actor?
4 Could you win a Nobel Prize one day?

newsreader – not old enough, not serious enough

7b **Tell your partner your answers.**

We aren't old enough to read the news.

No, we aren't, and my hair's too long! The men who read the news always have short hair!

Developing speaking *Negotiating*

1 SPEAKING Work with a partner. Imagine these programmes are on TV tonight. Which one(s) would you like to watch? Why?

7pm	7.00	**Cook off!** Twelve contestants take on the food challenge.	**The Real Shakespeare** Did Shakespeare really write all of the plays? Timothy Robinson investigates.	**Sunnydale** Bob tells Tracey it's all over between them.	**News**
	7.30	**The Daily Show** Topical magazine show.		**Station Street** Sarah is appalled by Hazel's behaviour.	NEW SERIES **No Place Like Home** The property renovation show returns.
8pm	8.00	PICK **Earthwatch** David Kent explores the wonders of the Amazon rainforest.	**You're Nicked!** An insight into the life of Britain's police force.	**Who Wants to be Incredibly Rich?** James Kay hosts the big money quiz.	PICK **Incredible Stories** Conjoined twins, Sarah and Louise Harmer, talk about their life together.
	8.30				
9pm	9.00	**The Informer** Smith is accused of murder. Last in the series.	**The Review Show** The week's cultural highlights.	**Dance Nation** Three couples remain in the competition and there's another routine to learn.	**Family-ville** Animated sitcom about America's most unusual family.
	9.30				**The Politics Slot** Panel discussion on current affairs.
10pm	10.00	**News**	FILM **Three's a Crowd** (2009) *** A young woman's life is turned upside down when her mother-in-law moves into the marital home.	PICK **Patterson's People** Interviews with the rich and famous.	**Criminal Intent** A businessman is shot dead.
	10.30	**Sports Roundup** Highlights from this afternoon's big match between Liverpool and Barcelona.			

2 LISTENING 1.37 Listen to two people deciding what to watch on TV tonight.

1 Tick the types of TV programme you hear.
2 Put two ticks for the programme they decide to watch.

chat show ☐☐ comedy ☐☐ documentary ☐☐
game show ☐☐ reality show ☐☐
soap ☐☐ sports programme ☐☐

3 Listen again and answer the questions.

1 What does the boy think about soaps?
2 What does the boy think about the Shakespeare programme?
3 What does the boy think about the crime programme?
4 What does the girl think about the dance programme?

4 Listen a third time. Tick the expressions that you hear.

Speaking Bank

Useful expressions for making suggestions

- Shall we (do something)?
- Why don't we (do something)? ✓
- Let's (do something).
- How about (doing something)?

Useful expressions for responding to suggestions

- Great!
- OK.
- Fine.
- Yes, let's …
- Good idea.
- You're right.
- Me too/Me neither.
- Yes, but …
- I'm not sure.
- I know what you mean, but …
- No, I prefer …
- Why don't we … ?
- But what about … ?

5 SPEAKING Work with a partner. Take it in turns to suggest watching a programme from 1 and respond to the suggestion.

Shall we watch the Shakespeare documentary?

I'm not sure. What about watching … ?

6 SPEAKING Look at these different ways of spending the evening. Work with a partner. Think of good and bad things about each activity.

a 

b 

c 

d 

e 

f 

EXAM SUCCESS

You are going to do an oral exercise called 'negotiating'. You usually work with another person. The examiner explains a situation where you and the other speaker need to come to a decision. What can you do if you can't think of anything to say? EXAM SUCCESS ▶ page 151

Practice makes perfect

7 SPEAKING Work with a partner. Do this role-play using your ideas from 6 and the Speaking Bank to help you.

You and your partner want to spend the evening together.

- Suggest an activity and explain why you think it is a good idea.
- Listen to your partner's suggestion and explain why you don't want to do this activity.
- Talk about different activities until you come to a decision about what to do.

Why don't we go for a walk? It's really nice outside, and we could take the dog.

I'm not sure. I'm a bit too tired to go for a walk. Sorry. How about …

1 **Read this email from a girl called Marina. Write a few words to describe what she talks about in the three main paragraphs of her email.**

Paragraph 1 ....

Paragraph 2 ....

Paragraph 3 ....

Message - TV in Spain

Reply | Reply to All | Forward | Delete | Print | Mark as Unread

From: Marina <nicenails@mailnet.com>
To: Matt <matt2389@realmail.com>
Subject: TV in Spain

Hi Matt,

You asked me to tell you about TV here in Spain. Well, there are lots of reality shows and lots of chat shows talking about famous people. Soaps are popular, either Spanish soaps or ones from South America. And we have lots of American TV series, particularly dramas and cartoons.

Personally, my favourite programme is a sports programme. It's called 'Football Crazy' in English. It's on the Canal + channel on Sundays, which is the day when Spanish teams usually play. The programme starts at 7pm and finishes at 10pm. In fact, it starts again at 11pm but I don't watch it then, it's too late because I have school the next morning.

I think this programme is cool because it tells you what's happened in all the matches that weekend. In my opinion, the best thing about the programme is that they show you all the goals and action from every match, not just in Spain but in all the best leagues in the world. As far as I'm concerned, it's much more interesting than other football programmes because the presenters always have funny comments to make about the matches, and they often find surprising things to show.

Why don't you tell me something about TV in your country? What's your favourite programme?

Best wishes,

Marina

2 **Read the email again and find out this information about Marina's favourite TV programme.**

1 Title of the programme: ....

2 Channel: ....

3 Day and time it's on: ....

4 Description of the programme: ....

5 Reasons why the writer likes it: ....

3 **Read the email again and complete the expressions in the Writing Bank.**

Writing Bank

Expressions of opinion

- *Personally*, my favourite programme is …
- .... this programme is cool because …
- ...., the best thing about the programme is …
- As .... concerned, it's …

4a **SPEAKING** **Work with a partner. Make a list of British or American TV programmes that are popular in your country at the moment.**

4b **Individually, write your opinion of the programmes. Use the expressions in the Writing Bank.**

4c **Tell your partner your opinion of the programmes. Are your opinions similar?**

5 **Look at the information in 2. Write information about your favourite TV programme.**

Practice makes perfect

6 **Look at this task and write the email. Use the paragraph plan from 1 and the Writing Bank to help you.**

Write Marina an email with information about your favourite TV programme. Tell her:

- basic information about the programme (title, channel, time, day)
- a description of the programme
- reasons why you like it

Language reference and revision

Grammar reference

Comparatives and superlatives

Form

	Adjective	Comparative	Superlative
One syllable	long short	longer shorter	the longest the shortest
One syllable ending in one vowel and one consonant	big fat	bigger fatter	the biggest the fattest
Two syllables ending in *-y*	lazy funny	lazier funnier	the laziest the funniest
Two or more syllables	important boring	more important more boring	the most important the most boring
Irregular	bad good far	worse better farther/further	the worst the best the farthest/furthest

Use

We use the comparative to compare two people, places or things.

We use the superlative to compare more than two people, places or things.

We use **than** in sentences that compare two people, places or things.
Soaps are worse than documentaries.

We use **the** before the superlative form of the adjective and we often use **in**.
He's the most famous actor in Hollywood.

Less … than, as … as

Use

Less is the opposite of **more**.
Badminton is less popular than football.
(= Football is more popular than badminton.)

We use **as … as** to say two things are the same.
Books are as good as films.

We use **not as … as** to say that the second person or thing is **more … than** the first one.
Badminton isn't as popular as football.
(= Football is more popular than badminton.)

Too

Form

The word **too** comes before the adjective.
The programme is too serious. People get bored when they watch it.

Use

We use **too** to say that something is excessive. It is not the same as **very** because it has a negative meaning.
He's very clever. (= positive)
Yes, but sometimes he's too clever. (= negative)

Enough, not … enough

Form

The word **enough** comes after adjectives and before nouns.
It's good enough.
It isn't good enough.
I haven't got enough time.

Use

We use **enough** to say that something is sufficient.
We use **not enough** to say that something is insufficient.
He's good enough to be a TV presenter.
I'm not fast enough to win a gold medal.

Vocabulary

1 TV programmes

advert (ad/advertisement)
cartoon channel chat show
comedy documentary
film game show reality show
remote control series soap
sports programme the news

2 Adjectives describing TV programmes

awful boring cool
funny informative
interesting moving
popular scary

3 Adjectives ending in *-ing* and *-ed*

bored boring confused confusing
disappointed disappointing embarrassed
embarrassing frightened frightening interested
interesting moved moving relaxed
relaxing surprised surprising tired tiring

4 Other words and phrases ▸ page 141

Grammar revision

Comparatives and superlatives

1 Correct the mistakes in these sentences.

1 Charlotte's school is more bigger than this school.
2 You look thiner than the last time I saw you.
3 Some people think that watching sport is more boring that playing it.
4 The Volga is longest river in Europe.
5 Ethan is much worst at German than Jake.
6 Do you think this exercise is most difficult in the book?
7 That's the sillyest thing you've said today.

WORKBOOK ▸ page 40

/7 points

Less … than, (not) as … as

2 Make true sentences using the words and *as … as, not as … as* or *less … than*.

1 Holland/big/the USA
2 A kilo of sugar/heavy/a kilo of iron
3 Knowing English/important/knowing anatomy
4 Jamie (born 1995)/old/Alex (born 1995)
5 I/good at maths/my best friend
6 Playing tennis/dangerous/parachuting

WORKBOOK ▸ page 43

/6 points

Too, (not) enough

3 Write sentences using the adjectives *too* or *(not) enough*.

1 Why is it difficult for most people to climb Mount Everest?
It .... (high).
2 Why can't your brother vote in the General Elections?
He's only 15. He .... (old).
3 Why can't you run a marathon?
My legs .... (strong).
4 Why can't you buy a sports car?
I .... (money).
5 Why can't Linda drive?
She's only sixteen. She .... (young).
6 Why can't palm trees grow in the Arctic?
It .... (warm).
7 Why don't you like that series?
I don't understand the story. It .... (confusing).

WORKBOOK ▸ page 43

/7 points

Vocabulary revision

TV programmes

1 Name these types of TV programme.

1 It tells you information about today's events. ....
2 They interview famous people. ....
3 It's based on a competition with prizes. ....
4 It looks at facts or historical events. ....
5 It follows the lives of fictional characters in a melodramatic style. ....
6 It goes between programmes to get you to buy something. ....

WORKBOOK ▸ page 38

/6 points

Adjectives describing TV programmes

2 Think of an example of something which *you* think is:

1 awful ....
2 boring ....
3 cool ....
4 informative ....
5 moving ....
6 popular ....
7 relaxing ....
8 scary ....

WORKBOOK ▸ page 38

/8 points

Adjectives ending in -ing and -ed

3 Complete the sentences with these words. There are ten words but only six sentences.

disappointed disappointing embarrassed embarrassing frightened frightening relaxed relaxing surprising tired

1 I thought I was going to get ten in the exam, but I only got five. I was ....
2 It's .... to see you because I thought you were on holiday.
3 I went out with one black shoe and one brown shoe. It was really ....
4 I hate high places. Yesterday we went up a really big tower. I was ....
5 The examiner was so nice. She made me feel .... before the exam.
6 I'm very .... after running. I can't move my legs!

WORKBOOK ▸ page 41

/6 points

Total /40 points

6 Living planet

Grammar	▸ *Be going to, will, may, might* ▸ Zero conditional and first conditional
Vocabulary	▸ Geographical features ▸ The environment ▸ Different uses of *get*
Speaking	▸ Making arrangements
Writing	▸ A formal letter

▸ Vocabulary

Geographical features

1 **Work with a partner and match the photos to these words.**

beach desert forest ice cap
mountain range rainforest and jungle

2 **2.01/2 Listen and repeat.**

a

b

c

d

e

f

The environment

3 **Work with a partner. Match the words with the definitions.**

drought environment flood global warming ~~greenhouse effect~~ nuclear disaster
oil spill ozone layer pollution recycle save waste

1 when heat cannot escape from the atmosphere and the temperature on earth goes up *greenhouse effect*
2 to use something again, or change something so that you can use it again ……
3 the natural world around us ……
4 to stop using something (for example water, money, electricity) or to use it less ……
5 a long period of time when there is no rain ……
6 the part of the earth's atmosphere which protects the earth from the sun ……
7 the process of making the air, water or land worse, with chemicals, for example ……
8 a large quantity of water that suddenly covers an area ……
9 the increase in the temperature on earth ……
10 to use something more than necessary, or in an incorrect way ……
11 an accident with nuclear power, usually causing radioactivity ……
12 an accident when oil comes out of its container, for example at sea ……

4 **SPEAKING Work with a partner. Use words from 3 to talk about the photos.**

You can recycle bottles here. It's good for the environment.

5 **LISTENING 2.03 Listen to four descriptions of environmental problems. Match each description to a photo in 4.**

1 …… 3 ……
2 …… 4 ……

6a **SPEAKING Look at the questions and make a note of your answers.**

1 How is global warming affecting your country?
2 Where and when do you have floods or droughts in your country?
3 What do you do to protect the environment?
4 What products or materials do you recycle?
5 How do people waste water or electricity in your country?
6 What do you do to save water or electricity?

6b **Work with a partner. Ask and answer the questions.**

Reading

1 You are going to read a text about things we can do to protect the environment. You have three minutes to read the four paragraphs and match them to these titles.

Paragraph .... a Young people can make a difference

Paragraph .... b Predictions for the future

Paragraph .... c What *is* a carbon footprint?

Paragraph .... d Your lifestyle and your carbon footprint

1 It's difficult to know exactly how our climate will change. Scientists think that the global temperature may go up by between 1.4°C and 5.8°C in the next fifty years. This global warming will definitely make a big change to life on earth. Most areas will become warmer. Some parts of the world might have terrible floods, but some may have droughts. This will probably be bad for plants and animals in all parts of the world. In the Arctic we can already see that the changing weather is going to make life very difficult for polar bears.

2 So what can we do about this? One thing we can do is to think about our 'carbon footprint'. A carbon footprint is a way of working out the difference that each person makes to the environment. It shows the pollution that we, as individuals, are responsible for. For example, when you go to school by car every day your carbon footprint gets bigger because you are adding to the pollution. When you walk to school or go by bike, your footprint is much smaller.

3 Your decisions in life make a difference to your carbon footprint. Do you fly when you go on holiday? Planes are much worse for the environment than trains. They leave a bigger carbon footprint. When you buy products that have a lot of plastic packaging, you are also making your carbon footprint bigger.

4 You are a teenager. Perhaps you think that you are not responsible for your own carbon footprint because your parents and your school are responsible. But you can help your family and others to change their habits. And you can watch less TV and turn off the light when you leave a room. Each small action will make your carbon footprint smaller. And that will help to slow down global warming and its dangerous consequences.

2 Choose the correct alternative. Write the number of the paragraph where you found the answer.

1 A carbon footprint works out the difference that each *human being/type of transport* makes to the environment.
Paragraph ....

2 The text suggests that teenagers can *take decisions for their parents/influence their parents' decisions*.
Paragraph ....

3 *Rail travel/Flying* is relatively good for the environment.
Paragraph ....

4 The effects of climate change *will probably/will probably not* affect nature all over the planet.
Paragraph ....

5 Everyday activities *make/don't make* a big difference to your carbon footprint.
Paragraph ....

6 Scientists *are/are not* sure what will happen in the next fifty years.
Paragraph ....

7 Scientists predict that the changes *will/won't* be the same in different places.
Paragraph ....

3 Match the underlined words in the text with their definitions.

1 cause (*v*) ....*are responsible for*....
2 the plastic that covers things you buy ....
3 deciding, calculating ....
4 results ....
5 routines ....
6 the mark that your foot leaves on the ground ....

4 Choose the six words in the text which you think are the most important. Compare your answers with a partner and explain your choices.

I chose 'climate' because the text is talking about how the climate is changing.

5 Use your words in 4 to write a short summary of the text.

6 SPEAKING What about *you*?

1 How important do you think global warming is? Why?
2 Do you think your carbon footprint is big or small? Why?

I think global warming is the most important problem in the world right now.

I don't agree. There are other big problems too.

GRAMMAR GUIDE

Be going to and *will*

1a Look at the sentences.

a I think global warming **will** get worse.
b Greenpeace began in 1971. In 2021 it **will** celebrate its 50th anniversary.
c What can I do to help? I know! I**'ll** keep a record of my carbon footprint.
d Yesterday I decided what to do in the summer. I**'m going to** work for Greenpeace.
e Look at the sky. It**'s going to** rain.

GRAMMAR REFERENCE ▸ page 80

1b Match these explanations of the use of *will* and *be going to* with example sentences a–e in 1a.

We use **will** . . .

1 for decisions that we take at the moment of speaking. ....*c*....
2 to talk about an objective truth. ....
3 to make a general prediction. We often use **think**, **hope**, **expect** with this use. ....

We use **be going to** . . .

4 to make predictions based on some sort of evidence. ....
5 to talk about plans or intentions. ....

2a PRONUNCIATION Look at these sentences. Why do you think some words are marked in bold?

1 The **situation** is going to get **worse**.
2 **Temperatures** are going to go **up**.
3 It's going to be a **hot summer**.
4 We're **all** going to have **problems**.
5 **I**'m going to **do** something to **help**.

2b 2.04 Listen to the sentences. What happens to the words in bold? What is the pronunciation of *be going to*?

2c Listen again and repeat the sentences with the correct stress.

3 Complete the sentences with the correct form of the verbs using *will* or *be going to*.

1 Experts expect that the ice cap .... (disappear) one day.
2 It's only 10am but the sun is already strong. It .... (be) a hot day.
3 A: What's the matter?
B: I'm really hot.
A: I .... (open) the window.
4 Next week .... (be) the anniversary of the world's worst oil spill.
5 My friends have decided they .... (write) a letter about the environment to the local newspaper.
6 People think that global warming .... (cause) lots of problems in the future.
7 A: Where are you going?
B: To see a documentary about the environment.
A: Wait! I .... (come) with you.
8 A: Come to my house this evening.
B: I can't. I .... (go) to a meeting about making our school 'green'.

4 Write down six different plans or intentions you have for the future. Write about these areas:

1 school 3 work 5 family
2 home 4 sport/hobbies 6 friends

I'm going to do a project about biology at school next week.

5 Now write down six predictions for the future. Write about these areas:

1 the environment 3 politics 5 sport
2 TV 4 clothes and fashion 6 medicine

I think the planet will get hotter in the future.

6 SPEAKING Work with a partner. Compare your plans and predictions from 4 and 5. Are they similar or different?

GRAMMAR GUIDE

Will, may, might

7a Look at the sentences and give an approximate percentage of certainty for each expression in bold.

1 This **will probably** affect plants and animals.
70–80% certain
2 Global warming **will definitely** make a big difference.
....
3 **Perhaps** some places **will** have more rain.
....
4 **It's possible that** other places **will** become drier.
....
5 Different parts of the world **might** have terrible floods or droughts. ....
6 The temperature **may** go up by 5ºC in the next fifty years.
....
7 The changes **probably won't** be immediate.
....
8 Things **definitely won't** get better until we do something.
....

7b Look at the position of the adverbs *definitely* and *probably* in sentences 1 and 2 and sentences 7 and 8. What do you notice?

GRAMMAR REFERENCE ▸ page 80

EXAM SUCCESS

You are going to do a sentence transformation activity. Read the instructions. What things are important to check when you finish an activity like this? EXAM SUCCESS ▶ page 151

8 Rewrite the sentences keeping the same meaning. Do not change the word given. Use between two and five words, including the word given.

1 It's possible that the sea level will go up in the next fifty years.
may
The sea level *may go up* in the next fifty years.

2 It's 100% certain that some parts of the earth will become deserts.
definitely
Some parts of the earth .... deserts.

3 There's a possibility that the consequences will be catastrophic.
perhaps
.... catastrophic.

4 It's 100% certain life on the planet won't end in the next twenty years.
definitely
Life on the planet .... in the next twenty years.

5 It's quite probable that people won't change their habits.
won't
People .... habits.

6 The situation might get worse before it gets better.
possible
It's .... get worse before it gets better.

9 How certain do you think these predictions are? Write sentences with the expressions in 8.

1 Summers will get hotter.
2 Polar bears will become extinct.
3 Cars of the future won't use petrol.
4 We will have another ice age.
5 One day there will be a terrible nuclear disaster in the USA.

I think summers will definitely get hotter.

10 SPEAKING Work with a partner. Compare your answers in 9.

I think summers will definitely get hotter.

I think they may get hotter. I'm not sure.

Different uses of *get*

1 Look at *get* in these sentences and match each one to the correct meaning (a–e).

1 Summers are *getting* very hot. *c*
2 I *got* your email yesterday. ....
3 Last week she *got* a book about pollution. ....
4 What time will you *get* to the meeting? ....
5 Can you *get* me the pen that's on the desk? ....

a arrive
b bring
c become
d obtain or buy
e receive

2 Complete the sentences with these words. What is the meaning of *get* in each sentence?

dark late ready red thin worse

1 I can see that you're hot. Your face is getting ....
2 My brother needs to eat more. He's getting very ....
3 Come on! You need to get .... for the meeting.
4 Scientists are very worried because they say the situation is getting ....
5 Come on! It's getting .... Time for bed.
6 I'll switch the light on. It's got very .... in here.

3 What usually happens in these situations? Write sentences with *get* and these words.

an email with news angry bread home late paper and a pen presents tired

1 Somebody is saying horrible things to you.
You get angry.
2 You run for an hour or more.
....
3 It's your birthday tomorrow.
....
4 You're out at 11pm and there are no buses.
....
5 You're in a supermarket because you want to make a sandwich for lunch.
....
6 Your friend in the USA writes to tell you about what happened to her last week.
....
7 Somebody is talking to you on the phone and wants to leave a message.
....

4a SPEAKING Work with a partner. Write a story where you use *get* as many times as possible.

4b Tell your story to the class. Who uses *get* the most?

Yesterday I got up at 7am and I got ready for school.

Click onto... Australia

International cultural knowledge
Australia – People, places, language

1 Work with a partner. Choose the correct answers in the quiz. If you don't know, guess!

2 Find the answers on page 159. How many did you get right?

The Australia quiz

1 What is the most common geographical feature in Australia?
a) jungle
b) rainforest
c) desert

2 What is the capital of Australia?
a) Sydney
b) Melbourne
c) Canberra

3 Who was the first European to make contact with the east coast of Australia?
a) Captain James Kirk
b) Captain James Cook
c) Magellan

4 Who were the first British people to go to live in Australia?
a) prison convicts
b) farmers
c) hospital patients

5 What is the Great Barrier Reef?
a) a long coral structure near the north-east coast of Australia
b) a big rock in the middle of Australia
c) a dangerous beach with sharks near Sydney

6 What does the word 'kangaroo' really mean?
a) jumping dog
b) wild animal
c) I don't understand you

7 What is a 'didgeridoo'?
a) an indigenous Australian musical instrument
b) an indigenous Australian dance
c) an indigenous Australian tribe

8 All these actors live or lived in Australia. Which of them have won an Oscar?
a) Nicole Kidman
b) Russell Crowe
c) Mel Gibson
d) Hugh Jackman

Cross-curricular – Geography

SOS Australia

3 Read the articles and match them with the photos.

a .... b .... c .... d ....

a Australians will need to stop singing in the shower. Why? To save electricity and water. A company has discovered that Australians are usually in the shower for seven minutes a day. This is because many Australians like singing in the shower. So the idea is to sing shorter songs to save water. Australia is the second driest continent in the world. There are frequent droughts, which is why there are water restrictions in all parts of the country.

b The recent drought in Australia has been terrible. Even Australia's wild camels have suffered. They are so thirsty that they are going mad. They are beginning to attack other animals and destroy plants to get water. Australians imported thousands of camels from India in the 19th century. Today, the total wild camel population is approximately one million, possibly the biggest in the world.

c Global warming is a big problem for Australia. The sea level is going up and this may have a very big impact on cities and towns on the coast. For Australia, this is very serious because 80% of the total population lives on or near the coast. If the ice cap melts faster than predicted, the consequences will be disastrous.

4 Read the articles again and write questions for these answers.

1 *How long are Australians usually in the shower?*
Seven minutes.

2 ....
Because they like singing in the shower.

3 ....
Because the camels haven't got enough water.

4 ....
Approximately one million.

5 ....
Because a lot of Australians live on or near the coast.

6 ....
Because they are very dry.

7 ....
Millions of tonnes.

5 What about *you*?

1 What information in the texts surprises you? Why?
2 Do you think Australia has more serious environmental problems than your country? Why?

The idea of singing short songs to save water surprises me.

Why?

Because I think it's silly!

d Many parts of rural Australia are incredibly dry and hot. Fires, called bushfires, are very common and dangerous there. These disasters sometimes begin by accident, but sometimes they are the result of arsonists, people who deliberately start fires. In February 2009 bushfires in the area of Victoria killed 173 people and millions of animals. Some bushfires have generated the power of more than 100 atomic bombs and created millions of tonnes of pollution. In fact, bushfires are responsible for more pollution than all of Australia's industry and cars together. You can see big bushfires from space.

1
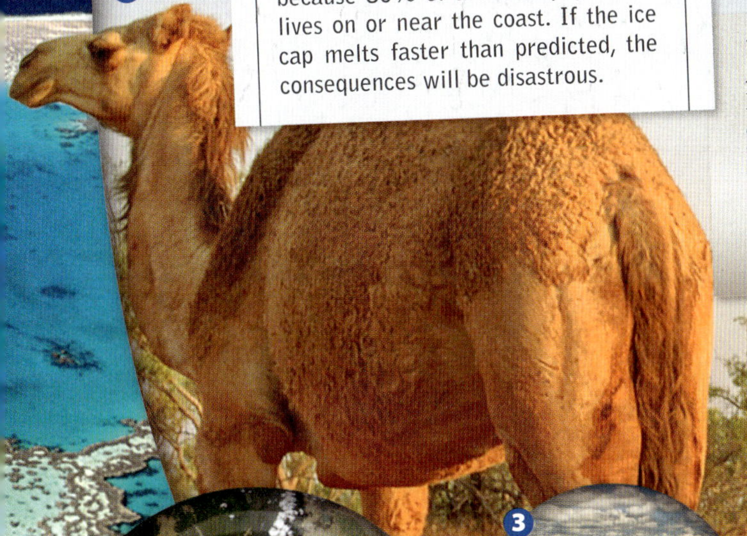

2

3

4
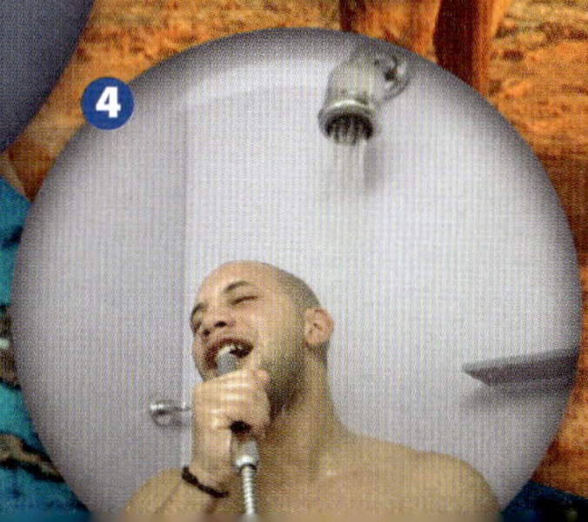

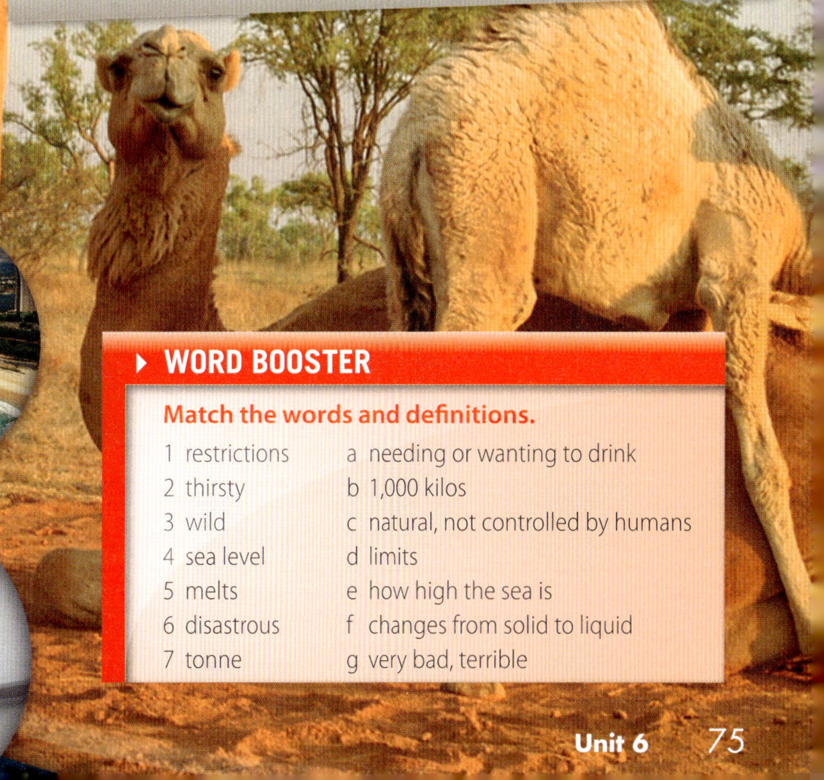

WORD BOOSTER

Match the words and definitions.

1 restrictions	a needing or wanting to drink
2 thirsty	b 1,000 kilos
3 wild	c natural, not controlled by humans
4 sea level	d limits
5 melts	e how high the sea is
6 disastrous	f changes from solid to liquid
7 tonne	g very bad, terrible

1 **SPEAKING** **Work with a partner. Look at the photos. What can you see in each one? Is the situation good for the environment or not? Why?**

2 **LISTENING** **2.05 You are going to listen to part of a meeting at a school. Listen and answer the questions.**

1 What is the meeting about?
2 How many ideas do they write down?

STUDY SKILLS

What is your main objective the first time you listen to a listening text? STUDY SKILLS ▸ page 147

3 **Listen again. Are these sentences true (T) or false (F)?**

1 The teacher has given the students time to think of ideas. T/F
2 The first student, William, wants to separate paper into different boxes. T/F
3 William wants only one person in the class to take paper for recycling. T/F
4 The school has already told students to switch lights off. T/F
5 Isabelle's idea is to help people remember to switch the lights off. T/F
6 The last idea, from Jack, is to save water in the school canteen. T/F

4 **Correct the false sentences. Listen again if necessary.**

5 **SPEAKING** **What about *you*?**

1 Do you do any of these things in your school?
2 How 'green' do you think your school is? Why?

We recycle paper.

Yes, and we always switch the lights off at the end of the day.

GRAMMAR GUIDE

Zero conditional

1a Look at the sentences in the zero conditional. Then choose the correct alternative.

1 If you **have** very long showers, you **waste** water.
2 You **die** if you **don't drink**.

We use the zero conditional to talk about *specific situations/things that are generally true*.

1b Look again at the sentences in 1a.

1 What tenses do we use in the zero conditional? *If* + ..., ...
2 Does the half of the sentence with *if* always come first?
3 When do we use a comma in conditional sentences?

GRAMMAR REFERENCE ▸ page 80

2 **Complete these sentences by putting the verb in the correct form.**

1 If it's sunny, people often .... (go) to the beach.
2 If it .... (not rain) for months, the result is usually a drought.
3 If it rains a lot for months, there .... (be) often floods.
4 If you don't water plants, they .... (die).
5 If it .... (be) very sunny, it's bad for your eyes.
6 If the sun .... (shine) all day, the temperature goes up.

3 **Write sentences to make general statements using the zero conditional.**

1 If I'm late for school, *my teacher gets angry with me*.
2 If you sit too close to the TV, ...
3 If you go to bed late, ...
4 I feel sad if ....
5 I enjoy English classes if ....
6 My parents are happy if ....

4 **SPEAKING** **Work with a partner. Compare your sentences from 3. Are any sentences the same?**

I feel sad if I watch a sad story on the news.

Me too. But I wrote that I feel sad if I argue with my friends.

GRAMMAR GUIDE

First conditional

5a Look at these sentences in the first conditional. Then choose the correct alternative.

1 If you **see** the poster, you**'ll remember** to switch the lights off.

2 It **won't be** so bad if we all **help**.

We use the first conditional to talk about *possible/impossible* situations and their consequences.

5b Look at the sentences again and choose the correct alternative.

1 In the part of the sentence with *if* we use the *present simple/ will or won't*.

2 In the other part of the sentence we use the *present simple/ will or won't*.

GRAMMAR REFERENCE ▸ page 80

6 Choose the correct alternatives.

1 If we *don't/won't* recycle paper, we *need/will need* to cut down more trees.

2 If we *cut/will cut* down more trees, the forests *disappear/will disappear*.

3 There *are/will be* more deserts if the forests *disappear/will disappear*.

4 If there *are/will be* more deserts, the planet *becomes/will become* hotter.

5 Many plants and animals *die/will die* if the planet *becomes/will become* hotter.

7 Put the verbs in the correct tenses using the first conditional.

'If we **(a)** .... (not do) something soon, electronic products **(b)** .... (create) serious problems for the environment. We use more and more energy because we buy more and more electronic gadgets. If this situation **(c)** .... (continue), each house **(d)** .... (need) an incredible quantity of energy. The popularity of computers and games consoles has created an enormous need for more power. In the 1970s homes contained, on average, just 17 electronic products. But now some people think that they **(e)** .... (not be) able to brush their teeth if they **(f)** .... (not have) an electric toothbrush. And if we **(g)** .... (forget) to switch off all these electronic gadgets we **(h)** .... (use) up all of our electricity for nothing.'

8 SPEAKING Work in groups. Begin with this sentence.

If I pass all my exams this year, I'll have a holiday in the summer.

Take it in turns to add conditional sentences. How many sentences can you make?

If I pass all my exams this year, I'll have a holiday in the summer.

If I have a holiday in the summer, I'll go with my friends.

If I go with my friends, I'll . . .

1 SPEAKING Work with a partner and answer the questions.

1 What places can you see in the photos?
2 How often do you go to these places?
3 Which is your favourite place to go at the weekend? Why?

2 LISTENING 2.06 Listen to two people making arrangements for the weekend and answer the questions.

1 Where are they going to go?
2 When and where are they going to meet?
3 What are they going to take?
4 What will they do if it rains?

3 Complete the dialogue. Listen again if necessary.

JAMIE: Hi, Danny.
DANNY: Hi, Jamie.
JAMIE: Listen. Are you up to anything this weekend?
DANNY: Not really. What about you?
JAMIE: If the weather's **(a)** ………………, Alex and I are going to go to the **(b)** ……………… . Do you fancy coming?
DANNY: Sure. What time shall we meet?
JAMIE: How about **(c)** ………………?
DANNY: OK. Why don't we meet at the **(d)** ………………?
JAMIE: Fine. I know. I'll bring some **(e)** ……………… and we can **(f)** ……………… .
DANNY: What will we do if it **(g)** ………………?
JAMIE: I'll give you a **(h)** ……………… and we'll go somewhere else.
DANNY: OK. Listen. I'll ring **(i)** ……………… too and see if she wants to come.
JAMIE: Good idea. See you tomorrow at **(j)** ………………?
DANNY: See you.

4 Tick the expressions in the Speaking Bank that appear in the dialogue.

Speaking Bank

Useful expressions for making arrangements

Asking about somebody's plans

- What are you up to at the weekend?
- Are you up to anything at the weekend? ✓
- Do you fancy verb + *-ing?*

Arranging to meet

- What time shall we meet?
- Where shall we meet?
- Why don't we meet at … ?

Responding to plans and arrangements

- Sure/Fine/OK/Great/Good idea.
- Not really/Sorry, I can't/I prefer …

Remember that we can use the present continuous as well as **be going to** to talk about future arrangements.

Where are we meeting tomorrow?
Where are we going to meet tomorrow?

5 SPEAKING Practise the dialogue in 3 with your partner.

6a PRONUNCIATION 2.07 Listen to the start of the dialogue again. How do the speakers use their voices to show enthusiasm?

6b Work with a partner. Practise the first six sentences of the dialogue again, remembering to show enthusiasm.

Practice makes perfect

7a SPEAKING Work with a partner. Practise the dialogue in 3, changing the information. Use a different place, time, etc.

7b Now change partners and practise again with your book closed.

1 **Read this newspaper article about recycling. What does the writer think about recycling? What reasons does he give?**

RECYCLING IS A WASTE OF TIME
Harry Macdonald's Viewpoint

Everybody is always telling us to recycle. In some countries it is a crime *not* to recycle! This just shows how stupid modern society has become. The fact is that it's more expensive to recycle paper and glass than to make them from new materials. Why don't we just burn our rubbish? If we burn it, we'll produce lots of energy. And another thing, recycling only really works if we separate plastic, paper, aluminium etc. Let's be honest, how many people really do that? Recycling? It's just a waste … of our time.

2 SPEAKING **Work with a partner. What do you think? Do you agree or disagree with Harry Macdonald? Why? Make a list of your ideas.**

1 Recycling may be expensive but it's better than using new materials.

3 **Here is a letter to the editor of the newspaper. Does the reader agree or disagree with Harry Macdonald? Are any of your ideas from 2 here?**

LETTERS TO THE EDITOR

Dear Editor,

I am writing in response to Harry Macdonald's article 'Recycling is a waste of time' which appeared in your newspaper last week. Personally I agree with many of the things that Mr Macdonald says.

Firstly, recycling is more expensive than we think. **Furthermore**, it is difficult or impossible to recycle some materials.

Next, some people say that burning rubbish is bad for the environment because of the fumes. **Nevertheless**, burning rubbish is a very efficient way to generate electricity.

Finally, many people say they recycle their rubbish. **However**, not many people take the time to separate glass, paper and plastics. **What's more**, I totally disagree with the idea of making people recycle.

I will be interested in hearing other readers' opinions on this question.

Yours faithfully,

Helen Horton, Manchester

STUDY SKILLS

Read the letter again. Why is it important to divide texts into paragraphs when we write? STUDY SKILLS ▸ page 147

4 **The words in bold in the letter are all linkers. Put them in the correct place in the Writing Bank below.**

Writing Bank

Linkers of sequence, addition and contrast

- Sequence: *Firstly*, ……………………, ……………………
- Addition: *Furthermore*, ……………………
- Contrast: *However*, ……………………

5 **Complete the sentences with linkers from the Writing Bank.**

1 I think recycling is easy. ……………………, it is cheap.

2 Let me explain what I think. ……………………, I want to explain my opinions about recycling paper. Next, I want to tell you what I think about recycling glass. ……………………, I want to talk about plastic.

3 In general, I agree with the article. ……………………, there are some things in it that I don't agree with.

Practice makes perfect

6a **Look at this topic and make notes.**

A newspaper journalist writes:

'Humans aren't responsible for climate change. It's just a natural process.'

Write a letter to the newspaper editor expressing your own opinion on this topic.

- Begin by explaining why you are writing.
- Express your opinion and explain your main reason for it.
- Give additional reasons for your opinion.
- End your letter.

6b **Write your letter using the model in 3, your notes and the Writing Bank to help you.**

EXAM SUCCESS

When you write in exam conditions, you cannot usually use a dictionary or grammar book. What can you do if you do not know a word or if you are not sure how to use a specific grammar structure? EXAM SUCCESS ▸ page 151

Language reference and revision

Grammar reference

Be going to

Use

We use **be going to** to talk about plans and intentions for the future. We use it for things that we have already decided to do in the future.

We've decided that we're going to join the WWF.

We can also use **be going to** to make predictions about the future, particularly when we have evidence for the prediction.

That car is going very fast. I think it's going to crash.

Will

Use

We use **will** and **won't** to make general predictions about the future. We often use **think**, **hope**, **expect**, **imagine**, etc. with **will** and **won't** to express our opinion about the future.

I don't think he will win the election.

We also use **will** and **won't** when we decide to do something at the moment of speaking, for example when we suddenly offer to do something for someone.

A: It's hot in here.
B: I'll open the window.

We use **will** and **won't** to talk about the future when we consider it to be an objective truth.

It's my birthday next week. I'll be 17.

We use **definitely**, **probably**, **perhaps**, **it's possible that** with **will** to say how certain we think something is. **Definitely** is when we are very certain, **probably** when we are quite certain, and **perhaps** and **it's possible that** when we think the situation is 50-50.

Definitely and **probably** come just after **will** but just before **won't**.

It'll definitely rain. It definitely won't rain.

May, might

Form

Affirmative	subject + **may/might** + verb in infinitive *Temperatures may get higher.*
Negative	subject + **may not/might not (mightn't)** + verb in infinitive *We may not be able to stop it.*

Use

May and **might** are used in predictions when we are not sure about something. They express approximately 50% certainty.

Zero conditional

Form

If + **present simple**, … **present simple**

If you take a fish out of water, it dies.
If we arrive late to school, the teachers get angry.

Use

We use the zero conditional to talk about situations that are generally or always true.

If you don't drink any liquids, you die.

(= This is not just a specific situation – it always happens.)

First conditional

Form

If + **present simple**, … **will** + **infinitive**

If the situation gets worse, it will be terrible.
If we don't recycle, we won't have enough resources.

The present simple comes in the part of the sentence with *if*. *Will* does not appear in this part of the sentence.

~~*If I will go to the shops, I will buy some bread.*~~

Use

We use the first conditional to talk about possible and probable situations in the future and their consequences.

If it doesn't rain, (possible future situation) *we won't have enough water.* (the consequence of this situation)

Vocabulary

1 Geographical features

beach desert forest ice cap jungle mountain range rainforest

2 The environment

drought environment flood global warming greenhouse effect nuclear disaster oil spill ozone layer pollution recycle save waste

3 Different uses of *get*

arrive bring become (= a process or change of state) obtain or buy receive

4 Other words and phrases ▶ page 141–2

Grammar revision

Be going to, will

1 Correct the mistakes in these sentences.

1 Scientists think that they'll to find a solution for this problem.
2 What are your plans? What do you do tomorrow?
3 They say it's raining next week.
4 I can't meet you tomorrow because I'll do an exam.

WORKBOOK ▶ page 48

/ 4 points

Will, may, might

2 Complete the sentences with these words.

definitely may perhaps probably will won't

1 My team will .... win tonight. I'm totally sure.
2 Paula .... go to see him next week but I don't really know.
3 .... the problem will disappear but we aren't certain.
4 They .... won't go out tonight because they have an exam tomorrow, but it's not impossible.
5 She definitely .... run tomorrow because she's got a broken leg.
6 It's possible that I .... see him tomorrow.

WORKBOOK ▶ page 48

/ 6 points

Zero conditional

3 Answer these questions with complete sentences.

1 What happens if you mix blue and yellow?
....
2 What happens if you study for an exam?
....
3 What happens if you never brush your teeth?
....
4 What happens if you eat too much?
....

WORKBOOK ▶ page 51

/ 4 points

First conditional

4 Complete the sentences with the correct form of the words.

1 If the sun .... (shine), we'll be able to go out.
2 We'll go shopping if my mum .... (finish) work early.
3 If you do the exercise carefully today, you .... (get) all the answers right.
4 It'll be great if she .... (come) tonight.
5 She'll leave hospital today if she .... (feel) OK.
6 I .... (not bring) the dog if you don't want me to.

WORKBOOK ▶ page 51

/ 6 points

Vocabulary revision

Geographical features

1 Look at the names. What are the geographical features?

1 Sahara _ _ _ _ _ _
2 The Amazon River and _ _ _ _ _ _ _ _ _ _
3 The Andes _ _ _ _ _ _ _ _ _ _ _ _ _
4 Ipanema in Rio de Janeiro _ _ _ _ _
5 Costa del Sol _ _ _ _ _
6 The North Pole _ _ _ _ _ _
7 Sherwood _ _ _ _ _ _

WORKBOOK ▶ page 46

/ 7 points

The environment

2 Complete the text with these words.

droughts floods global warming ozone layer recycle save waste

(a) .... is getting worse and worse – the temperatures keep going up and up. That's probably because of the big hole in the (b) ...., which protects us from the sun. In some parts of the planet there have been terrible (c) .... where the water has destroyed towns and cities. Meanwhile, in Africa there are terrible (d) .... where it hasn't rained for a long time. But in places like the USA and Europe people (e) .... water – they use too much, without thinking. It's important to (f) .... water, for example by having short showers, not baths. There are other things we can do to protect the earth. We can (g) .... things like bottles or newspapers.

WORKBOOK ▶ page 46

/ 7 points

Different uses of get

3 Decide on a synonym for *get* in these sentences.

1 I'm going to get some bread from the supermarket. ....
2 Did you get home late last night? ....
3 The book started off really well but then it got boring in the end. ....
4 Don't move. I'll get you a glass of water. ....
5 I got my exam marks yesterday. ....
6 She got an email from her best friend. ....

WORKBOOK ▶ page 49

/ 6 points

Total */ 40 points*

Gateway to exams *Units 5–6*

Listing

Tip for Listening Exams

In listening exams where you have to identify the speaker, remember …

Read the statements before you listen. But don't forget that the speakers will probably express the same ideas using different words and expressions. Thinking of synonyms for the words in the statements can help you to identify the answers. EXAM SUCCESS ▸ page 151

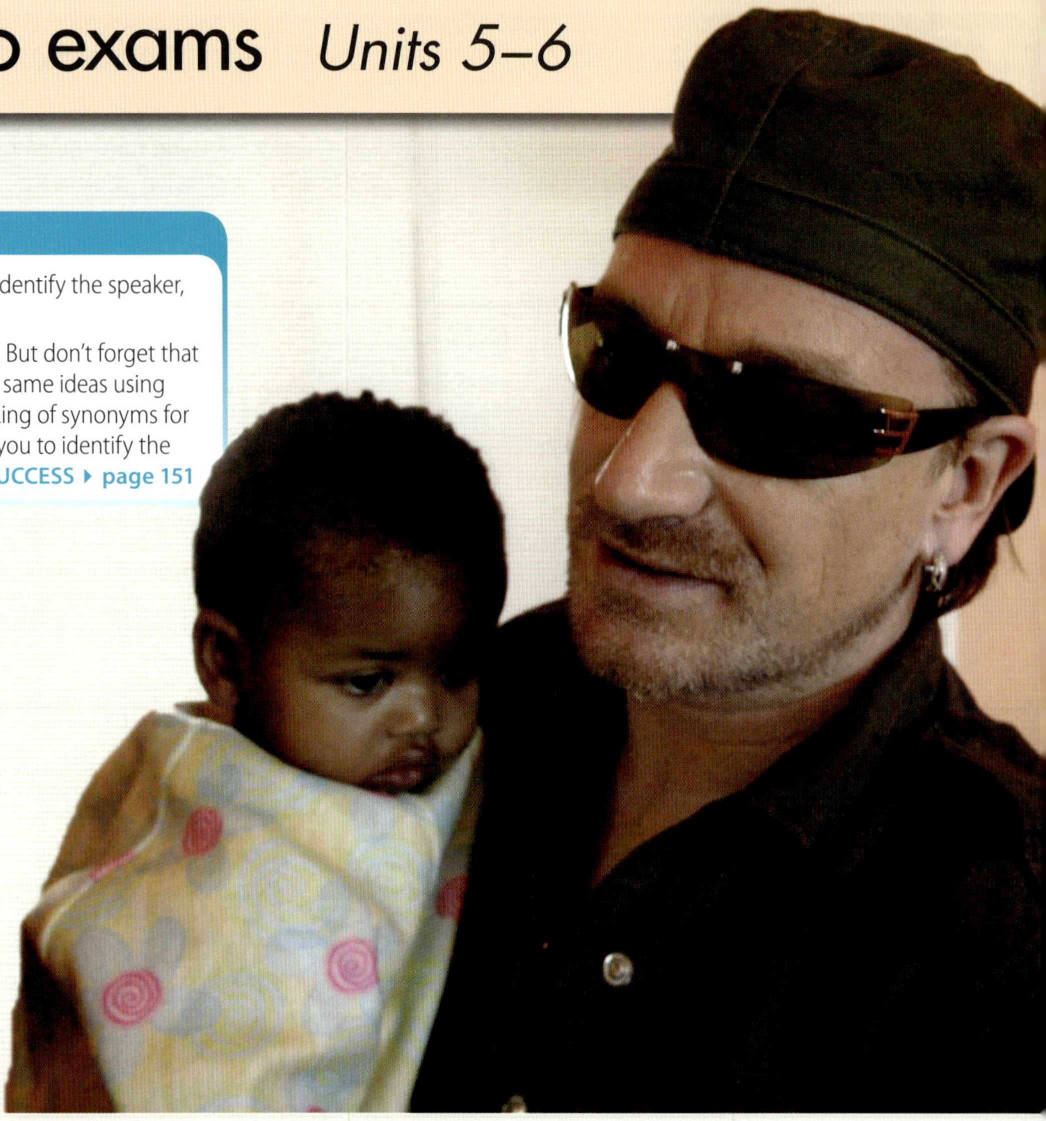

1 Work with a partner and answer these questions.

1 Look at the photo. Why do you think this person is famous?

2 What do you think he's doing in the photo and why?

2 **2.08** Listen to a radio programme. People are giving their opinions about famous people who speak on TV about the environment and other world problems. Match the speakers and their opinions.

A Famous people do a lot of good for environmental problems.

B Generally, the public isn't very interested in environmental questions.

C The most important thing is for people to know what they are good at.

D Famous people are just interested in getting attention for themselves.

E It's better for famous people to give a good example than to tell other people what to do.

F Famous people don't really spend much time talking about the environment.

Speaker	1	
Speaker	2	
Speaker	3	
Speaker	4	

3 What about *you*?

Do you think it's good or bad for famous people to talk about the environment or world problems? Why/Why not?

Writing

Tip for Writing Exams

When you are writing in exam conditions, remember …

If you don't know a word, think of a more general or basic word. If you aren't sure how to use a grammatical structure, change what you are going to say.

EXAM SUCCESS ▸ page 151

4 Write an email to a friend. Tell them about your favourite celebrity. It can be an actor, a singer or a sportsperson. Answer these questions:

- Who is it?
- Why are they famous?
- Do they do anything to help the environment or other people?
- Why do you like them?

Speaking

Tip for Speaking Exams

When negotiating, remember …

If you can't think of something to say, use fillers like *Well*, *Hmmm*, *Let me think* to give you time to decide what you can say next. And don't be afraid to say something that is obvious.

EXAM SUCCESS ▸ page 151

5 Work with a partner. Make a list of different ways of making and responding to suggestions. Use *Why don't we …?*

6 Work with a partner. Look at the situation below and act out the conversation. When you finish, change roles.

Your English friend wants to stay in and watch a nature documentary on TV tonight.

- Reject the idea of watching a nature documentary, giving your reasons.
- Suggest watching a film, giving reasons.
- Accept your friend's idea of watching a different type of programme.

Use of English

Tip for Use of English Exams

In sentence transformation activities, remember …

When you finish, check that you haven't changed the meaning of the original sentence and that you haven't used more than the maximum number of words permitted.

EXAM SUCCESS ▸ page 151

7 Rewrite the sentences keeping the same meaning. When you are given a word to use, do not change it. Use between two and five words, including the word given.

1. Africa is hotter than India. **as**
   India isn't ………………………… Africa.
2. Protecting the environment is more important than space exploration. **not**
   Space exploration is ………………………… protecting the environment.
3. Temperatures won't be warm enough for some types of animals. **too**
   Temperatures will ………………………… for some types of animals.
4. The situation in Europe isn't as serious as in Africa. **more**
   The situation in Africa is ………………………… in Europe.
5. It's possible that environmental problems will become more serious. **may**
   Environmental problems ………………………… more serious.
6. It's 100% certain that some animals will die. **definitely**
   Some animals ………………………….
7. You cannot be too young to help protect the environment. **never**
   You're ………………………… to help protect the environment.
8. I think that it's quite probable that things won't get better. **probably**
   I think that ………………………… get better.

'Can Do' Progress Check

CEF

1 How well can you do these things in English now? Give yourself a mark from 1 to 4.

1 = I can do it very well.
2 = I can do it quite well.
3 = I have some problems.
4 = I can't do it.

a I can compare two or more things using different structures (*more/less than*, *as … as*). ☐
b I can name and describe different types of TV programme. ☐
c I can identify information in a radio programme about the news. ☐
d I can make and respond to suggestions about what to do in my free time. ☐
e I can express my opinions in an informal email. ☐
f I can make predictions and talk about future plans and decisions using *will*, *may*, *might*, *be going to*. ☐
g I can talk about situations and their usual or future consequences using zero and first conditionals. ☐
h I can discuss the environment and pollution. ☐
i I can make arrangements for the weekend showing enthusiasm. ☐
j I can write a simple letter to a newspaper, organising my ideas with linkers and in paragraphs. ☐

2 Now decide what you need to do to improve.

1 Look again at my book/notes.
2 Do more practice exercises. ⇨ WORKBOOK pages 38–55
3 Other: ____________________

7 Odd jobs

Grammar ‣ Modal verbs of obligation, prohibition and advice *(must, have to, mustn't, don't have to, should, shouldn't)* ‣ Second conditional
Vocabulary ‣ Jobs ‣ Personal qualities ‣ Compound adjectives
Speaking ‣ Making polite requests
Writing ‣ A letter of application and CV

‣ Vocabulary

Jobs

1 Work with a partner and match the photos with these words.

builder computer programmer fashion designer journalist
mechanic police officer receptionist shop assistant

2 2.09/10 Listen and repeat.

3 Think of two or three jobs for these different categories. You can use your dictionary to help you.

1 People who work with children: *teachers, au pairs, doctors*
2 People who work outdoors: ....
3 People who do paperwork: ....
4 People who do manual work: ....
5 People who work with the public: ....
6 People who travel a lot: ....
7 People who work in a team: ....
8 People who work in an office, with numbers or with computers:
....

Personal qualities

4 Complete the sentences with these words.

ambitious calm caring clever
creative fit hard-working reliable
sociable strong ~~well-organised~~

1 I'm a very *well-organised* person. I always plan very carefully and I know exactly what I'm doing.
2 You need to be .... if you work with children. They need to know that you like them and will help them.
3 Police officers are usually .... and .... because in some situations they need to run fast and use force.
4 Top scientists are usually very .... They can find the answer to very complicated problems. They are also .... They need lots of imagination to think of new ideas.
5 Philip works in a bank. He's very ....; you can always depend on him and he always arrives on time. He's .... too – he always puts a lot of effort into his work.
6 Susan is very good at working in a team. She's very ...., she loves being with other people.
7 Fire fighters need to stay .... because they might make bad decisions if they get excited or angry.
8 Charles is really .... He won't be happy until he's the company director!

5 LISTENING 2.11 Listen to four people describing their jobs. What jobs do you think they are?

1 .... 3 ....
2 .... 4 ....

6 Write four sentences about yourself using the adjectives in 4.

I'm usually quite calm. For example, I don't panic in exams.

7 SPEAKING Work with a partner. Guess which adjectives your partner wrote in 6 and say why.

I think you put sociable because you're friendly with everyone in this class.

Yes, you're right!

1 Work with a partner and answer the questions.

1 What are the unusual jobs in the photos?
2 What do you think people do in these jobs?

2 Read a blog about four people who have unusual jobs. What are their jobs? Write a name or simple explanation for each one.

1 Lily Ann Lloyd ....
2 David Singleton ....
3 Stephen Redmond ....
4 Louise Perry ....

Do you have an unusual job? We want to hear from you!

Blog

[4 COMMENTS]

You don't have to be attractive to work on TV. If you watch any TV drama, you'll see normal people in the background, behind the main actors. TV or film directors don't want every scene to be full of George Clooneys or Keira Knightleys. They want things to look real, with normal people. That's my job. Some people call us 'background artists', but we're usually called 'extras'. Extras often have to be in the studio for long hours, but you usually only work for about two hours a day. So you should take a good book or a crossword because most of the time you're just sitting waiting. And if you're working with famous actors, you mustn't ask them for an autograph. They just want to do their job in peace.
Lily Ann Lloyd, Glasgow – 1 Mar 2011, 2:31 PM

When I tell people what my job is, they all think I'm lucky. I suppose I am. I test computer games, so basically I spend hours and hours playing them, to see if they're good or not. Sometimes we have to keep playing the game until it breaks. It can be fun but it can also get really boring, playing the same game again and again. We often have to work very fast too. What I really want to do one day is to design a computer game. I studied to be a computer programmer so I know about the technical side. But you have to be very creative to design a game that's original.
David Singleton, London – 1 Mar 2011, 2:57 PM

I'm a house sitter. You probably think that I just sit at home all day. Well, you're right. Except not at my own home. A house sitter is someone who looks after another person's house when they go away. Sometimes I stay for just a couple of weeks when someone goes away on holiday. But sometimes I have to stay for six months, when a family goes to live for a long time in another country for example. People say that I'm a 'living burglar alarm'. That's more or less true. It's an easy job, but you shouldn't do it if you love staying at home ... your own home, that is.
Stephen Redmond, Cornwall – 1 Mar 2011, 3:17 PM

My job isn't exactly unusual but I have to work with world issues, emotions, strange events, family problems, love, new pop groups, discipline, people who are too excited, people who are bored, lunch, chewing gum, fashion, pollution, history, sport, literature, A+, C-, all this and the future of the world ... In my job you have to be reliable, well-organised, hard-working, creative, clever, sociable, caring, calm ... I'm a teacher and I love my job.
Louise Perry, Oxford – 1 Mar 2011, 7:20 PM

EXAM SUCCESS

You are going to do a true or false reading activity. What should you do after reading the text quickly for the first time to get a general idea?

EXAM SUCCESS ▸ page 152

3 Read the texts in 2 again and decide if the statements are true (T) or false (F). Write down the number(s) of the line(s) where you found the answer.

1 Lily Ann is very attractive and this is why she works in TV. T/F ....
2 Background artists and extras are different names for the same job. T/F ....
3 Extras need to be patient. T/F ....
4 Stars don't like signing autographs for extras. T/F ....
5 David always enjoys his job. T/F ....
6 David thinks that technical knowledge is not enough to create a computer game. T/F ....
7 House sitters protect other people's property. T/F ....
8 Being a house sitter isn't a good job for people who like being away from their home. T/F ....
9 Louise needs to know about the past, present and future in her job. T/F ....
10 Louise thinks that she needs a variety of skills to do her job well. T/F ....

4 Match the underlined words in the text with their definitions.

1 takes care of, protects .... *looks after* ....
2 subjects, topics, questions ....
3 the place behind the main person or thing that you are looking at ....
4 handsome, beautiful ....
5 in a good situation, in a situation that other people want to be in ....
6 but ....

5 SPEAKING What about *you*? Discuss with a partner.

1 Which of the first three jobs in the text do you like the most? Why?
2 Would you like to be a teacher? Why/Why not?

GRAMMAR GUIDE

Modal verbs of obligation, prohibition and advice

1a Look at the sentences.

a You **don't have to** be attractive to work on TV.
b Extras often **have to** work long hours.
c You **should** take a good book with you.
d You **mustn't** ask famous actors for an autograph.
e You **must** wear a uniform.
f You **shouldn't** do this job if you like staying at home.

1b Which sentence(s) express:

1 obligation? b, e
2 no obligation? ....
3 prohibition? ....
4 advice or recommendation? ....

1c What type of word comes after *must, mustn't, should, shouldn't, have to, don't have to*?

GRAMMAR REFERENCE ▸ page 94

2a PRONUNCIATION The letter 'l' is silent in the word 'should' – we do not pronounce it. Look at these sentences. Which letters do you think are silent in each sentence? Cross the letter(s) out.

1 Firefighters should be calm.
2 You mustn't ask actors for autographs.
3 Discipline can be important.
4 My science teacher comes to school at half past eight.
5 Fashion designers shouldn't copy other people's designs.
6 Window cleaners often clean tall buildings.

2b 2.12 Listen, check and repeat.

3 Use *should* and *shouldn't* to give advice to these people.

1

2

3

4

4 Choose the correct alternative. If you think both alternatives are correct, choose both.

1 You must/have to learn to play an instrument if you want to be a professional musician.
2 Builders mustn't/don't have to work in an office.
3 Doctors mustn't/don't have to tell secrets about their patients' health.
4 Do you must/have to wear a uniform in your job?
5 People who work in banks must/have to do a lot of paperwork.
6 A fire fighter has to/have to work in a team.
7 A computer programmer mustn't/doesn't have to be fit to do his or her job.
8 My sister must deal/deals with the public in her job.

5 **Rewrite each sentence using a modal verb of obligation, prohibition or advice.**

1. It is not necessary to have experience to do the job.
   You *don't have to have experience to do the job*.
2. It is obligatory for builders to wear hard hats here.
   Builders ....
3. It is a good idea for Frank to work in the summer.
   Frank ....
4. In our school, teachers are not allowed to wear jeans.
   In our school, ...
5. It isn't a good idea to wear informal clothes for a job interview.
   You ....
6. It is not obligatory for our receptionists to speak French.
   Our receptionists ....
7. It is essential for Karen to be calm in her job.
   Karen ....

6a SPEAKING **Look at the photos and choose a job. Make a note of things you *have to/don't have to/must/mustn't/should/shouldn't do* in this job.**

6b **Work with a partner. Describe the job. Can your partner guess what it is?**

You have to work at the weekend. You have to work in a team. You should learn other languages in case you go to play in a different country. You shouldn't eat fast food. You must be ambitious if you want to win competitions.

Is it a football player?

Yes, it is.

Compound adjectives

1 **Look at these words. They are compound adjectives, adjectives made by joining two words. The two words are usually connected with a hyphen (-).**

well-organised hard-working

Complete the compound adjectives in the definitions with these words.

badly blue/brown/green easy full
good part right/left well

1. when you don't work all day in your job
   ....-time
2. relaxed and calm
   ....-going
3. when you don't get much money in your job
   ....-paid
4. when you work all day in your job
   ....-time
5. when you get paid a lot of money in your job
   ....-paid
6. with blue/brown/green eyes
   ....-eyed
7. when you write with your right/left hand
   ....-handed
8. attractive
   ....-looking

2 2.13 **Listen and check your answers.**

3a PRONUNCIATION 2.14 **Listen again and repeat. Where is the stress in the compound adjectives?**

3b **Practise saying the words with the correct stress.**

4 **How many compound adjectives from this page can you use to describe tennis-player Rafael Nadal?**

STUDY SKILLS

How do you learn new vocabulary? Which do you think is better: revising for a long time just once before an exam or revising for a shorter period more frequently? STUDY SKILLS ▸ page 147

Click onto... Working in the USA

International cultural knowledge

American teenagers and work

1 **Look at the jobs in the photos. How old do you think you have to be to do these jobs in the USA? Guess.**

2 **Read this information about work in the USA and answer the questions.**

1 Were your answers in 1 correct?

2 Do you think the answers are the same in your country?

3 Does any of the information surprise you?

What jobs can young people do?

Before you are 14 ...

You can work as a newspaper delivery boy/girl.
You can work as an au pair.
You can work as an actor.
You can work in your parents' business or farm.

When you are 14 ...

You can also work in ... offices, shops, restaurants, cinemas, theme parks or petrol stations.
You can't be ... a builder, a driver, a factory worker, or a miner.
You can work between 7am and 7pm. You can't work more than three hours on a school day.

When you are 16 ...

You can work in any job, except jobs that are especially dangerous (e.g. with explosives or radioactive substances).
You can work any day, any time of day and for any number of hours.

When you are 18 ...

You can work on any job for any number of hours.

3 **Read the article and write a title.**

4 **Read the article again and complete the sentences with the correct information.**

1 Vanessa works because ....
2 Vanessa's studies aren't going well because ....
3 Sometimes Vanessa doesn't do her homework because ....
4 Vanessa thinks that work is bad for her because ....
5 Steve works because ....
6 Steve thinks that the alternative to work is ....
7 Steve thinks that the good things about working are ....

5a **Make notes with your opinions on teenagers and work.**

5b **Work in small groups. Take it in turns to present your opinions.**

Title: ....

American teenagers who study often work as well. One report says that teenagers between 14 and 18 work an average of 16 hours a week. What do teenagers think about this? We asked two and this is what they told us.

Vanessa Hopkins, 18

Apart from my studies, I work about 20 hours a week. I wash dishes and serve food at a local restaurant. There's only one reason why I work – money. I need the money to pay for my studies. But the problem is that my studies aren't going so well at the moment because there are days when I just don't have time to do my homework. I have to work from 9 to 1 some nights. How can I find the time to do my homework after that? Some people say that working is good for teenagers because it gives you experience, it makes you more responsible and independent. No way! I'll have time to do all that when I'm older. Right now, I'm young and I'm at college. I have a great opportunity to learn and improve myself, but I'm just too tired to do it.

Steve Lacy, 15

I have a job at a fast-food restaurant. It isn't very exciting or creative but it gives me money. I'm saving up to buy a car. Most of my friends work too. It's a great way to become independent and not rely on your parents all the time. Sometimes it's difficult to find time to do everything, but I'm young, I can do it. If I wasn't working, I'd probably just be hanging out with my friends and playing basketball. This way, I'm doing something useful and making some money. I'm also learning about the 'real' world, the world outside the classroom, and I've met lots of people there and made some cool friends.

Popular culture

'I need a holiday' by *Scouting for girls*

6 **Read the words to a song about somebody who is tired of working. Can you guess any of the missing words?**

WORD BOOSTER

Match the words and definitions.

1 stuck inside
2 screen
3 drag
4 cheer up
5 home-time
6 hanging out
7 mates

a go slow
b with no possibility of going out
c part of the computer you look at
d friends
e be happy
f spending time
g time to go home

7 **Put these words in the spaces in the song.**

blue day dog five fly hate holiday mates money slow soon sun Sunday watch weekend working

8 **2.15 Listen to the song and check your answers.**

9 **What about *you*?**

1 How does this song make you feel?
2 Do you need a holiday? Why?

I think this song is really cool. I like the lyrics!

I need a holiday. I've worked really hard this term.

It's a beautiful (a) ...., but I'm stuck inside
Staring at this screen, working nine till (b) ....
How I (c) .... this job (how I (c) .... this job)
Because the days do drag (because the days do drag)
They work me like a (d) .... (they work me like a (d) ....)
And the (e) ....'s bad (and the (e) ....'s bad)

CHORUS
Cheer up, cheer up, don't be (f) ....
Don't forget it's home-time (g) ....
We'll make it through another (h) .... day
I need a holiday (I need a holiday)
I need a holiday with my friends.
I'm working every day (I need a holiday)
I'm working every day for the (i) ....

Looking at my (j) ...., for the millionth time
The days go (k) ...., and then the evenings (l) ....
When I'm out of this place (when I'm out of this place)
And the day's been won (and the day's been won)
I'm going out with my (m) .... (I'm going out with my (m) ....)
Hanging out in the (n) .... (hanging out in the (n) ....)

CHORUS
I wish it could be (o) .... when I wake up every day (x 8)

But I need you, yeah, I need you
Yeah I need you more than I can say
Yeah I need you, yeah, I need you
Yeah I need you more than I can say
More than I can say
Yeah I need you, I need you, I need you, I need you,
I need you, more than a (p) ....
Yeah I need you, I need you, I n-n-n-n-need you,
I need you more than I can say

1 **Look at the photos. They are connected to the conversation you are going to listen to. What do you think the conversation is going to be about? Guess.**

2 LISTENING 2.16 **Listen. Were your predictions correct?**

EXAM SUCCESS

You are going to do a multiple-choice listening activity. In this type of exercise you have to choose one of a number of statements which corresponds to the information in the listening text. What should you do if you don't hear the answer to one of the questions?

EXAM SUCCESS ▸ page 152

3 **Listen again and choose the correct alternative.**

1 Sarah doesn't know what to do because
a nobody has offered her a job for the summer.
b she doesn't want to go away.
c she doesn't know if she likes the job they've offered.

2 Sarah is worried because
a she doesn't have any experience of working with children.
b the last time she worked with children it didn't go very well.
c she doesn't like little children.

3 When Jim worked with kids he was
a tired.
b bored.
c angry all the time.

4 The family will
a pay Sarah something.
b pay for Sarah to go to New York but not to return.
c only give Sarah free food and a room.

5 Jim thinks Sarah should
a think hard before she takes the job.
b get experience of working with kids before taking the job.
c accept the job now and worry later.

4 SPEAKING **What about *you*?**

1 Do you think that looking after little children is a difficult job? Why/Why not?
2 Have you ever been to New York? Would you like to go? Why/Why not?

I don't think looking after little children is very difficult.

Why not?

Because you can play lots of games with them.

GRAMMAR GUIDE

Second conditional

1a **Look at these sentences. Then choose the correct alternative in sentences a–c.**

1 If I **took** the job, they **would pay** me.
2 If I **were** you I'd take the job.
3 I**'d take** the job if it **was** well-paid.

a We use the second conditional for *possible and probable/improbable and imaginary* situations and their consequences.
b We use the second conditional to talk about the *past/present* or *future*.
c We can use the expression **If I were/was you, I'd …** to give *advice/express obligation*.

1b **Choose the correct alternative.**

1 In the part of the sentence with *if* we use *the past simple/would(n't) + infinitive*.
2 In the other part of the sentence we use *the past simple/would(n't) + infinitive*.
3 We *can/can't* use **was** or **were** with **if I/he/she …**

GRAMMAR REFERENCE ▸ page 94

2 **Complete the sentences with the correct form of the words.**

1 If Mark was taller, he .... (play) basketball professionally.
2 If he .... (have) a job, he'd get up early in the morning.
3 If she didn't work, she .... (not be) able to buy a car.
4 We would get bored if we .... (play) computer games all day.
5 He wouldn't work in a restaurant if he .... (not like) cooking.
6 If they .... (know) more languages, they'd find it easier to get a job.
7 Frank .... (not do) much work if the boss wasn't there all the time.
8 If they needed a professional chocolate tester, I .... (offer) to do it.

3a SPEAKING **Look at these situations. Think of good advice to give somebody in these situations. Make notes.**

1 I need money.
2 I want to work in the USA one day.
3 I want to help to protect the environment.
4 I'm always tired in the morning.
5 I've got a toothache.
6 I can't sleep at night.
7 I make a lot of spelling mistakes in exams.
8 I haven't got many friends.

3b **Work with a partner. Take it in turns to ask for and give advice using *If I were you …***

I need money.

If I were you, I'd look for a job.

4 **Complete the text with the correct form of these verbs.**

brush eat frighten meet talk want wear

There are some very unusual jobs. For example, imagine if your job was to try new products for a fast-food restaurant. It sounds good at first. But if you **(a)** .... hamburgers all the time you'd soon get fat. Some people have to try new types of toothpaste all day. At least if you **(b)** .... your teeth all day they'd be white! Then imagine being an actor in a *House of Horrors* at a theme park. If you **(c)** .... people too much, they'd probably turn round and hit you. On the other hand, if you worked as a Father Christmas, people **(d)** .... presents from you all the time. A friend of mine once dressed up as a giant cheese to sell cheese at a supermarket. If you **(e)** .... a stupid costume like that, people would laugh at you! I also know someone who worked in a safari park looking after parrots. I suppose you **(f)** .... to the parrots if you were lonely and bored. And, finally, a good job for sports fans – collecting tennis balls at international championships like Wimbledon. If you did that job, you **(g)** .... the best tennis players in the world!

5 **Look at the situations and write sentences using the second conditional.**

1 I don't work because I'm still at school.
If I wasn't still at school, I'd work.

2 He isn't a pilot because he can't see very well.
....

3 They don't work in that restaurant because they're vegetarians.
....

4 She doesn't repair computers because she doesn't know how to.
....

5 I'm not a professional athlete because I'm not fast enough.
....

6 I don't work as an interpreter because I only speak two languages.
....

7 She can't take part in the concert because she doesn't sing very well.
....

8 We want to leave this company because we aren't happy here.
....

6a **SPEAKING** **Look at the situations and think about what you would do in each one and why. Make notes.**

1 You are in an exotic country staying with some friends. Your friends prepare a very special meal which is very expensive and only for people who are considered great friends – fried insects! What would you do?

2 You see a thin old woman stealing some bread from a supermarket. What would you do?

3 You and your family are going to buy a new house. It's perfect. But suddenly you discover that nobody wants the house because a murderer once lived there. What would you do?

4 You are walking past your local bank late at night and the door is open. What would you do?

5 You see two teenagers having a terrible argument. They start to fight. What would you do?

6 A man with a suit and tie says somebody has stolen all his money. He wants you to give him 20€. What would you do?

7 You open the door to your house and you find a burglar. What would you do?

8 You and a friend have just had a great meal in a restaurant. But you find out that you haven't brought any money. What would you do?

6b **Work with a partner. Compare your ideas for each situation.**

I would eat the insects.

Why?

Because I would want my friends to be happy. And maybe fried insects taste nice!

SUMMER JOB OFFERS

a

Sherwood Theme Park

We are looking for ride operators for the summer. If you're sociable and reliable, we want you to join our team. Good conditions. Perfect for students. Phone 0151 897 6543 for information about how to apply.

b

Grantham Gardens

We need assistant gardeners in the summer. Work outdoors in our beautiful park and gardens. A love of nature is essential! Phone 0181 754 6022 for more information about wages and conditions.

c

AUSSIE AU PAIRS

Ever wanted to visit Australia? Work as an au pair in Australia this summer. Free flights, food and accommodation! Phone 0121 977 2001 for inquiries and application forms.

d

Champions Camp

Like sports? Want to meet new people from different countries? Then come and work at our international sports camp this summer. Phone 0191 121 5533 for information about where to send your CV.

1 **Look at the adverts for summer jobs. Match the underlined words in the adverts with their definitions.**

1. questions to get specific information .... *inquiries* ....
2. money that you earn for your work, paid weekly or monthly ....
3. ask officially for ....
4. documents with a list of questions you answer to get a job ....
5. a document giving information about your education and jobs you've done ....
6. person who is in charge of an attraction at a theme park ....

2a SPEAKING **If you were looking for a job, which one would you be interested in and why? Work with a partner and compare your answers.**

2b **Work with a partner. Choose a job and make a list of questions that you would want to ask to find out more information about the job.**

Is the job full-time or part-time? What are the wages?

3 LISTENING 2.17 **Listen to a teenager calling about one of the adverts. Which advert is she calling about? Does she ask any of your questions from 2?**

Speaking Bank

Useful expressions for making polite requests

- Can you tell me what the wages are? ....
- Could I ask for some information first? ....
- Could you tell me if the job is full-time or part-time? ....

4 2.18 **All the expressions in the Speaking Bank are polite ways of requesting information. Listen to the dialogue again and put the requests in the order that you hear them.**

5 SPEAKING **Work with a partner. Take it in turns to use the table to make polite requests for information.**

Could you tell me Could I ask Can you tell me	if what when how how much	the job starts? I can apply? we have to do? you need experience? the basic wages are?

Practice makes perfect

6a SPEAKING **Work with a partner. Do this role-play using the polite requests from the Speaking Bank.**

You are speaking to somebody about a summer job. Find out:

- the dates and wages
- if the job is full-time or part-time
- necessary personal qualities
- if experience is necessary or not.

6b **Student A: Prepare questions to ask about the job at Grantham Gardens.**
Student B: You have information about the job at Grantham Gardens on page 159.
Invent any extra information you need.

Good afternoon. I'm calling about your job offer in the newspaper yesterday.

Yes. What would you like to know?

6c **Now change roles.**
Student B: Prepare questions to ask about the job at Champions Camp.
Student A: You have information about the job at Champions Camp on page 159.
Invent any extra information you need.

STUDY SKILLS

What should you do if you notice that you are making mistakes when you are speaking? **STUDY SKILLS ▸ page 147**

1 **Read this letter of application and CV. Which summer job offer on page 92 do you think this person is replying to? Why?**

34 Norton Road
Stoke
SO3 6HT

Ms Sheila Simpson
63 Mason Street
Brighton
ES9 5FN

14th February 2011

Dear Ms Simpson,

I am writing in response to your advertisement in *The Stoke Times*. I would like to apply for the job which you advertised in this newspaper on 10th February.

I enclose a CV with information about myself, including education and work experience. As you can see, I have experience of working with children and I also think that I am caring, patient and very hard-working.

I look forward to hearing from you.

Yours sincerely,

Diana Huxley

Diana Huxley

CURRICULUM VITAE
Diana Huxley

General information

Date of birth	2/8/1993
Nationality	British
Permanent address	34 Norton Road, Stoke, SO3 6HT
Telephone (home)	01333 455 3212
Telephone (mobile)	632 12 34 56
Email	dhuxley@surfnet.co.uk

Education and qualifications
Green Coat School, Stoke
A levels in Economics (Grade A), Sociology (Grade B) and English (Grade B)

Work experience
March 2008 – March 2010
Part-time teaching assistant at Sunnydale Kindergarten, Stoke
July – August 2007
Helper at Supersport Summer Camp, Brighton

Interests
Cookery, surfing
Good knowledge of computers – MS Office, PowerPoint, Excel, Word.

2 **Read the letter and CV again. Where does Diana give the following information: in her letter, in her CV or in both?**

1 where and when she saw the job offer *letter/CV/both*
2 her personal qualities *letter/CV/both*
3 her contact details *letter/CV/both*
4 her age *letter/CV/both*
5 her hobbies *letter/CV/both*
6 information about her experience *letter/CV/both*

3 **Read the letter and CV again and find the information listed in 2.**

1 Where and when she saw the job offer
The Stoke Times newspaper on 14th February

4 **Write your own CV. Use 1 as a model.**

5 **Look again at the letter in 1 and complete the information in the Writing Bank.**

Writing Bank

Useful expressions and conventions in formal letters

- In formal letters, we write *our address and the date* in the top right corner.
- We write the address of the recipient a little lower on the ....
- We write **Mr** for men, **Mrs** for married women and .... for women when we do not make any distinction if they are married or not.
- We can use the phrase **I** .... **to hearing from you** at the end of formal letters.
- When we know the name of the person we are writing to in a formal letter, we end the letter **Yours** ....
- We do not usually use .... in formal letters. We use **I would like** not **I'd like**.

6 **Work with a partner. Look at this job advertisement. What qualities, skills or experience would be useful for this job?**

THE MERSEY MIRROR 1 March 2011

Job Opportunity!
Coffee 'n' Cake Snack Bar
We need a young person to serve at our fantastic snack bar. We're always busy but always friendly!
Join our young and dynamic team!
Send a letter and CV to Gary Daly,
37 Wavertree Road, Southport, L76 3FP

You need to be sociable. Experience in another bar or restaurant would be useful.

Practice makes perfect

7a **Write a letter of application. Use the letter in 1, your ideas from 6, and the Writing Bank to help you.**

Write a letter to apply for the job at the Coffee 'n' Cake Snack Bar and:

- state which job you are applying for
- say what experience you have
- describe your personal qualities
- end your letter.

7b **Read letters by other students. Who would you give the job to? Why?**

Language reference and revision

Grammar reference

Have to, don't have to

Form

Affirmative	Police officers **have to** wear a uniform.
Negative	Teachers **don't have to** wear a uniform.
Question	**Do** police officers **have to** wear a uniform?
Short answers	Yes, they **do.**/No, they **don't**.

Use

We use **have to** to talk about things which are obligatory or necessary.

We use **don't have to** to talk about things which are not obligatory or necessary.

Must, mustn't

Form

Affirmative	Police officers **must** wear a uniform.
Negative	You **mustn't** smoke at school.

Use

We use **must** to talk about rules, regulations and obligations.

We use **mustn't** to talk about prohibitions.

Must is not very common in the question form. We usually use **have to**.

Should, shouldn't

Form

Affirmative	You **should** work hard.
Negative	You **shouldn't** worry if you make a mistake.
Question	**Should** you wear formal clothes for an interview?
Short answers	Yes, you **should**./No, you **shouldn't**.

Use

We use **should** and **shouldn't** to give and ask for advice and recommendations.

Second conditional

Form

If + **past simple**, … **would/wouldn't** + **infinitive**

If I worked outdoors, I'd be really happy.
If we didn't study, we wouldn't pass our exams.
If I was the president, I would do more to protect the environment.

The past simple comes in the part of the sentence with **if**. **Would** does not appear in this part of the sentence.

~~*If I would see the director, I would give him your message.*~~

The part of the sentence with **if** can go at the start of the sentence or at the end. There is no difference in meaning. However, if the part with **if** goes at the start of the sentence we must use a comma before the second half of the sentence.

If we had a crystal ball, we'd know the future.
We'd know the future if we had a crystal ball.

We can use **were** instead of **was** with **if**.

If I were/was the president, I would do more to protect the environment.

Use

We use the second conditional to talk about imaginary or improbable situations and their consequences.
The imaginary or improbable sentences are in the present or future, *not* in the past.

If I won an important competition (imaginary present situation), *I would be famous* (the consequence of this situation).

We use **If I were you, I'd…** to give advice and recommendations.

Vocabulary

1 Jobs

builder computer programmer fashion designer journalist mechanic police officer receptionist shop assistant

2 Personal qualities

ambitious calm caring clever creative fit hard-working reliable sociable strong well-organised

3 Compound adjectives

badly-paid blue/brown/green-eyed easy-going full-time good-looking part-time right/left-handed well-paid

4 Other words and phrases ▸ pages 142–3

Grammar revision

Must, mustn't, have to, don't have to

1 Choose the correct alternative. If two alternatives are correct, choose both.

1 You *must/mustn't/don't have to* smoke at school.
2 You *must/mustn't/have to* study a lot to be an architect.
3 People who work in a bank *doesn't have to/don't have to/mustn't* wear a uniform.
4 You *has to/have to/must* know how to use a computer to work in a bank.
5 Visitors to the museum *mustn't/must/don't have to* take photos. It is prohibited.
6 A professional football player *mustn't/doesn't have to/don't have to* work in an office.
7 You *must/don't have to/mustn't* drink and drive.

WORKBOOK ▶ page 58

/ 7 points

Should, shouldn't, If I were you

2 Choose the correct alternative.

SAM: I want to work in the States. Can you give me some advice?
TANYA: You should **(a)** *look for/to look for* job adverts on the Internet.
SAM: **(b)** *I should/Should I* send my CV?
TANYA: Yes, if I were you I **(c)** *sent/would send* a letter and a CV by email. But you **(d)** *should/shouldn't* worry if it takes a long time for them to answer. They probably have hundreds of people writing in and sending CVs. If I were you, I **(e)** *would be/should be* patient.

WORKBOOK ▶ page 58

/ 5 points

Second conditional

3 Write complete sentences in the second conditional.

1 I/see a ghost ➜ take a photo of it
If I saw a ghost, I'd take a photo of it.
2 the headmaster/be angry ➜ shout
....
3 my parents/win the lottery ➜ give me a present
....
4 I/not have a pen ➜ ask my friend for one
....
5 we/not have a TV ➜ talk more
....
6 he/not be very good at football ➜ not play in the first division
....
7 I/live in Italy ➜ speak Italian
....
8 we/have wings ➜ be able to fly
....

WORKBOOK ▶ page 61

/ 8 points

Vocabulary revision

Jobs

1 Write definitions of these jobs. Use these words to help you.

manual work
office outdoors
paperwork
team travel
work with the public

1 a builder
2 a journalist
3 a mechanic
4 a receptionist
5 a fashion designer
6 a nurse
7 a shop assistant
8 a computer programmer

WORKBOOK ▶ page 56

/ 8 points

Personal qualities

2 Complete the sentences in a logical way.

1 Alex is very ambitious because ....
2 He's very reliable. He ....
3 She's very caring. Do you remember when she ....?
4 Irene is very fit because ....
5 I think he's clever because ....
6 When you're creative you ....

WORKBOOK ▶ page 56

/ 6 points

Compound adjectives

3 Complete the compound adjectives with the appropriate word.

1 a job which gives you a lot of money: well-_ _ _ _
2 relaxed and calm: easy-_ _ _ _ _
3 with brown eyes: brown-_ _ _ _
4 when you write with your right hand: right-_ _ _ _ _ _
5 attractive: good-_ _ _ _ _ _ _
6 when you work all day in your job: full-_ _ _ _

WORKBOOK ▶ page 59

/ 6 points

Total / 40 points

8 Good friends

Grammar ‣ Past perfect ‣ Gerunds and infinitives
Vocabulary ‣ Relationships ‣ Feelings ‣ Noun suffixes *-ness, -ship, -dom*
Speaking ‣ Reporting a past event
Writing ‣ A personal description

Vocabulary

Relationships

1 Look at the pictures. Read the story and match the pictures with an appropriate phrase (a–k).

I've got an older brother called Dylan. Last July he went to a party and **(a)** *met* a girl called Sophie. He really **(b)** *liked* her and he started to **(c)** *chat to her*. They **(d)** *got on really well with each other* and at the end of the party Dylan **(e)** *asked her out*. She said yes and soon she was **(f)** *going out with him*. They **(g)** *fell in love* and it was really serious. But then one weekend they **(h)** *had a big argument* and Sophie **(i)** *split up with* my brother. Dylan felt terrible and stayed in all the time. One night I took him to a party. I knew Sophie was going to be there. When they saw each other they started chatting again and by the end of the party they'd decided to **(j)** *get back together* again. They're going to **(k)** *get married* next July!

1 ..*h*.. 2 .... 3 .... 4 .... 5 ....

2 Match the words in the story in 1 with their definitions.

1 to start to love somebody *g*
2 to make somebody your husband or wife
3 to have a good relationship with somebody
4 to end a relationship with somebody
5 to know somebody for the first time
6 to start a relationship with somebody again
7 to talk in a friendly way
8 to ask somebody to go somewhere with you
9 to have an angry disagreement with somebody
10 to have a romantic relationship with somebody

3 Complete these sentences with *up*, *with*, *to* or *out* if necessary.

1 John got on well .... Kate.
2 Kate asked John ....
3 John met .... Kate at university.
4 John got married .... Kate.
5 Kate chatted .... John.
6 John and Kate never split ....
7 John and Kate went .... with each other for two years.
8 John and Kate fell in love ....

4 2.19 **Listen, check and repeat.**

5a SPEAKING **Look at the sentences in 3 again. What do you think is the logical order? Make a note of your answers.**

5b Work with a partner. Take it in turns to tell the story of Kate and John.

Feelings

6 Write these words in two columns (nouns and adjectives) in your notebook.

afraid anger angry bored boredom
excited excitement fear happiness happy
loneliness lonely sad sadness

7 LISTENING 2.20 **Listen. Write down the feeling expressed by each speaker.**

1 .... 3 .... 5 ....
2 .... 4 ....

8 SPEAKING **Work with a partner. Ask and answer questions about the feelings in 6.**

When do you feel bored?

When I'm waiting for my friends.

Zhu Ying Tai was a beautiful, young girl who lived in ancient China. Zhu really wanted to study. But tradition said that only boys could go to school. Girls stayed at home and then got married. But Zhu was intelligent and determined. She dressed as a boy and went to the city of Hangzhou to join a school there.

When she was there, she met a boy called Liang Shan Bo. They got on well with each other and became great friends. Liang had no idea that Zhu was really a girl. But Zhu soon realised that she had fallen in love with Liang.

The years passed. When Zhu and Liang had finished their studies, they hated the idea of not seeing each other any more. Zhu had an idea. Liang should visit her family and meet her younger sister. Maybe he could marry her. But Zhu was really talking about herself. There was no younger sister. Liang, still not realising that Zhu was a girl, thought that this was a great idea.

Liang immediately got a job so that he could marry Zhu's 'sister'. A year later, when he had made enough money, he went to Zhu's house to speak to her father. When he got there, he met Zhu again. Finally, he realised that Zhu was a girl and he had been in love with her all along. They were so excited and happy to be back together again.

Their happiness did not last for long. Zhu's father was angry. He told them that he had already promised to marry Zhu to a wealthy businessman. The news broke Liang's heart. Lonely and sad, Liang left Zhu's home. But on the journey, he became ill and died.

Now Zhu was broken-hearted. She was on her way to get married when she passed Liang's grave. Suddenly, there was a terrible storm. Zhu jumped down onto the grave. Lightning hit it and it opened. Zhu jumped in. She wanted to be with Liang. The next minute, the storm stopped. Two beautiful butterflies flew out of the grave and danced happily together. Zhu and Liang had become butterflies. Nothing could separate them now.

1 Read this love story. Do you think the ending of the story is happy or sad?

STUDY SKILLS

To do the next exercise, you will need to read the text in a different way from exercise 1. How and why? STUDY SKILLS ▸ page 148

2 Put these events in the story in the correct order.

1 Liang realised Zhu was a girl. ....
2 Zhu's father told Liang that he couldn't marry his daughter. ....
3 Zhu began a journey to get married. ....
4 Zhu and Liang finished their studies. ....
5 Liang died because he was so sad and lonely. ....
6 Zhu went to school, dressed as a boy. ....1....
7 Zhu and Liang became friends. ....
8 Zhu and Liang became the 'butterfly lovers'. ....
9 Liang started work. ....
10 Liang went to Zhu's house. ....

3 Read the story again and answer the questions.

1 Why wasn't it easy for Zhu to study at school?
2 What was the relationship between Zhu and Liang at school?
3 What was Zhu's plan so that Zhu and Liang could continue to see each other?
4 Why didn't Liang see Zhu for one year?
5 Why was Liang's reunion happy but then sad?
6 Where was Zhu going when she passed Liang's grave?
7 What happened when the storm began?
8 What happened when the storm ended?

4 Match the underlined words in the story with their definitions.

1 rich ....
2 began to understand ....
3 from the start ....
4 not letting anything stop you from doing what you want to do ....
5 extremely sad ....
6 place where a dead body is put in a hole in the ground ....
7 bright flashes of light in the sky when there is a storm ....

5 What about *you*?

1 What do you think about this story?
2 Do you know any other love stories similar to this one?

GRAMMAR GUIDE

Past perfect

1a Look at these sentences. Which actions happened first, the green or the red?

1 Zhu and Liang had finished their studies before Liang visited Zhu's family.

2 Zhu's father had promised to marry Zhu to a businessman so Liang left Zhu's home, broken-hearted.

1b Choose the correct alternative.

We use the past perfect to talk about an activity in the past which happened *before/after* another activity in the past.

1c Complete the rule.

To make the past perfect, we use the past of ……………… + the ……………….

GRAMMAR REFERENCE ▶ page 106

2a PRONUNCIATION **The contracted form of *had* is *'d*. Look at these sentences. Some of them should be in the past perfect. Add *'d* to these sentences.**

1 She ……… fallen in love.
2 He ……… went to live in another town.
3 They ……… seen each other.
4 I ……… gone out.
5 We ……… always known each other.
6 He ……… took her flowers.

2b 2.21 **Listen and check your answers.**

2c 2.22 **Listen again and repeat the sentences with *'d*.**

3 Match the sentences.

1 The film ended.
2 She finished the shopping.
3 They finished their lunch.
4 He got out of the pool.
5 We finished the exam.
6 I put my pyjamas on.
7 I found my keys.

a They went out of the canteen.
b They left the cinema.
c I got into bed.
d I opened the door.
e She carried the shopping home.
f We gave it to the teacher.
g He dried himself with the towel.

4 Rewrite the sentences in 3 as one sentence. Put one verb in the past perfect and the other in the past simple. Use *when* or *after*.

1 *When the film had ended, they left the cinema.*
2 ………………
3 ………………
4 ………………
5 ………………
6 ………………
7 ………………

5 Complete these sentences in a logical way using the past perfect.

1 I was lonely because *everybody had left.*
2 I was feeling ill because ………………
3 They were very happy because ………………
4 She was bored because ………………
5 We were angry because ………………
6 He was feeling sad because ………………
7 Yesterday I was excited because ………………
8 They were afraid because ………………

6 Complete the text with the past perfect.

Before Ryan left school, he **(a)** ……………… (fall) in love with Ellie, one of the girls in his class. They **(b)** ……………… (be) good friends for the last three or four years. The second time Ryan asked Ellie out she accepted. When he **(c)** ……………… (ask) her the first time, she **(d)** ……………… (be) too surprised to accept! Five years later, they decided to get married. They had enough money because they **(e)** ……………… (finish) their university studies and they **(f)** ……………… (find) good jobs. They got married and were very happy together. When they **(g)** ……………… (be) married for a few years they decided to have children. They had a boy and a girl and called them Max and Holly. They were the names of the best friends that Ryan and Ellie **(h)** ……………… (have) at school.

7a SPEAKING **Work with a partner. Find out which of these things your partner had done by the age of seven.**

1 begin to learn English
2 learn to ski
3 travel to a different country
4 learn to read
5 swim in the sea
6 start to ride a bike
7 go on holiday without his/her parents
8 use a computer

Had you begun to learn English by the age of seven?

Yes, I had. And you?

Yes, I had too.

7b Now tell the class about your partner.

By the age of seven Bea had begun to learn English but she hadn't learnt to ski. She had used a computer but she hadn't swum in the sea.

Noun suffixes *-ness*, *-ship*, *-dom*

1 Look at these words. Which suffix, *-ness*, *-ship*, or *-dom*, can we add to them? Does the spelling of any of the words change?

bored free friend happy ill
lonely mad relation sad weak

bored – boredom

2 2.23 **Listen, check and repeat.**

3 Complete the sentences using the noun form of the appropriate word in 1.

1 That's a crazy idea. It's ....!
2 .... is a question of giving and taking, a question of being there for the other person when they need you.
3 To beat the other team we need to find their .... There must be something that they aren't very good at.
4 He loves the .... of being able to do what he likes, when he likes.
5 What's the .... between Lucas and Hannah? Are they family or friends?
6 Flu is a very common ....
7 The worst thing about being ill is the .... You can't do anything or go anywhere.
8 Many people say that money doesn't buy you ....

4a SPEAKING **Complete the questions with the correct noun suffix.**

1 What is important for a good *friend*...............?
2 What is your biggest *weak*...............?
3 How much *free*............... do you think you have?
4 What do you think is the secret of *happ(y)*...............?
5 How do you stop *bore*...............?
6 Have you ever had a moment of *mad*...............?

4b Think about your answers to these questions. Make notes.

a good friendship – always telling the truth

4c Work with a partner. Ask and answer the questions.

What is important for a good friendship?

I think it's important to always tell the truth and be loyal.

Click onto... Famous romances

Cross-curricular – History
The King and Mrs Simpson – A royal love story

1 Work with a partner. Do you know anything about the two people in the photo? If you don't know, make guesses based on the photo.

I think he was the King of England.

But I don't think she's the Queen.

2 Read the text. Why was King Edward VIII's story unusual?

3 Find out what happened:

on 20th January 1936:
Edward VIII became the King of England.
in October 1936
on 16th November 1936
on 10th December 1936
on 3rd June 1937
in 1972

4 Complete these sentences with information from the text.

1 It was difficult for Edward and Mrs Simpson to get married because
Mrs Simpson had already been married twice.
2 American and European newspapers started to write about Edward and Wallis when …
3 The British press didn't write about the romance because …
4 The British government didn't want Edward and Wallis to get married because …
5 King Edward VII stopped being the king because …

What happened on this day … 10th December?

1936: THE ABDICATION OF KING EDWARD VIII OF ENGLAND.

HOW DID IT HAPPEN?

Edward VIII became the King of England on 20th January 1936. He was not married but he spent a lot of time with a woman called Mrs Wallis Simpson. Mrs Simpson was an American who had been married twice. She had divorced her first husband, but she was still married when she and Edward began their relationship. Now that Edward was the King, people often saw him with Mrs Simpson. In the summer, they went on holiday together in the Mediterranean. Newspapers from America and continental Europe started to write about the relationship. But the British press wrote nothing because they did not want a scandal. At the end of October Mrs Simpson asked for a divorce from her second husband. The American press said that Edward and Wallis were going to get married soon. The British government was not happy. On 16th November, the King spoke to his Prime Minister, Stanley Baldwin. He told him that he was going to marry Wallis Simpson. Baldwin told the King that the British people would not allow it. There were religious reasons for this, and also legal, moral and political reasons. But King Edward did not change his plans to marry Mrs Simpson. The only thing that King Edward could do was to stop being the King, to abdicate. He did this on 10th December 1936. He had been King for less than a year.

i INSIDE INFORMATION

Edward became the Duke of Windsor. His younger brother became King George VI of England. King George VI was the father of Queen Elizabeth II. On 3rd June 1937 Edward married Mrs Simpson. They lived mainly in France for the rest of their lives. Edward died in 1972 and Mrs Simpson in 1986.

WORD BOOSTER

Match the words and definitions.

1 abdication (n.)/ abdicate (v.)	a generally
2 press	b permit, let
3 allow	c stop being the king or queen
4 mainly	d newspapers and news magazines in general

P PROJECT

5a Work in groups. Choose one of these members of the British royal famil

King Henry VIII — Queen Elizabeth I — King Charles I
Queen Victoria — Queen Elizabeth II

5b Each member of the group should find information and illustrations for one of these topics:

life — family — important events during their lifetime

5c In your group, decide how to present your information to the rest of the class. Prepare it and present it.

Cross-curricular – Literature

Romeo and Juliet by William Shakespeare

INSIDE INFORMATION

- William Shakespeare lived from 1564 to 1616.
- Shakespeare probably wrote his first version of Romeo and Juliet in 1595.
- There were other versions of the story, and a poem, before Shakespeare's version.

6 Look at the pictures. They illustrate the story of Romeo and Juliet. In which picture(s) can you see:

1 people fighting?
2 a priest?
3 two people getting married?
4 a potion?
5 poison?
6 a knife?
7 somebody killing himself or herself?

7 Work with a partner. Say what you think is happening in each picture.

8 With your partner, can you put the pictures in the correct order? If you aren't sure, guess!

1 *c* 2 ...... 3 ...... 4 ...... 5 ...... 6 ...... 7 ......

9 2.24 Listen to two students telling the story. What is the correct order of the pictures?

10 Listen again. Are these statements about the story true or false?

1 Romeo is a Capulet.
2 When Romeo meets Juliet, he knows which family she's from but it doesn't matter to him.
3 Romeo and Juliet get married almost immediately.
4 Romeo's friends are there with him when he gets married.
5 Romeo has to leave the city because he murdered somebody.
6 Juliet's parents know that Juliet married Romeo.
7 Romeo drinks a special potion.
8 Romeo doesn't know what Juliet and Friar Lawrence have planned.

11 Work with a partner. Take it in turns to tell the story of Romeo and Juliet. Use the pictures to help you.

There are two important families.

And they are always fighting.

12 What about *you*?

1 Have you ever read *Romeo and Juliet*, or seen the play or a film version? What did you think of it?
2 Why do you think the story of *Romeo and Juliet* is still famous today?

I saw the film with Leonardo DiCaprio.

Was it good?

STUDY SKILLS

Readers often come with an audio component that you can listen to outside the classroom. What other things can you listen to in English out of class?

STUDY SKILLS ▸ page 148

a

b

c

d

e

f

g

1 Do this questionnaire. When you finish, compare your results with a partner.

Discover your secret self!

Put a tick next to any statements which you think are true for you.

Section 1

- ☐ I feel I have to be right all the time.
- ☐ If I don't do my best, I get angry with myself.
- ☐ When I go shopping I don't buy anything if I'm not 100% happy with it.
- ☐ I enjoy criticising other people but I hate people criticising me.
- ☐ Understanding other people's opinions isn't easy for me.

Section 2

- ☐ I love giving presents to my friends and family.
- ☐ I'm good at drawing, writing and acting.
- ☐ I find it easy to talk about how I feel.
- ☐ When I feel sad or lonely I feel very sad or lonely.
- ☐ I hate rules and obligations because my freedom is the most important thing.

Section 3

- ☐ My idea of excitement is doing sudokus and crosswords.
- ☐ I always think hard before making a decision.
- ☐ I'm usually very hard-working at school.
- ☐ I stay calm in difficult situations.
- ☐ I learn by watching and reading more than by doing.

Section 4

- ☐ In a group, I'm the person who makes decisions.
- ☐ I hate being with people who can't make decisions.
- ☐ I love having a good argument.
- ☐ I'm not afraid of telling people what I think.
- ☐ I find it hard to say sorry.

2 Now count how many ticks you have in each section. Turn to page 159 to discover what each section means. Do you agree with the result?

3 LISTENING 2.25 Listen to Jessica talking to Jack about the questionnaire. Answer the questions.

1 Which section do they talk about?
2 Does Jessica agree with the results?
3 Does Jack agree with them?

4 Listen again and choose the correct alternative.

1 Last week Jessica decided *where they went/what they saw*.
2 Jack thinks Jessica isn't very good at *waiting/listening*.
3 Jessica and Jack have an argument about *why/how long* he waited last week.
4 Jessica *agrees/doesn't agree* that she likes arguing.
5 Jessica didn't like the *service/quality of the food* last night.
6 Jessica *often/never* apologises.

GRAMMAR GUIDE

Gerunds and infinitives

1a Look at these sentences.

1 When I go shopp**ing**, I don't buy anything.
2 I love giv**ing** presents.
3 Understand**ing** other people's opinions isn't easy for me.
4 I find it easy **to talk** about my emotions.
5 I learn by watch**ing**.
6 Nobody wanted **to make** the decision.
7 A: Why did you shout at the waiter?
B: **To tell** him the food was no good.

1b Put rules 1–7 below in the correct column.

We use the gerund …	We use the infinitive …
5	

1 … as the subject of a sentence.
2 … to explain why somebody does something.
3 … immediately after adjectives.
4 … after certain verbs like *want*.
5 … with *go* to talk about physical activities.
6 … after prepositions.
7 … after verbs of liking or disliking.

GRAMMAR REFERENCE ▶ page 106

2 Look at these statements. Which rule in 1b explains why we use the gerund or infinitive in each one?

Section 5

- ☐ I find it difficult to say no if someone asks me to do something. ....
- ☐ I love making other people feel good. ....
- ☐ People often come to me to get advice. ....
- ☐ I always want to help my friends and family. ....
- ☐ I'm interested in becoming a doctor or a nurse one day. ....

Section 6

- ☐ I hate having arguments. ....
- ☐ When I have a problem, I don't fight, I go running. ....
- ☐ I think it's stupid to disagree about small things. ....
- ☐ Shouting is horrible, in my opinion. ....
- ☐ I make problems disappear by not thinking about them. ....

3 Tick the statements in 2 that are true for you. Where do you have more ticks, in Section 5 or in Section 6? Now find out what each section means on the next page.

4 **Complete the texts with the gerund or infinitive form of the verbs.**

Mostly Section 5: You're a helper

Personality:
You're warm and caring and you think it's easy **(a)** .... (make) friends. You do many things **(b)** .... (make) your friends' lives better. But **(c)** .... (be) helpful can sometimes get you into trouble because you want **(d)** .... (know) what problems people are having.

Ideal jobs:
Nurse, Doctor, Primary school teacher

Romance:
You like **(e)** .... (show) your emotions but you can be possessive. Don't go **(f)** .... (fall) in love too fast!

Advice:
Learn to say no and don't be afraid **(g)** .... (make) it clear what you want from life.

Mostly Section 6: You're a pacifist

Personality:
You never want **(a)** .... (argue) about anything. You're calm and open-minded. You enjoy **(b)** .... (listen) to other people and you think it's important **(c)** .... (hear) different opinions. But **(d)** .... (do) what other people want all the time can be tiring.

Advice:
(g) .... (Defend) your own opinions isn't the same as being aggressive. Do it more often. Why? **(h)** .... (Get) the respect of other people.

Romance:
By **(e)** .... (accept) your partner's ideas, you seem an ideal partner. But it's important **(f)** .... (spend) time doing what you want.

Ideal jobs:
Social worker, Receptionist, Gardener

5 **Do you agree with the results? Why/Why not?**

6 **Look at these sentences. Then use appropriate words to complete the sentences below.**

Falling in love is easy.
Falling in love is like falling into an ocean.
Falling in love can be dangerous.
Falling in love stops loneliness.

1 Being a student …
2 Listening to music …
3 Spending time with friends …
4 Walking in the country …
5 Doing sport …

7 **Finish these questions using a gerund or an infinitive.**

What type of person are you?

1 Are you interested in *meeting new people*?
2 Do you enjoy ....?
3 One day do you want ....?
4 Do you ever go ....?
5 Do you find it easy ....?
6 Is it important for you ....?
7 Do you hate ....?
8 Why do you go ....?
9 Do you think .... is a good idea?
10 Are you excited about ....?

8a SPEAKING **Ask your partner your questions from 7.**

8b **Tell the class some things you discovered about your partner.**

I discovered that my partner is interested in collecting old manga comics.

1a SPEAKING **Work with a partner. Look at the photos. What can you see in each photo? Which of the two types of party do you prefer and why?**

a

b

1b What are typical things that you can do at a party? Make a list with your partner.

eat, talk with friends ...

2 LISTENING 2.26 **Listen to a conversation about a party. Tick any activities in your list that the two people mention.**

3 SPEAKING **Work with a partner. Can you complete these sentences? Listen again to the conversation if necessary.**

1 Joe had a party because he had ....
2 The party was at ....
3 There were .... people there.
4 .... had made lots of food.
5 Lee thought that one of the best things about the party was ....
6 At the party Lee met a(n) ....

4 Look at the sentences in the Speaking Bank. Match the verb forms in bold with the correct name of the tense and the explanation of its use.

Speaking Bank

Using different past tenses

1 I **went** to a great party.
2 They**'d made** lots of food.
3 When I **was dancing** I met George.

a Past perfect
b Past continuous
c Past simple

i An activity in progress at a moment in the past. We often use it to describe scenes in the past.
ii A completed action in the past.
iii An activity that happened before another action in the past.

5 Think of a party with family or friends that you went to. Prepare to talk about the party by looking at these questions. Make notes but do not write complete sentences.

1 Whose party was it?
2 Why did they have the party?
3 Who did you go with?
4 Where was the party?
5 How many people were there?
6 Did you know all the people there?
7 Was there any food? What was it like?
8 Was there any music? What was it like?
9 Did you dance?
10 Did you meet anybody?
11 What time did the party end?

Practice makes perfect

6 SPEAKING **Work with a partner. Do this task. Use your notes from 5 and the Speaking Bank to help you.**

Tell your partner about a party you went to. Tell them:

- whose party it was
- what you did at the party
- your opinion of the party, giving reasons.

EXAM SUCCESS

What language is useful in tasks where you have to report past events?

EXAM SUCCESS ▸ page 152

1 SPEAKING **Work with a partner. Describe the people in the photos.**

a

b

c

2 Read this email from a boy called Luke and answer the questions.

1 How and where did Luke meet Ethan?
2 Which photo in 1 shows Ethan?
3 Why does Luke get on well with Ethan?

Message – Hi Thomas!

From: Luke Smith (lsmith@anymail.com)
To: Thomas Ashfield (thomasjashfield@anymail.com)
Subject: Hi Thomas!

Hi Thomas,

How are things? Are you still doing exams or have you already finished?

Last weekend I met someone who knows you. His name is Ethan. Does the name sound familiar? He's got short fair hair and he's tall – very tall! He met you at a basketball camp last summer. You played together in the same team.

I met Ethan on Saturday night when I was out bowling with Steve and Jake. At first he was with two friends. Then his friends left and we started chatting. I got on well with him. He's really funny. And he's like us – he loves playing basketball but he hates football!

Anyway, Ethan had an idea. He wanted the three of us to meet this weekend. How about it? Are you free? We could go bowling or do something else if you like.

Write back and let me know!

Luke

3 The email in 2 is answering this exam task. Does it include all the information?

A few weeks ago you made a new friend. In an email to another friend write:

- your new friend's name and general appearance
- how and where you met the person
- the person's personality and likes and dislikes.

4 Look at the useful words and expressions in the Writing Bank. Circle the ones you can find in the email in 2.

Writing Bank

Useful words and expressions of sequence and time

- At first
- First of all
- Next
- Then
- After that
- Finally
- In the end
- Last weekend
- Two weeks ago
- On Friday
- On Saturday night

Practice makes perfect

5 Do the task in 3. You can write about a real or imaginary person or event. Use the email in 2 as a model and remember to use words and expressions from the Writing Bank.

EXAM SUCCESS

Why is it important to read the question carefully in writing exams? EXAM SUCCESS ▸ page 152

Language reference and revision

Grammar reference

Past perfect

Form

Affirmative	subject + **had ('d)** + **past participle** *She had finished the exam.*
Negative	subject + **had not (hadn't)** + **past participle** *They hadn't finished the exam.*
Question	**Had** + subject + **past participle** *Had you finished the exam?*
Short answers	Yes, subject + **had.** No, subject + **hadn't.** *Yes, I had.* *No, they hadn't.*

We often use time expressions such as **when**, **after**, **by the time**, **as**, **as soon as** with the past perfect.

Use

We use the past perfect to talk about actions that happened before another action or actions in the past.

I had finished working when Jamie called.
(= First I finished working and then Jamie called.)

Gerunds and infinitives

Use

We use the gerund:	We use the infinitive:
as the subject of a sentence. *Shopping is great.*	to explain why somebody does something. *Why did he go to university? To study art.*
after **prepositions.** *I'm interested in studying law.*	immediately after adjectives. *It's good to express your feelings.*
after **verbs of liking or disliking** e.g. *like, love, enjoy, can't stand, don't mind, hate.* *I enjoy being with friends.*	after certain verbs e.g. *want, learn, agree, decide, expect, hope, seem, try, would like.* *I want to work for a newspaper.*
with **go** to talk about physical activities. *go running, swimming, cycling, shopping, swimming, fishing*	

Spelling

We usually add *-ing* to the verb to form the present participle.
start – starting

Verbs which end in one *-e* lose the last *-e* and add *-ing.*
have – having

When a verb has only one syllable and ends with one vowel and one consonant, we double the consonant and add *-ing.*
put – putting, swim – swimming, run – running

If the verb ends in *-y, -w,* or *-x,* we add *-ing* but do not double the last consonant.
play – playing, mix – mixing, snow – snowing

When verbs finish in *-ie,* we change the *-ie* to *-y* and add *-ing.*
lie – lying, die – dying

Vocabulary

1 Relationships

to ask somebody out
to chat to somebody
to fall in love (with somebody)
to get back together (with somebody)
to get married (to somebody)
to get on well (with somebody)
to go out (with somebody)
to have an argument (with somebody)
to meet somebody
to split up (with somebody)

2 Feelings

afraid anger angry
bored boredom excited
excitement fear happiness
happy loneliness
lonely sad sadness

3 Noun suffixes *-ness, -ship, -dom*

boredom freedom friendship
happiness illness loneliness
madness relationship
sadness weakness

4 Other words and phrases ▶ page 143–4

Grammar revision

Past perfect

1 Complete the sentences in a logical way. Put one verb in the past perfect and the other in the past simple.

1 When I .... (finish) my breakfast, I .... (brush) my teeth.

2 When the students .... (do) the exam, the teacher .... (say) they could go.

3 He .... (go) to bed after he .... (put) his pyjamas on.

4 She .... (dry) her hair after she .... (wash) it.

5 They .... (take) her to the hospital because she .... (have) an accident.

6 They didn't see the start of the film. When they .... (arrive) at the cinema it .... (start).

7 When he .... (write) the email, he .... (send) it.

8 They .... (go) into the museum when they .... (buy) the tickets.

WORKBOOK ▸ page 66

/8 points

Gerunds and infinitives

2 Choose the correct alternative. Why do we use the gerund or infinitive in each case?

1 I went to the shops *buying/to buy* food for the weekend.

2 Are you interested in *seeing/to see* that film?

3 *Smoking/To smoke* is bad for your health.

4 Why don't we go *fishing/to fish* this weekend?

5 Richard and Sarah really enjoy *riding/to ride* their bikes in the park.

6 I want *listening/to listen* to that new group in concert.

7 The burglar got into the house by *opening/to open* the window.

8 Are you ready *helping/to help* me?

WORKBOOK ▸ page 69

/8 points

Vocabulary revision

Relationships

1 Match words from each column to make expressions about relationships.

1	to get on	a	out with somebody
2	to go	b	up with somebody
3	to ask	c	somebody
4	to have	d	well with somebody
5	to split	e	an argument with somebody
6	to like	f	in love with somebody
7	to fall	g	back together with somebody
8	to get	h	somebody out
9	to chat	i	to somebody
10	to get married	j	to somebody

WORKBOOK ▸ page 64

/10 points

Feelings

2 Write the nouns for these adjectives. Is each feeling generally positive (+), negative (-) or it depends (=)?

1 sad → ....
2 afraid → ....
3 lonely → ....
4 bored → ....
5 angry → ....
6 excited → ....
7 happy → ....

WORKBOOK ▸ page 64

/7 points

Noun suffixes -ness, -ship, -dom

3 Read the definitions and write words ending with *-ness*, *-ship*, or *-dom*.

1 A relationship between people who are friends:
f _ _ _ _ _ _ _ _ _

2 The opposite of strength:
w _ _ _ _ _ _ _

3 The feeling when nobody is with you and you feel bad:
l _ _ _ _ _ _ _ _ _

4 Something that affects people and makes them do crazy things:
m _ _ _ _ _ _

5 The connection between two people:
r _ _ _ _ _ _ _ _ _ _ _

6 Something which makes you feel bad or unhealthy:
i _ _ _ _ _ _

7 Being able to do what you want, with no obligations:
f _ _ _ _ _ _

WORKBOOK ▸ page 67

/7 points

Total /40 points

Gateway to exams Units 7–8

Reading

1 Work with a partner. What jobs can teenagers do in your country? How old do they have to be to do them?

2 You are going to read a text about a British teenager. First, match the words and the pictures.

1 jam 3 recipe
2 grapes 4 factory

a

b

c

d

3 Read the text. How has Fraser Doherty become a millionaire?

Fraser Doherty is a very hard-working, ambitious teenager. In fact, he's so hard-working and ambitious that he's already a millionaire! Fraser was 14 when he started making jam. There had been a special way of making jam for generations and generations in the Doherty family. One day his grandmother told Fraser the secret and, with her help, he began to invent his own unusual jams, all called SuperJam.

The jam was obviously good because soon Fraser was making it and selling it to his friends and neighbours after school. Within four years he was producing 1,000 jars of jam a week from his parents' home in Edinburgh, Scotland.

Now he has just won a contract to produce 120,000 jars of jam a week for a big British supermarket. That means that he will have to start producing jam in a factory, not at home.

Fraser is now 18 and he's studying business at Strathclyde University in Glasgow. Yesterday he said: 'If things continue to go well I'll need more people to work at my factory. I would love to have my jams in other supermarkets, too.'

Traditional jams are often 80 per cent sugar, but Mr Doherty, whose company is called Doherty's Preserves, has created a healthy alternative. He uses grape juice, not sugar. He said: 'I wanted to make jam as healthy as possible. Traditional jam is quite unhealthy. It was quite frightening to change a product that people have made the same way for hundreds of years, but I wanted to add a new dimension.' A food expert said: 'Fraser has taken an old product and he has made it young, exciting and modern.' Fraser has done this by being creative with new ingredients like kiwi and lime.

Mr Doherty's father, Robert, said that he was sad that Fraser was moving to a factory because he liked watching Fraser making the jams at their family home in Edinburgh. 'For a long time now, Fraser has used our kitchen to experiment with new recipes and to produce jam to sell. When he is in the kitchen, we can only go in there if we promise to help. People who visit our home all have to help!'

4 Read the text again and decide if the statements are true or false. Write down the number(s) of the line(s) where you found the answer.

1 Fraser Doherty's jams are a mixture of tradition and new ideas. T/F
2 At first Fraser made and sold the jam in his free time. T/F
3 Fraser started by producing 1,000 jars of jam a week. T/F
4 Fraser will continue to make jam at home. T/F
5 Fraser wants to sell his product to more and more people. T/F
6 Fraser has a totally positive opinion of typical, old jam. T/F
7 Fraser wanted to make a new type of jam but he didn't know what people would think. T/F
8 Fraser's dad invites people to his kitchen to help make jam. T/F

5 What about *you*?
Would you like to be Fraser Doherty? Why/Why not?

Tip for Reading Exams

In true/false activities, remember …

Read the sentences that you need to check and find the section of the text which includes the information. Read those sections again in more detail.

EXAM SUCCESS ▸ page 152

Writing

Tip for Writing Exams

In writing exams, remember ...

You lose marks if you do not answer the question and include all the information that appears in it.

EXAM SUCCESS ▸ page 152

6 You see an advertisement for a summer job at Fraser Doherty's new jam factory. You want to write a letter to apply for the job. In your letter, should you do the things below or not?

1 Write Fraser Doherty's address in the top right corner. ☐
2 Write your address in the top right corner. ☐
3 Write the date on the right. ☐
4 Begin *Dear Mr Doherty,* ☐
5 Write contractions like *I'm*, *It's*, etc. ☐
6 Say which advertisement you are writing about. ☐
7 Say why you are a good person for the job. ☐
8 Write expressions like *I look forward to hearing from you.* ☐
9 Finish *Yours faithfully,* ☐

7 Write your letter and include this information. You can invent it.

- Why you are writing
- What other information you are sending with the letter (CV, photo, other)
- Personal qualities you have that could help you to get the job
- What experience you have

Speaking

Tip for Speaking Exams

In activities where you report past events, remember ...

Use different past tenses (such as the past perfect for activities that happened before another activity in the past) and use expressions of time and sequence (*first*, *next*, *then*, *later*).

EXAM SUCCESS ▸ page 152

8 Work with a partner. Look at this exam task. You have a few minutes to make a note of things you are going to say or questions you are going to ask. Do not write complete sentences.

> Yesterday evening you worked as an au pair looking after your neighbour's two children (aged 8 and 10). Tell your partner:
> - what you did
> - what the children did
> - what the best and worst parts of the experience were.

Listening

Tip for Listening Exams

In multiple-choice listening activities, remember ...

If you don't hear the answer to one question, start listening immediately for the answer to the next question. Don't panic. You will probably be able to hear the text again.

EXAM SUCCESS ▸ page 152

9 2.27 Listen to a man talking about British teenagers and work. Which jobs do you hear mentioned?

10 Listen again and choose the correct alternative.

1 British teenagers
  A can't work legally when they are thirteen.
  B can only work two hours a day.
  C can work more hours on Saturday.

2 The most common job for teenagers is
  A working for a newspaper.
  B taking newspapers to where people live.
  C after school.

3 To be an au pair
  A you need different personal qualities.
  B is easy because you just watch TV.
  C you need to work in the morning.

4 British teenagers
  A don't usually cook.
  B can't prepare food very well.
  C aren't legally able to work in kitchens.

'Can Do' Progress Check

CEF

1 How well can you do these things in English now? Give yourself a mark from 1 to 4.

1 = I can do it very well.
2 = I can do it quite well.
3 = I have some problems.
4 = I can't do it.

a I can express obligation, prohibition and advice using modal verbs like *must* and *should*. ☐
b I can talk about imaginary situations and their consequences using the second conditional. ☐
c I can describe jobs and the personal qualities you need to do them. ☐
d I can ask about jobs, making polite requests. ☐
e I can write a simple job application. ☐
f I can describe past events using the past perfect. ☐
g I can talk about relationships and feelings. ☐
h I can understand information in a newspaper story about a relationship. ☐
i I can make nouns using the suffixes *-ness*, *-ship*, and *-dom*. ☐
j I can write about a friend in an informal email. ☐

2 Now decide what you need to do to improve.

1 Look again at my book/notes.
2 Do more practice exercises. ⇨ WORKBOOK pages 56–73
3 Other: ....

9 Read on

Grammar	▸ Reported speech – statements and questions
Vocabulary	▸ Fiction ▸ Non-fiction ▸ Phrasal verbs connected with reading and writing
Speaking	▸ Making offers
Writing	▸ A questionnaire

▸ Vocabulary

Fiction

1 **Work with a partner and match seven of these words with the book covers.**

comic crime novel fairy tale fantasy
graphic novel historical fiction horror
play romance science fiction thriller

d
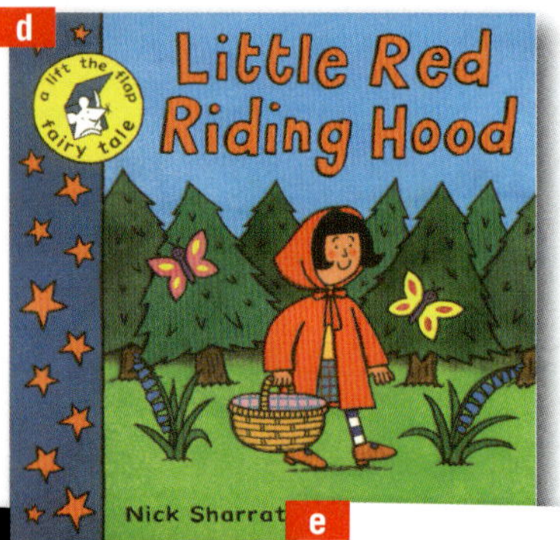

f

a

b

c

e

g

2 2.28/29 **Listen, check and repeat.**

3 SPEAKING **Work with a partner. Ask and answer these questions.**

1 Do you like reading fiction?
2 How often do you read fiction?
3 Which types of fiction do you enjoy reading the most? Why?
4 Which types of fiction do you dislike? Why?

Non-fiction

4 **Match these words with the book titles in 1–10.**

atlas autobiography biography cookbook
dictionary encyclopedia ~~guidebook~~ manual
newspaper textbook

1 *Discover Venice* ..... *guidebook*
2 *How to Get the Most From Your Digital Camera* .....
3 *My Life* by Bill Clinton .....
4 *Shakespeare* by Bill Bryson .....
5 *My Grandmother's Chinese Kitchen: 100 Family Recipes* .....
6 *Europe (World in Maps)* .....
7 *The Times* .....
8 *Gateway* .....
9 *English-French, French-English* .....
10 ..... *Britannica*

5a PRONUNCIATION **Practise saying the words in 4 and put them in the correct column, according to their stress.**

●•	●••	•●••	•••●••
atlas			

5b **Look at the words in 1 again. Can you put any of them into these columns?**

5c 2.30 **Listen, check and repeat.**

6 LISTENING 2.31 **Listen to the conversations. What types of book or publication are the people talking about? They can be fiction or non-fiction.**

1 .....
2 .....
3 .....
4 .....
5 .....

7a SPEAKING **Think about how often, and in what situations, you read non-fiction. Make notes.**

cookbooks – sometimes, to find new things to make, enjoy cooking

7b **Work with a partner. Compare your answers.**

I read cookbooks sometimes because I enjoy cooking. I read them to find new things to make.

I never read cookbooks because I never cook. I prefer reading history.

1 **Look at these photos then read the article. Number the photos in the order that they appear in the text.**

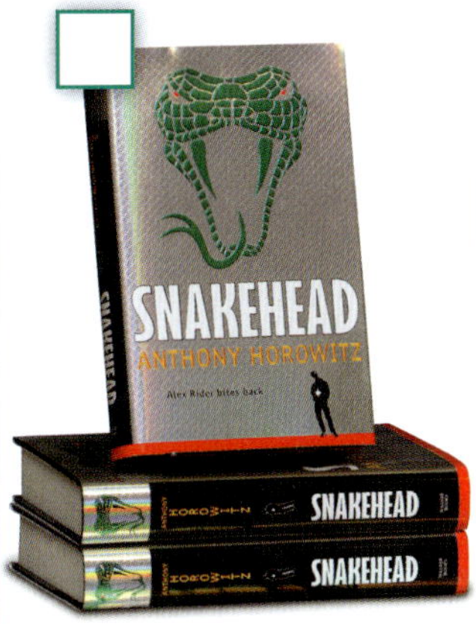

Top Teen Author: Anthony Horowitz

1............ But, like J. K. Rowling and her 'Harry Potter' novels, his books are so good that people of all ages read them. Telling stories has always been Horowitz's passion. He once told an interviewer that he had wanted to be an author since the age of eight. 2............

3............ He hated living and studying there. Once the headmaster told him to stand up in front of all the other students. The headmaster said: 'This boy is so stupid he will not be coming to the Christmas games tomorrow.' 'I have never totally recovered,' says Horowitz. To escape from these experiences, Horowitz started making up his own stories.

4............ Since then, he has written more than 30 novels, including horror stories, fantasies, detective stories and thrillers. His most famous books are almost certainly the Alex Rider series with titles such as *Snakehead* and *Scorpia*. Alex Rider is a teenage super-spy, like a young James Bond. Rider was the star of the popular film, *Stormbreaker*, based on the first novel in the series. The Alex Rider books have made English teachers very happy because they have helped to get a whole generation of teenage boys reading, instead of playing computer games.

5............ He has walked over part of the Andes, been scuba-diving and climbed a 150-metre tower in London, all just to be able to write his novels in sufficient detail.

6............ And another place where he gets inspiration for his stories is the cinema. He goes to see films three or four times a week. His favourite films are thrillers. Perhaps that explains why his own thrillers are so good!

▸ EXAM SUCCESS

You are going to do a missing sentences activity with this reading text. In this type of activity you have to find the best place to put various sentences taken from a text. How can you check this activity when you finish? EXAM SUCCESS ▸ page 152

2 **Read the article again and put these sentences into gaps 1–6 in the text.**

a Anthony's first novel was published in 1979.
b He's also worked as a cowboy in Australia, but that was just for fun!
c Anthony Horowitz is a best-selling author of books for teenagers.
d Horowitz is very serious about investigation for his novels.
e For birthdays, he always asked for just notebooks and pens.
f Perhaps Horowitz wanted to start writing at the age of eight because that was when his parents sent him to a boarding school.

3 **Look at the photos in 1 again. Explain why each one is significant for Anthony Horowitz.**

The Alex Rider books are Horowitz's most famous books. They're about a young spy.

4 **Match the underlined words in the text with their definitions.**

1 inventing *making up*
2 in the place of ....
3 enough ....
4 very popular ....
5 complete ....
6 new ideas that help you to create something ....

5 **SPEAKING What about *you*?**

1 Who is your favourite author?
2 Would you like to read a book by Anthony Horowitz? Why/Why not?

GRAMMAR GUIDE

Reported speech – statements

1a Look at what Anthony Horowitz said to a journalist.

1. **My** favourite films **are** thrillers.
2. **I go** to see films three or four times a week.
3. **I hated** living and studying there.
4. **I've written** more than 30 novels.

Now look at what the journalist wrote.

a Horowitz said **his** favourite films **were** thrillers.
b He told an interviewer **he went** to see films three or four times a week.
c He said that **he had hated** living and studying there.
d He told them that **he had written** more than 30 novels.

1b Answer the questions.

1. What happens to the verbs when they go into reported speech?
2. What happens to most pronouns and possessive adjectives when they go into reported speech?
3. What is the difference between *say* and *tell*?
4. After *say* and *tell* do we always need to use *that*?

GRAMMAR REFERENCE ▸ page 120

2 Match these sentences in direct and reported speech. One of the reported speech sentences can go with more than one of the sentences in direct speech.

1. I write novels. *d*
2. I'm writing a novel. ....
3. I wrote a novel. ....
4. I've written a novel. ....
5. I'll write a novel. ....
6. I can write novels. ....
7. I may write a novel. ....
8. I have to write a novel. ....

a He said he'd write a novel.
b He said he might write a novel.
c He said he was writing a novel.
d ~~He said he wrote novels.~~
e He said he had written a novel.
f He said he could write novels.
g He said he had to write a novel.

3 Look at the examples in 2 and put the tenses and verbs in the correct places in the table.

could had to might past continuous
past perfect past perfect ~~past simple~~ would

Direct speech	Reported speech
1 present simple →	*past simple*
2 present continuous →	
3 past simple →	
4 present perfect →	
5 will →	
6 can →	
7 may →	
8 must/have to →	

4 There are other words which we often change when we put statements into reported speech. Look at this example.

'I read this book last week.'
She said she had read that book the previous week.

Use these words to complete the table.

a (week/month/year) ago here
last (week/month/year) next (week/month/year)
~~this~~ today tomorrow tonight yesterday

Direct speech	Reported speech
1 *this*	that
2	there
3	that day
4	the day before
5	the next/following day
6	that night
7	the following (week/month/year)
8	the previous (week/month/year)
9	a (week/month/year) before

5 Complete the sentences with *said* or *told*. Which fictional character is 'he'?

1. He .... me he wasn't very tall.
2. He .... he had a friend called Sam.
3. He .... us that he had a ring.
4. He .... that he and Sam had travelled a long way.
5. He and Sam .... they needed to destroy the ring.
6. He .... that Gollum wasn't his friend.
7. He .... that he was from Middle Earth.
8. He .... me that he was a hobbit.

6 Rewrite the sentences in 5 as direct speech.

1. *'I'm not very tall.'*

7 **Report what this writer said in an interview. Use *say* and *tell*.**

1 She said that her name was Emma Maree Urquhart.

1 My name is Emma Maree Urquhart.

2 I'm thirteen years old.

3 I've already written two novels.

4 I sold more than 100,000 copies of my first novel.

5 I'm not writing anything at the moment.

6 I'll write another book one day.

7 I've got a sister but she doesn't write.

8 My first novels were about a virtual world.

9 My books are for young readers, but adults have read them too.

8a **Write a true sentence about yourself and the summer. It can be about last summer, next summer, or the summer in general.**

I went to Brighton in England last summer.
I usually go to the beach in the summer.

8b **Read out your sentences to the other people in your class or group.**

8c **When everybody has read out their sentence, write down what different people said. Can you remember everyone's sentence?**

Mia said that she had gone to Brighton the previous summer.
Jack told us that he usually went to the beach in the summer.

9a SPEAKING **Prepare five personal statements to tell your partner. Make three of your statements true. Make the other two false.**

9b **Tell your partner your statements.**

9c **Report back to your partner and tell him/her which statements you think are false.**

You said you'd read a novel in French, but I don't believe you!

9d **Tell the class your partner's false statements.**

Andrei told me he'd read a novel in French, but it wasn't true.

Phrasal verbs connected with reading and writing

1 **Read these sentences. Can you guess the meaning of the phrasal verbs in *italics*?**

1 I don't want to stop now. I want to *read on* to the end.
2 Can you *read out* your answer to the next question so that we can all hear it?
3 I don't understand some of these words. I'm going to *look* them *up* in my dictionary.
4 I want you all to *turn over* the page and continue reading.
5 Read the sentences and then *fill in* the gaps.
6 He *flicked through* the book quickly to see if he liked it before he bought it.
7 It doesn't look good when you make lots of mistakes and then you *cross* them *out*.

2 **Match the phrasal verbs in 1 with these definitions.**

a Read so that other people can hear you.
b Draw an X or a line through some writing to show that it's not correct.
c Write information in empty spaces.
d Try to find a particular piece of information in a book.
e Continue reading.
f Turn a page or piece of paper to see the other side.
g Turn the pages of a book quickly, not looking carefully.

3 **Complete the text with these words.**

cross   flick   look   on   out   over

The other day I was in a bookshop. I picked up a novel by a new writer and began to **(a)** .... through it. I didn't really read any of it, but I decided to buy it and take it home. When I started to read it carefully I didn't like the start much. But I decided to read **(b)** .... There were lots of unusual words that I had to **(c)** .... up in the dictionary. I turned **(d)** .... another page and then another but I still didn't like it. I told my friend and he asked me to read **(e)** .... a section so that he could hear. He said that the writer was using too many words to say something simple and that it was repetitive. He could **(f)** .... out half the words because they were unnecessary. In the end I stopped reading the book!

Click onto... Reading for pleasure

Literature

Maximum Ride: The Angel Experiment by James Patterson

1 Read the prologue to the novel and answer the questions.

1 What type of novel is it – historical fiction, crime, fantasy/science fiction or romance?

2 What does the prologue tell us about the 'angel experiment'?

2 Read the text again and make notes about these characters.

1 Max
14 years old, ...

2 Max's 'family'

3 the 'Erasers'

3 The author of this novel, James Patterson, is an expert at making people want to read on to find out what happens next in the story. He does this in different ways. Find a sentence from the text for each of these techniques.

1 The character talks directly to *you*, the reader.
Yes, you standing there, flicking through these pages.

2 Generally, the sentences are short and direct.

3 Reading the text is like a dangerous adventure.

4 The reader is part of the adventure.

5 The writer introduces the characters in the story quickly and dramatically.

6 The language is informal and natural, like listening to a person talking.

7 There is intrigue – you want to know more information.

4 What about *you*?

Would you like to continue reading the book? Why/Why not?

I'd like to read on because I want to know why Max and her friends are special.

INSIDE INFORMATION

- *Maximum Ride: The Angel Experiment* is a novel by American writer James Patterson.
- This text is the prologue to the novel and starts to explain what the story is about.

PROLOGUE

Congratulations. The fact that you're reading this means you've taken one giant step to surviving till your next birthday. Yes – you standing there, flicking through these pages. Do not put this book down. I'm really serious – your life could depend on it.

This is my story, the story of my family, but it could easily be your story too. We're all in this together, believe me.

I've never done anything like this, so I'm just going to jump in, and you try to keep up.

Okay, I'm Max, I'm fourteen. I live with my family, who are five kids not related to me by blood, but still totally my family.

We're – well, we're kind of amazing. We're like nothing you've seen before.

Basically, we're pretty cool, nice, smart – and very special. The six of us – me, Fang, Iggy, Nudge, the Gasman, and Angel – were made by the worst, most horrible 'scientists' you could possibly imagine. They created us as an experiment. An experiment where we ended up only 98% human. That other 2% has had a big impact, let me tell you.

We grew up in a science laboratory/prison called the School. There was one other School experiment that survived. Part human, part wolf – all predator: they're called Erasers. They're tough, smart and hard to control. They look human, but when they want to, they can change into wolf men. The School uses them as guards, police – and murderers.

This story could be about you – or your children. If not today, then soon. So please, please, take this seriously. I'm risking everything that matters by telling you – but you need to know.

Keep reading – don't let anyone stop you.

Max

WORD BOOSTER

Match the words and definitions.

1	jump in	a	part of the same genetic family
2	keep up	b	finally became
3	related by blood	c	go as quickly as another person
4	smart	d	putting in danger
5	ended up	e	strong
6	tough	f	intelligent
7	risking	g	start quickly

5 You are going to listen to a radio programme about books. They are talking about best-selling author James Patterson. Before you listen, work with a partner and answer these questions.

1 Do you think authors who write best-sellers usually write slowly or quickly?

2 Do you think they usually write only a few novels or a lot of novels?

3 Do you think they usually write serious works or not very serious works?

4 Do you think they write alone or do they sometimes write with other people?

6 2.32 Listen to the programme and choose the correct alternative.

1 James Patterson ***has/hasn't*** written more than 60 books.

2 James Patterson ***thinks/doesn't think*** he writes very serious literature.

3 When Patterson works with another writer, he writes ***a complete plan/the first version*** of the story.

4 Patterson ***has/hasn't*** written love stories.

5 Patterson has ***created/won*** a prize called the Page Turner Prize.

6 The Maximum Ride series is really for ***young people only/young people and adults***.

7 Listen again and complete the sentences.

1 Patterson has written approximately .... novels.

2 He has .... ideas for stories.

3 Often his books have his name and .... on the cover.

4 Some of his crime novels and thrillers have become ....

5 In .... his books are almost as popular as *Harry Potter*.

6 Patterson has spent .... on ideas to get people to read more.

INSIDE INFORMATION

- James Patterson is the American author of *Maximum Ride*.
- In 2007 people called him the world's best-selling author. He has sold more than 150 million books globally.
- In 2006 two of James Patterson's books were in the Top 10 books borrowed from British Libraries.
- Patterson is so famous in the USA that he once appeared in an episode of *The Simpsons*.

Literature

The Ides of March by Valerio Massimo Manfredi

8 Look at this book cover, read the website review and answer the questions.

1 What type of book is *The Ides of March*?

2 What is the book about?

3 If you saw this book in a book shop, would you pick it up and buy it? Why/Why not?

STUDY SKILLS

'Reading for pleasure' is when you read without any questions, exercises or tasks. The only objective is to enjoy yourself. What do you think is the best thing to do with new words when you read for pleasure? STUDY SKILLS ▸ page 148

9 What about *you*?

1 Do you ever read best-sellers?

2 What are the best-sellers in your country?

The Ides of March, Valerio Massimo Manfredi – Reviews

72 of 102 people found the following review helpful:

Loved this book! 14 February 2011

By J. Smith (UK) – See all my reviews

(TOP 500 REVIEWER)

The new international best-seller from the great Italian writer The Ides of March is an incredible book. I really enjoyed it! It combines the best elements of historical fiction with the most exciting features of a political thriller. The story starts in Rome in 44 BC. Julius Caesar is 56 years old and is the most powerful man in the Roman World. But he has enemies and they are working against him. Something happens that will change Rome, and the whole world, forever. The author manages to make the story really gripping from beginning to end and you learn a lot about Roman history along the way. All in all, a very good read!

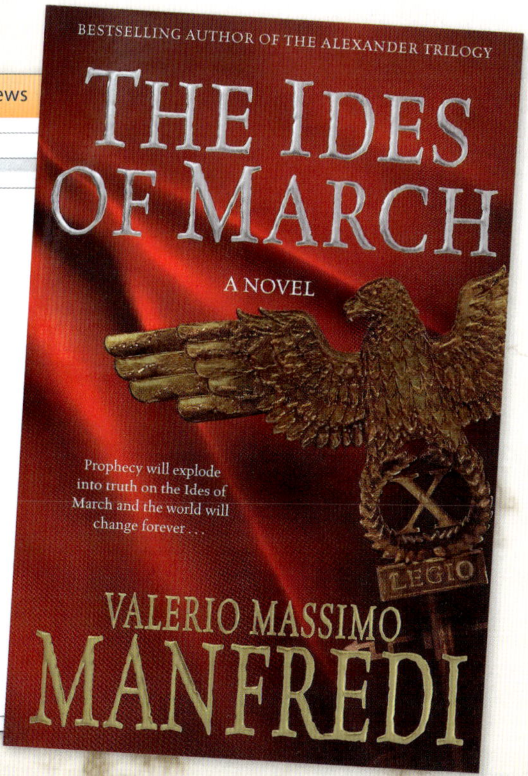

1 SPEAKING **Look at these questions and make notes. Then work with a partner and compare your ideas.**

1 Can you think of any books that have become films, like *The Lord of the Rings*?
2 What are the good things about books?
3 What are the good things about films?

EXAM SUCCESS

In the next activity you will listen to and complete gaps in notes or a text with the word(s) you hear. Is it possible to predict the type of words that are missing? How? EXAM SUCCESS ▸ page 152

2 LISTENING 2.33 **You are going to hear a woman being interviewed for a magazine survey on reading, watching films and film adaptations of books. Listen and complete the notes.**

Culture Vulture Magazine
Book vs. Film Survey
Male ☐ Female ☐

Comments
Reads one or two books a (a)..........
At the moment reading a (b).......... book.
Goes to cinema two or three times a (c)..........
(d).......... goes to see film adaptations of books.
Thinks that with books you know what the characters (e).......... The characters are almost like (f).......... Sometimes gets a shock watching films because characters (g).......... to the way she imagined.

3 **Are these statements true (T) or false (F)? Listen again if necessary.**

1 He asked her how often she bought books. T/F
2 He wanted to know how often she read historical fiction. T/F
3 He asked her what she was reading at that moment. T/F
4 The man asked the woman how often she went to the cinema. T/F
5 He asked her if she had seen *The Lord of the Rings* films. T/F
6 He asked her whether she preferred reading books or watching TV. T/F

GRAMMAR GUIDE

Reported speech – questions

1a Look at these questions and statements. Which are direct questions (DQ) and which are reported questions (RQ)?

1 He asked her what she was reading at that moment. ....
2 He wanted to know if she had seen *The Lord of the Rings* films. ....
3 How often do you go to the cinema? ....
4 Have you seen *The Lord of the Rings* films? ....
5 He asked her how often she went to the cinema. ....
6 What are you reading at the moment? ....
7 Do you prefer reading books or watching TV? ....
8 He asked her whether she preferred reading books or watching TV. ....

1b Choose the correct alternative.

1 We *change/don't change* tenses, pronouns and words like *this* and *here* in the same way in reported statements and reported questions.
2 We *use/don't use* question marks in reported questions.
3 We *use/don't use* the auxiliary verb *do* in reported questions.
4 We *put/don't put* the verb before the subject in reported questions.
5 We *use/don't use* *if* or *whether* in reported questions when there is no question word (who, what, why, etc.) in the original question.

GRAMMAR REFERENCE ▸ page 120

2 Complete the sentences with a question word or *if/whether*.

1 They asked the novelist .... her favourite writer was. She said Kafka.
2 Greg asked Jenny .... she wanted to do.
3 Paul wanted to know .... I had come by bus or by car.
4 Hannah asked me .... I wanted a coffee and I said yes.
5 They asked me .... I had brothers or sisters and I said no.
6 My teacher asked me .... I hadn't been at school the day before.
7 Karen's mum asked her .... she had had a good time.

3 **Write what the people actually said in each situation.**

1 The journalist asked the film director if he was making a film at that moment. He said that he wasn't but that he was going to start a new one soon.

Journalist: ....

Film Director: ....

2 The writer asked the man if he had enjoyed her book. He said that he thought it was the most beautiful thing he'd ever read.

Writer: ....

Man: ....

3 The reporter asked the singer why she wouldn't answer any of his questions. She told him that she only wanted to talk about her new CD and that she wasn't going to talk about anything else.

Reporter: ....

Singer: ....

4 The teacher asked the class whether they could write an essay for the next day, but they replied that they couldn't because they had to study for an exam and they wouldn't have enough time.

Teacher: ....

Students: ....

5 Julie wanted to know what my favourite book was. I said it was *1984* by George Orwell. She asked me how many times I'd read it and I told her that I'd read it three times.

Julie: ....

Me: ....

4a PRONUNCIATION **Match the diagrams with the questions. In which type of questions, *Wh-* or *Yes/No*, does the intonation usually go up?**

Diagram A **Diagram B**

1 How often do you read? ....

2 Do you like reading? ....

4b **Do you think the intonation will go up or down in reported questions?**

4c 2.34 **Listen to these reported questions. Check your answer to 4b and repeat the sentences.**

1 She asked me what my name was.

2 She wanted to know where I was from.

3 They asked me why I'd come.

4 I asked her where she'd been.

5 **Write this conversation in reported speech. Practise reading it aloud with the correct intonation.**

KEIRA: What did you do last night?

MATTHEW: I didn't do much. I just watched TV with my parents.

KEIRA: Did you study for the literature exam?

MATTHEW: When do we have the exam?

KEIRA: We're doing it today.

MATTHEW: Why didn't you remind me?

KEIRA: I told you but you weren't listening. Why do you never pay attention to me?

6a SPEAKING **Try to remember questions that people have asked you so far today. Write down five reported questions.**

1 My mum asked me what time I would come home.

2 My teacher asked me if I had done my homework.

6b **Compare your sentences with a partner. Are they similar?**

7a SPEAKING **As a class, choose a famous person who you would like to interview. It can be an actor, politician, sports personality or singer.**

7b **Imagine that this famous person is coming to your school. With your partner, prepare five questions to ask them.**

7c **Choose a student to be the famous person. Interview them and make a note of their answers.**

7d **Now take it in turns to report the interview.**

First we asked him why he had decided to come to our school. He said that he'd been a student here.

1a SPEAKING **Work with a partner.**

1 How often do you go to bookshops?
2 What type of books or other things do you buy there?

1b Look at the photo. Talk about what you can see.

2 LISTENING 2.35 **Listen to a customer in a bookshop speaking to a shop assistant and answer these questions.**

1 What type of book does the customer want to buy?
2 Which section should the book be in?
3 Where should she go to find this section?

3 LISTENING 2.36 **Listen to the same customer speaking to another shop assistant.**

1 In the end, does the customer find the book she wanted?
2 Does she order any books?
3 How much does she spend in the bookshop?

4 2.37 **Complete this dialogue with the correct information in 3. Listen again if necessary.**

SHOP ASSISTANT: Yes, can I help you?

CUSTOMER: Yes, please. I'm looking for a book called **(a)** .... It's a **(b)** .... book. They told me that it would be in the **(c)** .... section.

SHOP ASSISTANT: Right. Have you looked there?

CUSTOMER: Yes, I have, but I can't see it.

SHOP ASSISTANT: OK, I'll just check on the computer. Do you know the name of the author?

CUSTOMER: Yes, it's **(d)** ....

SHOP ASSISTANT: OK, let's see. Ah, no, I'm sorry, it isn't in stock at the moment. Would you like me to order it for you?

CUSTOMER: How long will it take?

SHOP ASSISTANT: It should be here in **(e)** ....

CUSTOMER: That's **(f)** .... I'll take these two books then.

SHOP ASSISTANT: Certainly. That's **(g)** ...., please.

CUSTOMER: Can I pay by credit card?

SHOP ASSISTANT: Of course.

5 SPEAKING **Practise the dialogue in 4 with a partner. Include the correct information.**

6 **Tick the expressions in the Speaking Bank that appear in the dialogue. Which are more formal ways of offering help?**

Speaking Bank

Useful expressions for making offers

- Can I help you?
- Do you want me to ... ?
- Would you like me to ... ?
- Shall I ... for you?
- How about if I ... for you?

Practice makes perfect

7a SPEAKING **Student A: Work with a partner. Do the role-play, using the Conversation Guide to help you.**

Student A: you are the shop assistant.

Student B: you are the customer.

Conversation Guide

SHOP ASSISTANT: *Say hello to the customer and offer to help.*

CUSTOMER: *Tell the shop assistant what book you are looking for.*

SHOP ASSISTANT: *Ask the customer what type of book it is.*

CUSTOMER: *Tell the shop assistant what type of book it is.*

SHOP ASSISTANT: *Tell the customer which section to look in.*

CUSTOMER: *Tell the shop assistant that you've looked there but can't find it.*

SHOP ASSISTANT: *Tell the customer you'll check on the computer if it is in stock. Ask for the name of the author.*

CUSTOMER: *Tell the shop assistant the name of the author. Spell it if necessary.*

SHOP ASSISTANT: *Tell the customer that you don't have the book but offer to order it.*

CUSTOMER: *Ask how long it will take and the price.*

SHOP ASSISTANT: *Tell the customer how long it will take and the price of the book.*

CUSTOMER: *Agree to order the book.*

SHOP ASSISTANT: *Ask for the customer's name and address.*

CUSTOMER: *Tell the shop assistant your name and address. Then tell the shop assistant that you want to buy the three books in your hand.*

SHOP ASSISTANT: *Tell the customer how much the three books cost.*

CUSTOMER: *Ask if you can pay by credit card.*

SHOP ASSISTANT: *Say yes.*

7b **Now change roles. Cover the Conversation Guide.**

1 **Look at the magazine covers. What type of magazines are they? Use these words to help you. Which covers are not shown?**

car celebrities computer film games
music nature science sports

2 **Complete the questions about magazines with these question words.**

how much how often when
where which who why

1 .... do you read magazines?
often/sometimes/never

2 .... magazine(s) do you read?

3 .... buys the magazines you read?
you/your parents/your brother(s) or sister(s)/other

4 .... do you spend on magazines a month?

5 .... do you read magazines?
at home/on the bus or train/in waiting rooms/other

6 .... do you read magazines?
to relax/to learn new things/other

7 .... do you usually read magazines?
from Monday to Friday/at the weekend/any day

3 **Put the words in order to make more questions about magazines.**

1 favourite/is/your/which/magazine/?
2 magazines/you/like/what/do/about/?
3 reading/long/spend/you/do/how/magazines/day/each/?
4 buy/magazines/you/where/do/?
5 read/you/online/do/magazines/?

4 SPEAKING **Work with a partner. Take it in turns to ask and answer the questions in 2 and 3.**

5 **Look at these questions and match each one with one of the rules in the Writing Bank.**

1 What are you reading at the moment?
2 Who gives you money to buy magazines?
3 What type of magazines do you like?

Writing Bank

Writing questions

- In subject questions, the *question word (who, what, etc)* is the subject of the verb. *The auxiliary verb (do, does, did)* is not necessary.
- In object questions, the *question word (who, what, etc)* is the object of the verb. The *auxiliary verb (do, does, did)* is necessary.
- When we have *to be* or a *modal verb (can, will, should)*, we do not need the *auxiliary verb do* to make questions.

6 **You are going to write a questionnaire about newspapers. Work with a partner and write down any ideas for things that you could ask. Look at this example:**

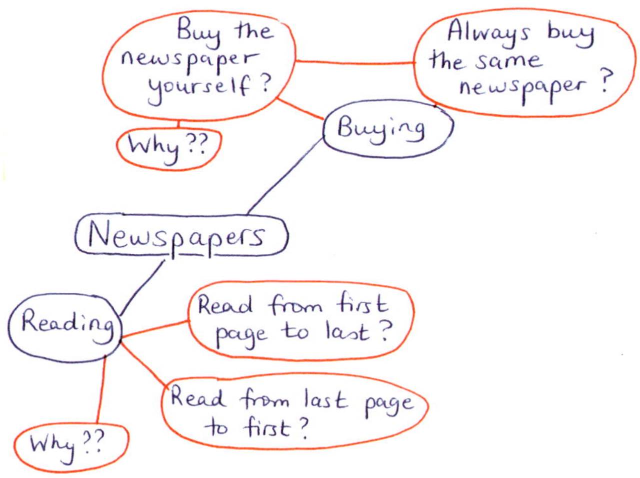

STUDY SKILLS

The activity in 6 is called brainstorming. The idea is to come up with as many ideas as possible, without stopping to analyse them. Why is this a good thing to do before writing? STUDY SKILLS ▸ page 148

Practice makes perfect

7a **Look at the task.**

- Prepare a questionnaire about newspapers with 6–8 questions.
- Use the questions in 2 and 3 as a model and include the ideas that you brainstormed in 6.
- Ask different students the questions in your questionnaire.

7b **Write a report about what you discovered from your questionnaire.**

Most people said they bought newspapers but Leo told me that he only read the sports section of the newspaper. Ava told me she never bought newspapers – she always read other people's.

Language reference and revision

Grammar reference

Reported speech – statements

Form

When the reporting verb (*say, tell*) is in the past, the tense of the verb in reported speech usually changes, going one tense 'back'.

Direct speech – tenses	Reported speech – tenses
'I **work** at home.' *Present simple*	She said she **worked** at home. *Past simple*
'I'**m working**.' *Present continuous*	She said she **was working**. *Past continuous*
'I **have worked**.' *Present perfect*	She said she **had worked**. *Past perfect*
'I **worked**.' *Past simple*	She said she **had worked**. *Past perfect*
'I **had worked**.' *Past perfect*	She said she **had worked**. *Past perfect*
'I **will** work.' *will*	She said she **would** work. *would*
'I **can** work.' *can*	She said she **could** work. *could*
'I **may** work.' *may*	She said she **might** work. *might*
'I **must/have** to work.' *must/have to*	She said she **had to** work. *had to*

Could, **would**, **should** and **might** do not change from direct to reported speech.

When the reporting verb is in the present simple, the tense of the verb in reported speech usually stays the same.
'I love cycling'. → *She says she loves cycling.*

When the reporting verb is in the past but the statement is something which is still true, or is and will always be true, the tense of the verb in reported speech usually stays the same.
'I'm from Poland.' → *Monika said she's from Poland.*

In reported speech, pronouns and possessive adjectives also change.
'I like your jacket.' → *Mary said she liked my jacket.*

Here are some other words which change from direct to reported speech.

Direct speech	Reported speech
this/these	these/those
here	there
today	that day
yesterday	the day before
tomorrow	the next/following day
last night	that night
next (week/month/year)	the following (week/month/year)
last (week/month/year)	the previous (week/month/year)
a (week/month/year) ago	a (week/month/year) before

Use

We use reported speech to report the words spoken by another person.
'I came, I saw, I conquered,' said Julius Caesar. → *Julius Caesar said that he'd come, he'd seen and he'd conquered.*

Reported speech – say and tell

Use

With **say** you do not need to use a personal object to say who you are saying something to.
He said (...) he wanted to go.

With **tell** you *must* use a personal object to say who you are saying something to.
He told John he wanted to go.

Reported speech – questions

Form

The same changes occur with tenses, pronouns and other words as with reported statements. We do not use the auxiliary verb **do** in reported questions.
'Do you like this newspaper?' → *He asked me if I liked that newspaper.*

There is no inversion of subject and verb in reported questions.
'Where is he?' → *They asked me where he was.*

Reported questions are not real questions so they do not need question marks.

When there is no question word (*who, what, how, why,* etc.), we use **if** or **whether**.

'Will you go to the party?' → *They asked me if I would go to the party.*

Vocabulary

1 Fiction

comic graphic novel
crime novel fairy tale
fantasy historical fiction
horror play romance
science fiction thriller

2 Non-fiction

atlas autobiography
biography cookbook
dictionary encyclopedia
guidebook magazine
manual newspaper textbook

3 Phrasal verbs connected with reading and writing

cross out fill in flick through look up
read on read out turn over

4 Other words and phrases ▶ page 144–5

Grammar revision

Reported speech – statements

1 Write these sentences in reported speech.

1 'I'm going to a conference next week,' my sister said.
2 'I'll be late tomorrow,' Daniel told the teacher.
3 'This is my book,' said Holly.
4 'I've always wanted to write stories,' said the novelist.
5 'There is going to be a concert in this room,' they told the public.
6 'The talk will start at 9 o'clock tomorrow,' they said.
7 'We haven't read any of your books,' the students told the writer.
8 'I wrote the article yesterday,' said the journalist.

WORKBOOK ▶ page 76

/ 8 points

Reported speech – questions

2 Write these questions in reported speech.

1 'Are you from Manchester?' she asked me.
2 'What time are you going to leave?' Joe asked Jessica.
3 'Why were you crying?' I asked Katie.
4 'Have you read this book?' the teacher asked the students.
5 'Will you help me tomorrow?' Sandra's dad asked her.
6 'Did the doctor see Mike yesterday?' Abigail asked her mum.
7 'Do you know the answer to this question?' our teacher asked us.
8 'How many pages has that book got?' I asked Stephen.

WORKBOOK ▶ page 79

/ 8 points

Vocabulary revision

Fiction

1 Complete the sentences with the correct words.

1 A _ _ _ _ _ _ _ story is often about elves, dragons, trolls or other imaginary creatures.
2 A _ _ _ _ _ _ _ _ is an exciting story about spies, murders and assassinations.
3 You can either read a _ _ _ _ or see it at a theatre.
4 A _ _ _ _ _ _ _ is a story about people who fall in love.
5 A _ _ _ _ _ _ _ _ _ is usually about a prince, a princess or a witch.
6 In _ _ _ _ _ _ _ _ _ _ _ fiction, the story takes place at a particular moment in the past.
7 A _ _ _ _ _ _ _ _ _ _ _ _ _ is a type of book which combines writing and art, like 'manga' for example.
8 A _ _ _ _ _ _ story should be frightening.

WORKBOOK ▶ page 74

/ 8 points

Non-fiction

2 Which type of book or publication is best in these situations?

1 You want to find the meaning of a word. ....
2 You want to find out about the geography of a country. ....
3 You want to read about the life of a person, in his/her own words. ....
4 You want to find new ideas for dinner. ....
5 You want to learn how to use your computer well. ....
6 You're going to Prague and want to know what to visit. ....
7 You want to know what's happening in the world at the moment. ....
8 You want to revise maths for an exam. ....
9 You want to find out information about lots of different topics to write a quiz. ....

WORKBOOK ▶ page 74

/ 9 points

Phrasal verbs connected with reading and writing

3 Match the sentence halves.

1 I love this book, I want to read
2 When you finish that page, turn
3 You have to fill
4 Because the text was difficult, I had to look
5 I can't read what he wrote because he crossed
6 I looked at the magazine quickly. I flicked
7 I want to hear your answers so please read

a them out to me in a loud voice.
b it out with a big X.
c over and read the next one.
d through it looking at the pictures.
e up lots of words.
f in the answers on your sheet.
g on tonight until I get to the end of it.

WORKBOOK ▶ page 77

/ 7 points

Total / 40 points

10 Cyberspace

Grammar ▸ The passive – present simple and other tenses
Vocabulary ▸ Computers and computing ▸ The Internet ▸ Collocations with *email*
Speaking ▸ Talking about photos
Writing ▸ Text messages

▸ Vocabulary

Computers and computing

1 **Work with a partner. Match these words with the parts of the computer in the photo.**

hard drive keyboard laptop mouse mouse pad printer screen ~~speaker~~ USB port webcam

2 2.38/9 **Listen, check and repeat.**

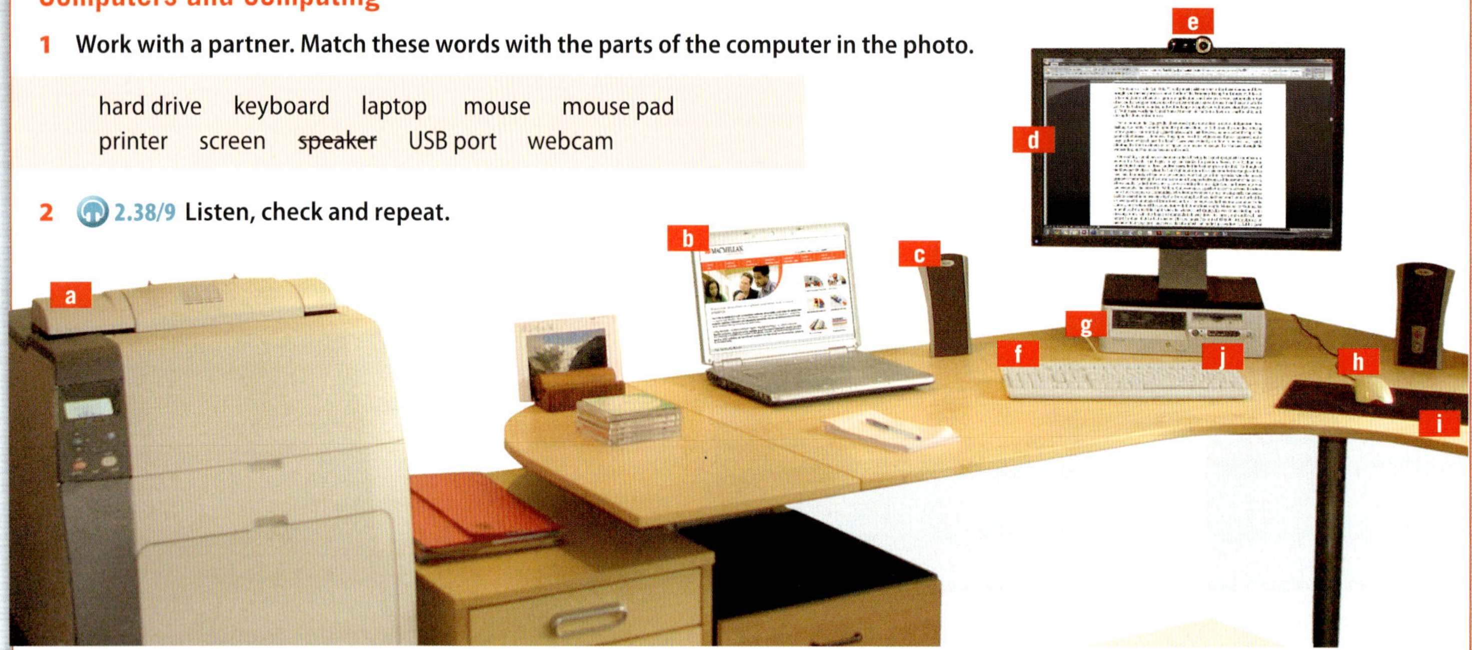

3 **Read these sentences. Which word in 1 does each sentence describe?**

1 You use it to hear things like music. *speaker*
2 You move it and click on the buttons to do things on a computer. ....
3 It's the part of the computer where you can see words and pictures. ....
4 You use it to write with a computer. ....
5 You move the mouse on this. ....
6 You use it to record images that you can see and send on the Internet. ....
7 It's the part inside a computer which has the information that the computer needs to work. ....
8 You use it to make hard copies of documents that you have created on a computer. ....
9 It's a place on a computer where you can connect a keyboard, printer, camera, etc. ....
10 It's a small computer that you can carry with you. ....

The Internet

4 **Read this description by a teenager of how she uses the Internet. Underline any words that you don't understand and then look them up in your dictionary.**

'I've got broadband so my connection to the Net is quite fast. I usually go online in the evenings, after I've finished my homework, but sometimes I use the Net for schoolwork too. The first thing I do is check my emails. I surf the Net and look at my favourite websites. My favourite search engine is Google. I sometimes download music and films, but not often. I haven't got a blog but I chat online with my friends.'

5a PRONUNCIATION **Look at these two sentences. Is *download* a verb or a noun in each sentence? Where do we place the stress?**

1 I want to *download* this song.
2 The *download* didn't work.

5b 2.40 **Listen to the two sentences. Is the pronunciation of *download* the same in each sentence?**

5c 2.41 **Listen again and choose the correct alternative.**

1 In two-syllable verbs the stress is usually on the *first/second* syllable.
2 In two-syllable nouns the stress is usually on the *first/second* syllable.

6 **Here are some other words which are both nouns and verbs. Check that you understand the meaning of the words. Say the words first as a verb and then as a noun.**

export import increase protest record

7a SPEAKING **Work with a partner. How often do you do these things on a computer (never, sometimes, often, very often)?**

1 do schoolwork
2 print documents or photos
3 use a webcam
4 go online and surf the Net
5 send emails
6 download music or films
7 read or write blogs
8 chat online
9 participate as a member of an online community (e.g. MySpace, Facebook)

7b **Take it in turns to ask how often you do the different things. Are your answers similar?**

1 Work with a partner. Discuss these questions.

1 How often do you have to write essays or prepare presentations at school?
2 Do you know any websites where you can buy essays written by other people?
3 What happens in your school if you cheat in an exam or doing homework?

2 Read this text about buying essays for school or university online. Does the text give the:

1 teachers' side of the argument? Yes/No
2 students' side of the argument? Yes/No
3 arguments of the companies that sell online school work? Yes/No

You can answer *yes* more than once.

Internet cheating

1 Millions of pounds are spent each year on Internet cheating. There are tens of thousands of websites where you can buy essays. With most essay-writing companies, students pay per word. Sometimes they pay per page. Some companies offer to write a special, personalised essay, but at an extra cost. You can also pay extra for faster essays.

2 Barclay Littlewood is the owner of one online essay-writing organisation. 3,500 specialists are employed by his company. They have written more than 15,000 essays for students. The company made £90,000 in just one week in May. Thanks to his company, Littlewood has a Ferrari and a Lamborghini in his garage.

3 However, Internet cheating is now an enormous problem for schools and universities. One education expert predicted that schools would have to stop continuous assessment and start doing more exams again. Universities and schools say that the UK's academic reputation is going down because of online essay companies.

4 Barclay Littlewood, on the other hand, says he doesn't help students to cheat. He says he simply offers them a guide. 'The essays are a starting point. Students use them to create their own work. Students analyse our answers and then they write their own. We're just showing them how to write a great essay.'

5 But as one teacher replied: 'The suggestion that these essays are used by students as "guides" is crazy and dishonest. We need to do something to stop it.' Many colleges and universities now have software which allows teachers to check if students are copying from five billion web pages. Many universities have somebody doing this full-time. 'It's not a question of catching people and punishing them. It's a question of helping students to understand what education really is. Education is research and investigation. In the end, the students who are using these services are just not learning the skills they need for their studies or for the rest of their lives.'

3 Read the text again and choose the best answers.

1 The price of a basic online essay usually depends on
a who writes it.
b what the subject is.
c how long it is.

2 Barclay Littlewood is
a a businessman.
b a writer of online essays.
c an ex-teacher.

3 An educational specialist thinks that online cheating will
a change the way teachers teach.
b change the way teachers assess students.
c make it easier for students to pass exams.

4 Barclay Littlewood says
a students shouldn't just give teachers the essay that they buy.
b he is helping students to copy work.
c his objective is to help students get the best marks.

5 The text says that teachers
a have no way of knowing if students are copying essays.
b are using technology to find people who are cheating.
c want to make cheats suffer.

4 Answer these questions using your own words.

1 Why does Barclay Littlewood think online essays are good?
2 Why do teachers think online essays are bad?

5 Guess the type of word (noun, verb, adjective, preposition, etc) and the possible meaning. Then use your dictionary to see if you were correct.

1 per *preposition – for each*
2 personalised ....
3 owner ....
4 continuous assessment ....
5 starting point ....
6 crazy ....
7 punishing ....
8 research ....

STUDY SKILLS

Why is it important and useful to guess difficult words from their context?

STUDY SKILLS ▶ page 148

6 SPEAKING What about *you*?

1 What do you think about buying online essays?
2 Would you ever buy an online essay? Why/Why not?

GRAMMAR GUIDE

The passive – present simple

1a Look at these sentences. Which are active and which are passive?

1 Millions of pounds **are spent** each year on Internet cheating.

2 People **spend** millions of pounds on Internet cheating.

3 His company **employs** 3,500 specialists.

4 3,500 specialists **are employed** by his company.

1b Are these statements true (T) or false (F)?

1 We use the passive when we are more interested in the action than in the person who does it. T/F

2 We use the passive when we don't know who exactly does the action. T/F

3 We use the passive when it is obvious who does the action. T/F

1c Complete the rules.

1 To make the present simple passive we use .... + the past participle.

2 We use the preposition .... to introduce the agent, the person or thing which does the action.

GRAMMAR REFERENCE ▶ page 132

2 Complete the sentences with *is* or *are*.

1 The Internet .... used by approximately 67% of the British population.

2 Every day approximately 183 billion emails .... sent around the world.

3 That means more than 2 million emails .... sent every second.

4 Email .... used by around 1.3 billion people.

5 Some people calculate that 56.4% of web pages .... written in English.

6 A new blog .... created each half-second of every day.

7 The biggest percentage of Internet users in the world .... found in Asia.

3 Put the verbs in the correct form of the present simple passive.

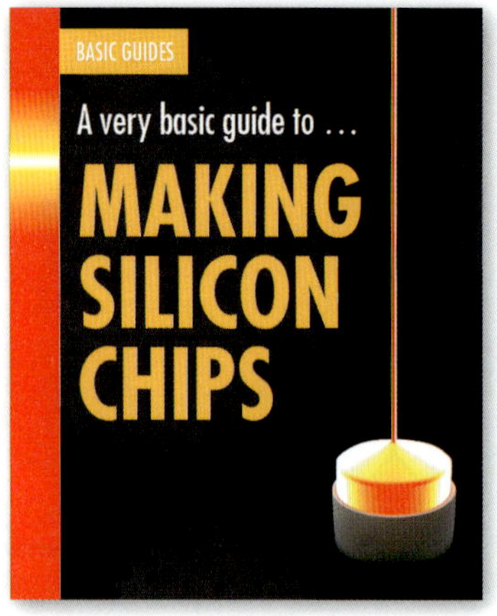

1 Silicon .... (find) in sand.

2 The silicon .... (refine) to be 100% pure.

3 The pure silicon .... (heat) and .... (make) into small blocks called ingots.

4 The ingots .... (cut) into thin slices called wafers.

5 The wafers .... (wash) in various chemicals and metal layers .... (add).

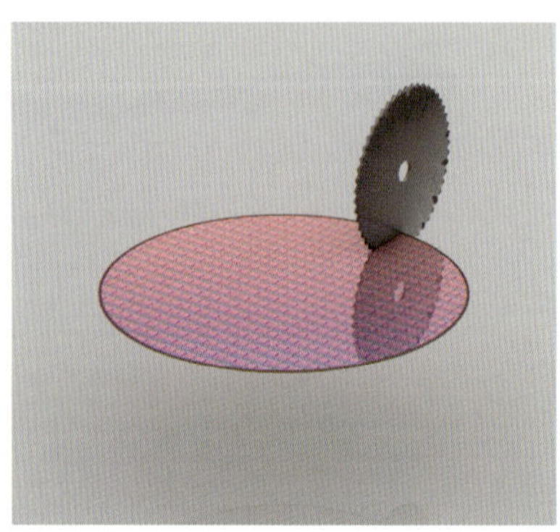

6 The wafers .... (cut) into smaller pieces called dies.

7 The dies .... (add) to a cooling plate to form a micro-processor. They are then .... (send) to computer factories.

4 **Change these sentences from active to passive, or from passive to active. Include *by* plus the agent only when necessary.**

1 They make a lot of silicon chips in India.
2 They employ many people in the computer industry.
3 They invent new technology every day.
4 Most new games consoles are created by Sony and Nintendo.
5 Millions of kids play computer games every day.
6 People do a lot of shopping online nowadays.
7 Some governments control the use of the Internet.
8 You don't need a password to enter this site.

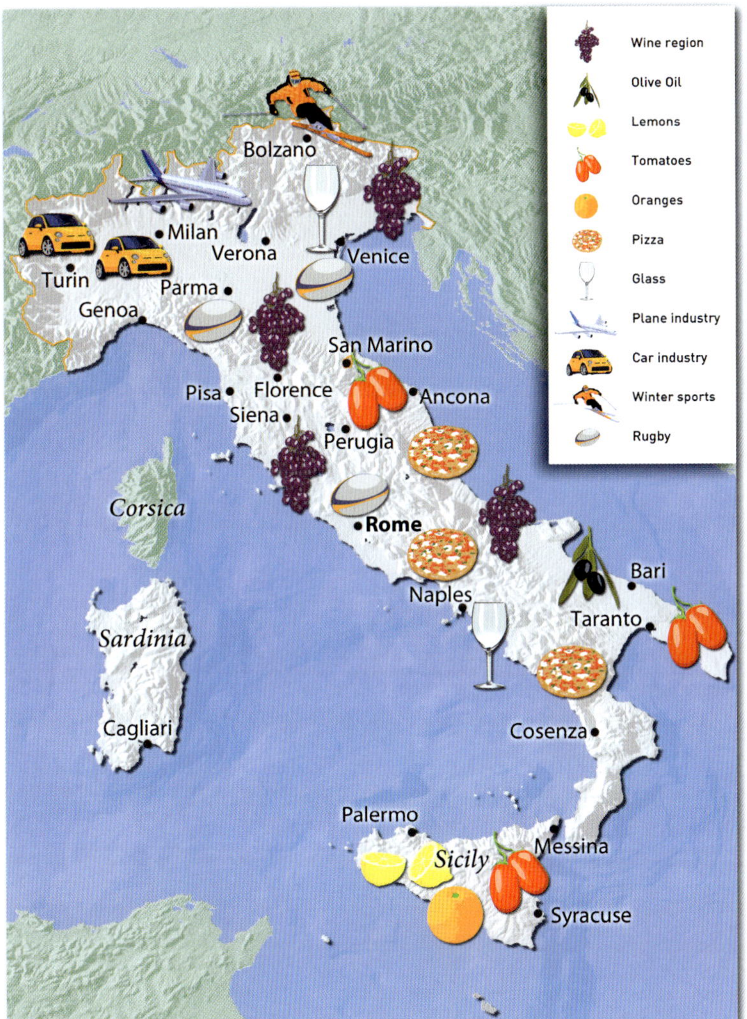

5a SPEAKING **Work with a partner. Look at the map of Italy and answer these questions.**

1 What things are made there?
2 What things are exported?
3 What fruit and vegetables are grown?
4 What fruit and vegetables are *not* grown?
5 What typical food is eaten?
6 What sports are played?
7 What sports are *not* played?

Cars are made in Italy. They're made in the north, in Turin and Milan.

5b **Now use the questions to help you prepare a presentation about your country. Give as many details as possible.**

5c **Give your presentation to the class.**

Collocations with *email*

1 **Read the text. The words in *italics* frequently go with the word *email*. Which of these words match the icons below?**

The other day I tried to **(a)** *send* an email to my cousin but it **(b)** *bounced back*. The email **(c)** *address* wasn't correct. The problem was that my cousin had recently changed his email **(d)** *account*. He'd sent me a message with his new email address but I had accidentally **(e)** *deleted* it, so I didn't have it any more. I knew that one of my friends had my cousin's new email address so I sent my original email to my friend and asked her to **(f)** *forward* it to my cousin. The next day I was **(g)** *checking* my email and I saw that my cousin had **(h)** *replied to* my message.

1 ....

2 ....

3 ....

2 **Match these definitions with the correct words in 1.**

1 an arrangement you have with an Internet company to use email ....*account*....
2 when an email doesn't go to the person you send it to and it comes back to you ....
3 the letters, numbers and symbols you need to write to send someone an email ....
4 to see if you have any email ....
5 to send an email on to somebody ....

3a SPEAKING **Think about these questions. Make a note of your answers.**

1 Have you got an email address? If so, do you know how to say it in English?
2 Do you have a free email account or do you pay?
3 Who do you send most emails to?
4 How fast do you usually reply to the emails you receive?
5 How often do you delete the emails you receive?
6 When do you usually check your email?
7 Have any of your emails ever bounced back? Do you know why?
8 How much spam do you get via email?

3b **Work with a partner. Ask and answer the questions.**

3c **Now tell another student what you discovered about your partner.**

Click onto... New technologies

Cross-curricular – Science

The inventor of the World Wide Web

1 LISTENING 2.42 **Listen to a radio programme about Sir Tim Berners-Lee, the inventor of the WWW. Does the presenter say anything about …**

1 when Berners-Lee was a child? Yes/No
2 when he was at university? Yes/No
3 his life now? Yes/No

2 **Listen again and choose the correct alternative.**

1 Berners-Lee was born in the south-west of England/London/Switzerland.
2 Berners-Lee liked riding on trains/building model trains/watching trains.
3 Berners-Lee's first contact with electronic gadgets was making a model train/making something for his model trains/repairing the TV.
4 Berners-Lee made a TV program/computer/computer program when he was at university.
5 Berners-Lee studied physics at university because he thought it was more practical than maths/he didn't like maths/his parents taught physics.

3 **You are going to read some Frequently Asked Questions from the website of Sir Tim Berners-Lee, the inventor of the World Wide Web. Match the questions with answers 1–4 in the text.**

a Was it easy to invent the WWW?
b Where were you when you invented the WWW?
c Why do you always say everything is simple?
d What made you think of the WWW?

1 ....
I was working in a physics laboratory called CERN. CERN is in Geneva, Switzerland. At CERN, people study High Energy Physics. That is the physics of really, really small particles – particles much smaller than atoms. If you want to investigate really, really small things, you need enormous machines called accelerators. That's what they have at CERN.

2 ....
Well, things were very frustrating in the past. There was different information on different computers, but you couldn't get all the information with just one computer. People at CERN came from universities all over the world. They brought all types of computers with different types of software. Sometimes you had to learn a different program for each computer. So I wrote some programs to take information from one computer system to put it in another system. And then I thought "Can't we connect all these different information systems and make just one imaginary information system? Everybody could read the same system." And that became the WWW.

3 ....
Actually inventing it was simple. The difficult part was to persuade everybody to use the same system. It's incredible that so many people now use it.

4 ....
Well, because it is, basically. I want you to know that you too can make new programs which create new, fun ways of using computers and using the Internet. I want you to know that, if you can imagine a computer doing something, you can program a computer to do that. The only limit is your imagination. And a couple of laws of physics. Of course, what happens with computers is that you have a basic, simple idea. Then you have to add things on to it to make it work. But all good computer programs are simple inside.

4 Read the text again and answer the questions.

1 What is high energy physics?
2 What is an accelerator?
3 Why did people have to learn different programs for different computers at CERN?
4 What was Sir Tim Berners-Lee's solution to the problem with computers at CERN?
5 What was the hardest part about making the World Wide Web work?
6 How can you create a new computer program, in Berners-Lee's opinion?

5 What about *you*?

1 How important are the Internet and the World Wide Web for you? Why?
2 What information about the inventor of the World Wide Web did you find interesting?

I think the Internet is really important for me.

Why?

It's very useful for finding information for schoolwork, for example.

Cross-curricular – Geography
Silicon Valley

6 Work with a partner. Do you know anything about Silicon Valley? Make a list with ideas.
We think it's in California, USA.

7 Read the facts about Silicon Valley. Did any of your ideas in 6 appear? Were your ideas correct?

8 Read the facts again and classify the information into these categories. Some numbers can go in more than one category.

Geography	Population	Economy/Industry	Other
1			

9 Complete the notes.

10 What about *you*?
Would you like to live or work in Silicon Valley? Why/Why not?

I'd like to go there because I'm really interested in computers.

I'd prefer to go to San Francisco.

Eight facts about ... Silicon Valley

1 Silicon Valley is in North California, USA, near San Francisco.
2 The name Silicon Valley is used to describe a geographical area (its real name is the Santa Clara Valley), but also to describe all the high-tech companies in this area. Many of these companies originally designed and made silicon chips.
3 2.43 million people live in Silicon Valley.
4 38% of the population of Silicon Valley was born outside the USA. These people are usually top engineers and scientists who have gone there to work.
5 There are 16 different cities in Silicon Valley. The biggest is San José. It is called the capital of Silicon Valley.
6 The area has had a great reputation for new ideas and technology. Many rich businessmen have gone there to invest money in new projects, especially in computers and the Internet.
7 Many engineers and scientists went to live in Silicon Valley because there was a lot of space and prices were relatively cheap. Now it is one of the most expensive places in the USA to buy a house.
8 Silicon Valley is the home of Apple, eBay, Google, Yahoo!, HP, Intel and many other world-famous computer and Internet businesses.

SILICON VALLEY
1 How did it get its name?
2 Who works there?
3 How much did/does it cost to live there?
4 Where is it?
5 What is the correct name for its location?
6 Why is it famous?

Listening

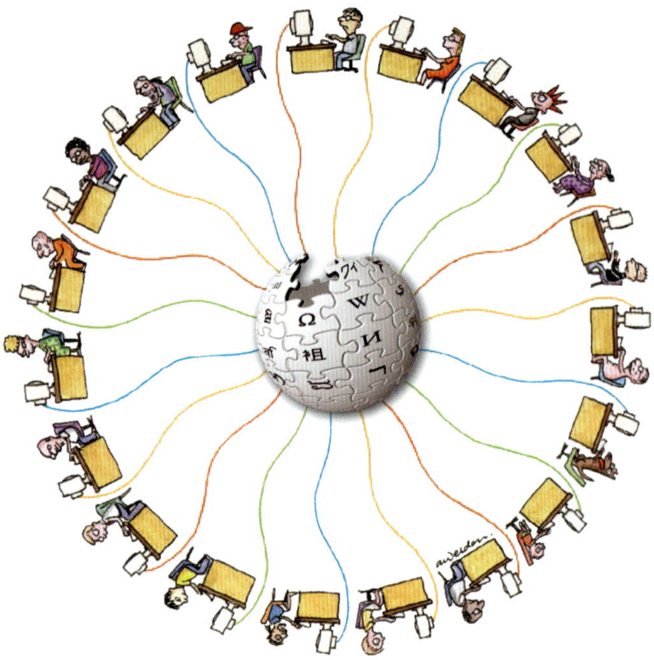

1 SPEAKING **Work with a partner. Can you answer these questions? If you don't know the answers, guess!**

1 What is Wikipedia?
2 Who is Wikipedia written by?
3 How many languages does Wikipedia appear in?

2 LISTENING 2.43 **Listen to a radio programme about Wikipedia and check your answers in 1.**

3 **Look at this text about Wikipedia. It contains six mistakes. Listen again to the radio programme and find the mistakes.**

Wikipedia is the fifth most popular website in the world. It was started in 2001 by two Australians but it isn't written by them. Their first encyclopedia was an incredible success. Then the website became a 'wiki', a website that visitors can change and add information to. Approximately 170 articles are being added every day. 'Wiki wiki' is an African expression which means 'quick', and one of the reasons that Wikipedia is so popular is that articles can change quickly when things change in the world. Wikipedia has offices in many countries, including Poland. One of the five most popular editions of Wikipedia is the Polish edition.

4 SPEAKING **What about *you*?**

1 Do you ever use Wikipedia? When and what for?
2 Would you like to write an article for Wikipedia? What would you write about?

I sometimes use Wikipedia for projects at school.

Me too. I usually use it to find out about famous people, especially for history classes.

Grammar in context

GRAMMAR GUIDE

The passive – other tenses

1a Look at these passive sentences. Match them with the correct tenses (a–c).

1 *It was started in 2001.* ....
2 *Hundreds of articles are being added every day.* ....
3 *Articles have been written by hundreds of thousands of people.* ....

a present continuous passive
b present perfect passive
c past simple passive

1b To change the tense in a passive sentence, do we change the verb *be* or the past participle?

GRAMMAR REFERENCE ▸ page 132

2 **Change these sentences from active to passive.**

1 Wikipedia has transformed traditional encyclopedias.

....

....

2 Sir Tim Berners-Lee didn't start Wikipedia.

....

....

3 They are changing Wikipedia articles at this moment.

....

....

4 Normal people have written most of the articles for Wikipedia.

....

....

5 'Vandals' have ruined some Wikipedia articles.

....

....

6 A 14-year-old boy from Puerto Rico is checking many Wikipedia texts.

....

....

7 A famous scientist wrote an article in 2007.

....

....

8 A lot of students have used Wikipedia.

....

....

▸ EXAM SUCCESS

The next exercise is a cloze activity. You have a text with gaps, but they do not give you words to fill in the gaps. How do you decide which word is missing?

EXAM SUCCESS ▸ page 153

3 Complete the text by filling in each space with one word.

Second Life is a virtual world. It **(a)** *was* created in 2003 by a company called Linden Lab. Some people call it the future of entertainment, social interaction and business. In fact, business **(b)** .... important in Second Life because you can buy and sell almost anything. People **(c)** .... for things with Linden dollars. You can buy Linden dollars with real US dollars. In September 2006 a **(d)** .... of money **(e)** .... spent in Second Life ($6.6m!), mostly on designer clothes. Officially there **(f)** .... more than two million residents in Second Life at the moment but many of these residents are not active. People under 18 can't join Second Life because you **(g)** .... be 18. So now a place called Teen Second Life has **(h)** .... created **(i)** .... Linden Lab for young people **(j)** .... 13 to 17.

4 Write questions in the passive for these answers.

1 *Who was Second Life created by?*
Second Life was created by Linden Lab.

2 .... ?
The first Nobel Prize was given in 1901.

3 .... ?
A supercomputer is being created by the University of California.

4 .... ?
The DS Lite™ is made by Nintendo™.

5 .... ?
Wikipedia has been used by millions of people.

6 .... ?
The first computer mouse was made in 1964.

7 .... ?
Brave New World was written by Aldous Huxley.

5a SPEAKING Look at these trivia questions. Do you know the answers?

5b Work with a partner. Write five trivia questions in the passive. You must know the answers to all your questions.

5c Join another pair and ask them your questions. Who gets the most correct answers?

1 SPEAKING Work with a partner. Each choose a different photo. Make notes for what you can say about your photo. Use these questions for ideas: Who? What? Why? Where? When? Take it in turns to say what you can see in your photo. Speak for two or three minutes.

In the second photo I can see a group of people in a café. They are talking and laughing ...

a

b

2 SPEAKING Work with a partner. Imagine the photos are from a speaking exam and that you are the examiners. What questions would you ask about photo b? Make a list.
Where are the people in this photo?

STUDY SKILLS

What is the best way to improve your speaking?

STUDY SKILLS ▶ page 148

3 LISTENING 2.44 Listen to a student talking about photo c in an exam. Do they ask any of your questions? Do you think the student does the exam well or not? Why?

c

d

4 Listen again. Tick the expressions in the Speaking Bank that you hear. Why are these expressions useful to talk about photos and pictures?

Speaking Bank

Useful expressions for speculation

- I think ...
- It looks as if ...
- I imagine that ...
- It's not clear if ...
- I'm not sure, but I think that ...
- It looks like ...
- It may/might/could be ...
- They're probably ...

EXAM SUCCESS

In conversations based on photos, what should you do if you aren't 100% sure of what you can see in the photo(s)?

EXAM SUCCESS ▶ page 153

Practice makes perfect

5a SPEAKING Work with a partner. Look at photos c and d above and each choose a different photo. Make notes to describe your photo.

5b Prepare questions to ask about your partner's photo and then take turns to ask and answer questions.

Who is in this photo?

It looks as if they are a group of students in a computer class.

1 Match the words and the abbreviations used in text messages.

1	are	a	2nite
2	at	b	2
3	before	c	YR
4	great	d	L8R
5	later	e	@
6	please	f	C
7	see	g	PLS
8	to/too	h	U
9	tonight	i	WOT
10	what	j	R
11	you	k	B4
12	your	l	GR8

2 Read these five text messages. What order were they sent in?

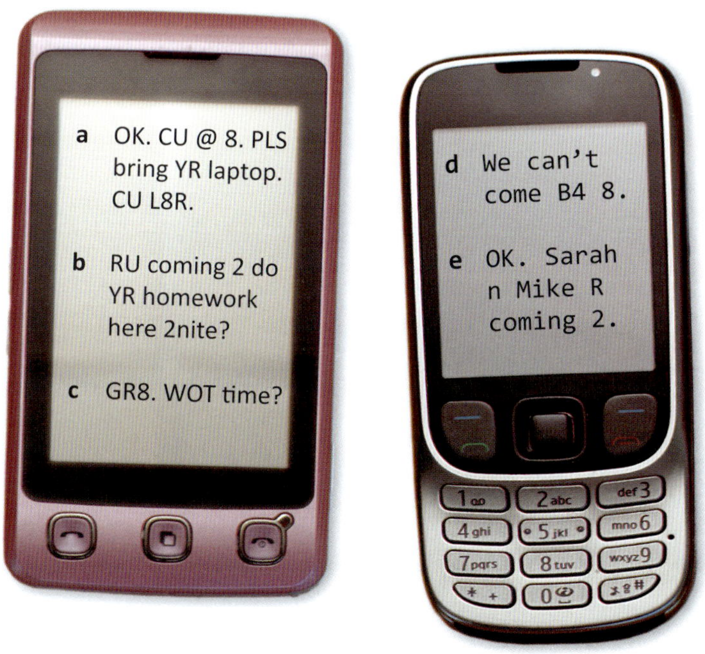

1 *b*...... 2 .... 3 .... 4 .... 5 ....

3 Write out the text messages in 2 as full sentences. Use the information in 1 to help you.

a *OK. See you at 8. Please bring your laptop. See you later.*
b ....
c ....
d ....
e ....

4 Read the information in the Writing Bank. What do you think the complete words are?

Writing Bank

How to write text messages

- We often use abbreviations instead of writing the complete word.
- To make abbreviations, we sometimes take away vowels from the word (e.g. PLS = please) or we replace words with symbols (e.g. @ = at) or numbers (e.g. L8R = later).
- Here are some more common examples:
  B BCZ L8 MSG SPK THX
  2DAY 2MORO WKND XLNT HMWK
- Remember! It is not correct to use these abbreviations in other types of writing like essays, formal letters, etc.
- We can also use emoticons like ☺ or ☹ in text messages to show emotions.

5 Use abbreviations to make these text messages shorter.

1 What are you doing at the weekend?
WOT R U doing @ the WKND?

2 Thanks for helping me with my homework.
....

3 Can you come tomorrow to fix my computer?
....

4 You should be happy because your exam results are excellent.
....

5 Don't forget to send me a message later tonight.
....

6 I want to see you and Peter before I speak to the teacher tomorrow.
....

Practice makes perfect

6a Look at this task and write a text message. Use abbreviations and the Writing Bank to help you.

> You need to use the Internet tomorrow to do a piece of work for school, but your connection at home doesn't work. Write a text message to a friend asking if you can go to their house tomorrow to use the Net.

6b Now give your message to your partner and write a reply to their message. Keep sending messages until you both know exactly when, where and why you are meeting and what you can do later.

Language reference and revision

Grammar reference

The passive

Form – Affirmative/Negative

Tense	Subject	Be	Past participle	(by + agent)
Present simple	Silicon	**is**	**used** to make computer chips.	
	Olive oil	**is**	**produced**	by Italian farmers.
	Computers	**are**	**made** in China.	
Present continuous	This game	**is being**	**played**	by millions of people.
	Essays	**are being**	**written**	by Internet companies.
	Billions of emails	**are being**	**sent** every day.	
Present perfect	Teen Second Life	**hasn't been**	**created**	by Wikipedia.
	Many things	**have been**	**invented**	by women.
	Wikipedia articles	**have been**	**ruined**	by vandals.
Past simple	The Internet	**wasn't**	**invented** in 1930.	
	The last World Cup	**was**	**played** in South Africa.	
	A lot of songs	**were**	**written**	by George Gershwin.

We make the passive with the appropriate tense and form of the verb **be** and the past participle of the verb.
We use the preposition **by** to introduce the person or thing which does the action.

Form – Questions

Tense	Be	Subject		Past participle	(by + agent)
Present simple	**Are**	computers		**made** in the USA?	
Present continuous	**Is**	this game	**being**	**played**	by millions of people.
Present perfect	**Has**	a new console	**been**	**created**?	
Past simple	**Was**	that film		**made** in 1986?	

To make object questions in the passive, we put the first auxiliary verb before the subject.

Use

We use the passive when:

1 we are more interested in the action than the people who do the action.
The new hospital was opened yesterday.

2 we do not know exactly who does the action.
My bag has been stolen.

3 it is obvious or understood who did the action.
The criminal was arrested at 5.30pm.

Vocabulary

1 Computers and computing

hard drive, keyboard, laptop, mouse, mouse pad, printer, screen, speaker, USB port, webcam

2 The Internet

blog, broadband, chat online, connection, download, online, search engine, surf the Net, website

3 Collocations with *email*

bounce back, check email, delete an email, email account, email address, forward an email, reply to an email, send an email

4 Other words and phrases ▶ page 145

Grammar revision

The passive – present simple

1 Write sentences in the present simple passive.

1 Computers/use/everywhere.
....

2 Chocolate eggs/eat/at Easter in the UK.
....

3 Christmas/celebrate/in many countries.
....

4 Shoes/not wear/in mosques.
....

5 Portuguese/speak/in Brazil.
....

6 Fish/not sell/at the butcher's.
....

7 Cars/make/by robots in this factory.
....

8 This programme/watch/by thousands of people.
....

WORKBOOK ▸ page 84

/ 8 points

The passive – other tenses

2 Each sentence contains a mistake. Find the mistake and rewrite the sentence correctly.

1 The song *Blue Suede Shoes* was sang by Elvis Presley.
2 *The Lord of the Rings* is written by J.R.R. Tolkien between 1937 and 1949.
3 London is visited for hundreds of people every day.
4 The radio invented Marconi.
5 Many products made in China nowadays.
6 Yesterday the eclipse was saw by many people around the world.
7 Oh no! His car has stolen.
8 My friend have been given a computer for her birthday.
9 The dog was been hit by a car yesterday.
10 New types of computers are being invent right now.

WORKBOOK ▸ page 87

/ 10 points

Vocabulary revision

Computers and computing

1 Match to make words or phrases.

1	hard	a	port
2	key	b	pad
3	USB	c	top
4	down	d	cam
5	lap	e	load
6	web	f	drive
7	mouse	g	board

WORKBOOK ▸ page 82

2 Write the correct names next to these objects.

1 ....

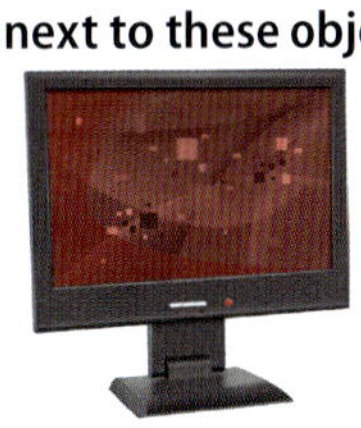

2 ....

3 ....

/ 10 points

The Internet

3 Read the definitions. What are the words?

1 look at various places on the Net one after another
_ _ r _

2 a computer program used for looking for information on the Internet
_ _ _ r _ _ _ _ g _ _ _

3 a type of diary on a website that changes regularly
_ l _ _

4 connected to the Internet o _ _ _ _ _

5 move information to your computer from the Internet _ _ w _ _ _ _ _

6 a type of connection to the Internet that allows you to receive or send a lot of information very quickly _ _ _ _ _ b _ _ _

WORKBOOK ▸ page 82

/ 6 points

Collocations with email

4 Complete the sentences with six of these words.

account address bounce check
delete forward reply send

1 When somebody sends you an email you should .... to it quite quickly.
2 When somebody sends you an email that you want to send to another person, you .... it.
3 When you don't want to keep an email, you .... it.
4 When emails don't go to the correct address they .... back.
5 My email .... is fredbloggs@bloggs.co.uk.
6 The first thing I do when I go online is to .... my email to see if any new ones have arrived.

WORKBOOK ▸ page 85

/ 6 points

Total ***/ 40 points***

Gateway to exams *Units 9–10*

Reading

Tip for Reading Exams

In reading activities where you complete a text with missing sentences, remember …

When you finish, check the activity by reading the text with your answers in the correct place. Do the sentences go together logically? Do words like *this* or *it* make sense?

EXAM SUCCESS ▸ page 152

1 Work with a partner. Discuss these questions.

1 How often do you read novels?

2 Do you like reading novels? Why/Why not?

3 How often do you read text messages?

4 What type of text messages do you receive?

2 Read the text quickly. What is the connection between novels and mobile phones in the text?

1 ____________________

Maybe that situation is going to change soon. It's already changed in Japan, where thousands and thousands of people are reading. The only thing is that they aren't reading books, they're reading mobile-phone novels. They are older teenagers and young adults, the first generation to spend their childhood with email.

2 ____________________

Some authors' novels are downloaded 260,000 times a day. A lot of the people downloading these novels never buy traditional books, maybe because books are too big for their bags or pockets. And another advantage of mobile-phone novels is that you can read them in the dark!

3 ____________________

Some publishers have made mobile-phone versions of old, well-known novels but these haven't been as successful as new stories. The most popular types of books are thrillers and romance. Some of the most popular mobile-phone novels have been made into traditional books. One of these books, by a writer called Yoshi, sold a million copies. Now it is being made into a film. Other mobile-phone novels have also been turned into TV series, films or manga comics.

4 ____________________

But Yoshi found it easy and it helped him to write in an exciting, fast, natural way. He also used modern technology in a different way. Readers sent him emails with their opinions and ideas and Yoshi used some of these ideas in future chapters. There was real interaction between the readers and writer.

3 Put these sentences in the correct place in the text. There is one extra sentence that you do not need.

A One interesting thing about this new fashion is that readers want new, original novels.

B People often say that teenagers and young adults don't read.

C Some Japanese teachers aren't happy about the success of mobile-phone novels.

D In Japan, it's common to download and read books on your mobile phone.

E The difficult part of writing a mobile-phone novel is that each episode or chapter has to be short.

4 Read the text again and choose the best answers.

1 In the text it says that one day in the future
- **A** young Japanese people are going to read mobile-phone novels.
- **B** young Japanese people are going to read traditional books.
- **C** people in other countries may read more mobile-phone novels.

2 One reason why these mobile-phone novels are popular may be because
- **A** you can carry them and read them easily in different situations.
- **B** traditional books are boring.
- **C** you can receive them by email.

3 Classic novels
- **A** have never become mobile-phone novels.
- **B** will never become mobile-phone novels.
- **C** aren't very popular mobile-phone novels.

4 Mobile-phone novels
- **A** have been changed into other types of entertainment.
- **B** are only popular with a small part of the population.
- **C** are similar to comics and films.

5 Yoshi
- **A** didn't like writing short paragraphs.
- **B** found out what his readers thought of his story while he was writing it.
- **C** couldn't write quickly because he didn't have ideas.

5 What about *you*?

Would you like to read a mobile-phone novel? Why/Why not?

Listening

Tip for Listening Exams

In listening activities where you complete notes, remember …

Read the notes before you listen and predict what type of word (noun, verb, adjective, adverb) goes in each space

EXAM SUCCESS ▸ page 152

6 2.45 Listen to a programme with information about the history of SMS text messages and complete the notes.

The first SMS was sent in **(1)** __________. SMS means **(2)** __________. An SMS text can only have **(3)** __________ characters, or letters, from the Roman alphabet. The first SMS was sent by a man who was working for Vodafone. He sent it to **(4)** __________. The first ever SMS message was '**(5)** __________'. At first you couldn't send SMS messages to people who were with a **(6)** __________. **(7)** __________ made SMS texts popular because it was **(8)** __________ to send a message than to make a phone call.

Use of English

Tip for Use of English Exams

In activities where you have to complete gaps in a text, remember …

Look carefully at the words just before and after the gap. Do these words need a special preposition or an article or an auxiliary verb, for example?

EXAM SUCCESS ▸ page 153

7 Complete the text about the magazine *National Geographic*. Use one word in each gap.

Every year their magazines and TV programmes **(1)** ________ read and watched by millions of people around the world. The National Geographic Society began in 1888 with just a few members and now it is one of the largest scientific and educational organisations **(2)** ________ the world. It was created **(3)** ________ a group of 33 teachers, explorers, and businessmen **(4)** ________ 13 January 1888 in Washington, D.C. They met to talk about their interest in geography. Later that year the first edition of the *National Geographic* magazine was published. The articles and reports were **(5)** ________ by professors but they weren't very interesting for people **(6)** ________ weren't experts in geography. But then **(7)** ________ magazine became easier to read and included more and more photos, especially in colour. Some amazing photos have **(8)** ________ printed in the magazine from all corners of the planet. So if one day you need to **(9)** ________ up some information about geography for a school project, why not start by picking up a copy of the *National Geographic*?

Speaking

Tip for Speaking Exams

In conversations based on photos, remember …

If you aren't 100% sure of what you can see, speculate by using language like *I'm not sure but I think, It may/might/could be, It looks like …*

EXAM SUCCESS ▸ page 153

8 Look at this photo for a few minutes and think of things you can say about it. Make notes if you want, but do not write complete sentences.

9 Work with a partner. Describe the photo and then discuss these two questions.

What are the good things about buying in a shop like this?

Is it better to shop online? Why/Why not?

'Can Do' Progress Check

CEF

1 How well can you do these things in English now? Give yourself a mark from 1 to 4.

1 = I can do it very well.
2 = I can do it quite well.
3 = I have some problems.
4 = I can't do it.

a I can report what other people have said or asked using reported speech. ☐
b I can talk about books and reading. ☐
c I can identify information in an interview about books and films. ☐
d I can ask for things in a bookshop. ☐
e I can write a questionnaire about magazines and newspapers. ☐
f I can describe different stages of a process using different forms of the passive. ☐
g I can talk about computers and the Internet. ☐
h I can identify information in a newspaper article about the Internet. ☐
i I can describe and make speculations about photos. ☐
j I can write a simple text message. ☐

2 Now decide what you need to do to improve.

1 Look again at my book/notes.
2 Do more practice exercises. ⇨ WORKBOOK pages 74–91
3 Other: ____________________

Wordlists

(adj) = adjective (adv) = adverb (conj) = conjunction (n) = noun (pron) = pronoun (v) = verb	The most common and useful words in English are marked according to the Macmillan Dictionary 'star rating'. This is so that you can easily recognize the vocabulary you need to know especially well. ★★★ = very common words ★★ = common words ★ = fairly common words If there is no star next to the word, this means that it is not very common.

Unit 1

Ages and stages of life

adolescence (n)	/ˌædəˈles(ə)ns/
adult (n) ★★★	/ˈædʌlt/
baby (n) ★★★	/ˈbeɪbi/
birth (n) ★★★	/bɜː(r)θ/
child (n) ★★★	/tʃaɪld/
childhood (n) ★★	/ˈtʃaɪldˌhʊd/
death (n) ★★★	/deθ/
middle-aged (adj)	/ˈmɪd(ə)l ˌeɪdʒd/
old age (n) ★	/əʊld ˈeɪdʒ/
senior citizen (n)	/ˌsiːniə(r) ˈsɪtɪz(ə)n/
teenager (n) ★★	/ˈtiːnˌeɪdʒə(r)/
young adult (n)	/ˌjʌŋ ˈædʌlt/

The family

aunt (n) ★★★	/ɑːnt/
born (adj) ★★★	/bɔː(r)n/
brother (n) ★★★	/ˈbrʌðə(r)/
brother-in-law (n)	/ˈbrʌðə(r) ɪn ˌlɔː/
cousin (n) ★★	/ˈkʌz(ə)n/
daughter (n) ★★★	/ˈdɔːtə(r)/
divorced (adj)	/dɪˈvɔː(r)st/
father-in-law (n)	/ˈfɑːðə(r) ɪn ˌlɔː/
grandfather/mother (n) ★★	/ˈɡræn(d)ˌfɑːðə(r)/, /ˌmʌðə(r)/
grandson/daughter (n) ★	/ˈɡræn(d)ˌsʌn/, /ˌdɔːtə(r)/
husband (n) ★★★	/ˈhʌzbənd/
mother-in-law (n)	/ˈmʌðə(r) ɪn ˌlɔː/
nephew (n) ★	/ˈnefjuː/
niece (n) ★	/niːs/
one-parent family	/ˌwʌn peərənt ˈfæm(ə)li/
only child (n)	/ˌəʊnli ˈtʃaɪld/
partner (n) ★★★	/ˈpɑː(r)tnə(r)/
single (adj) ★★★	/ˈsɪŋɡ(ə)l/
sister (n) ★★★	/ˈsɪstə(r)/
sister-in-law (n)	/ˈsɪstə(r) ɪn ˌlɔː/
son (n) ★★★	/sʌn/
stepfather/mother (n)	/ˈstepˌfɑːðə(r)/, /ˌmʌðə(r)/
uncle (n) ★★	/ˈʌŋk(ə)l/
wife (n) ★★★	/waɪf/

Noun suffixes *-ment, -ion, -ence*

adolescence (n)	/ˌædəˈles(ə)ns/
difference (n) ★★★	/ˈdɪfrəns/
equipment (n) ★★★	/ɪˈkwɪpmənt/
improvement (n) ★★★	/ɪmˈpruːvmənt/
independence (n) ★★★	/ˌɪndɪˈpendəns/
information (n) ★★★	/ˌɪnfə(r)ˈmeɪʃ(ə)n/
invention (n) ★★	/ɪnˈvenʃ(ə)n/
movement (n) ★★★	/ˈmuːvmənt/
protection (n) ★★★	/prəˈtekʃ(ə)n/

Other words and phrases

alone (adj) ★★★	/əˈləʊn/
approximately (adv) ★★	/əˈprɒksɪmətli/
behaviour (n) ★★★	/bɪˈheɪvjə(r)/
boil (v) ★	/bɔɪl/
care (n) ★★★	/keə(r)/
celebrity (n) ★	/səˈlebrəti/
chance (n) ★★★	/tʃɑːns/
company (n) ★★★	/ˈkʌmp(ə)ni/
computer technician (n)	/kəmˈpjuːtə(r) tekˈnɪʃ(ə)n/
connected (adj) ★	/kəˈnektɪd/
constant (n) ★★★	/ˈkɒnstənt/
cost (v) ★★★	/kɒst/
cultural values (n)	/ˈkʌltʃ(ə)rəl ˌvæljuːz/
dangerous (adj) ★★★	/ˈdeɪndʒərəs/
decision (n) ★★★	/dɪˈsɪʒ(ə)n/
difficult (adj) ★★★	/ˈdɪfɪk(ə)lt/
discipline (n) ★★★	/ˈdɪsəplɪn/
discuss (v) ★★★	/dɪˈskʌs/
enter (v)	/ˈentə(r)/
e-pal (n)	/ˈiːpæl/
experiment (n) ★★★	/ɪkˈsperɪˌmənt/
(v) ★	/ɪkˈsperɪˌmənt/
explore (v) ★★★	/ɪkˈsplɔː(r)/
extra-curricular (adj)	/ˌekstrə kəˈrɪkjələ(r)/
fair (= just) (n) ★★★	/feə(r)/
fashion (n) ★★★	/ˈfæʃ(ə)n/
fast (adv) ★★★	/fɑːst/
female (n) ★★★	/ˈfiːmeɪl/
fortunate (adj) ★★	/ˈfɔː(r)tʃənət/
free (adj) ★★★	/friː/
fridge (n) ★	/frɪdʒ/
government (n) ★★★	/ˈɡʌvə(r)nmənt/
GPS system (n)	/ˌdʒiː piː ˈes sɪstəm/
grow up (v)	/ˌɡrəʊ ˈʌp/
health (n) ★★★	/helθ/
helmet (n) ★	/ˈhelmɪt/
hide (v) ★★★	/haɪd/
inform (v) ★★★	/ɪnˈfɔː(r)m/
jacket (n) ★★★	/ˈdʒækɪt/
late (adj & adv) ★★★	/leɪt/
later (adj)	/ˈleɪtə(r)/
(adv) ★★★	/ˈleɪtə(r)/
leave (v) ★★★	/liːv/
lie (= not tell the truth) (v) ★★★	/laɪ/
limit (n) ★★★	/ˈlɪmɪt/

look after (v) /lʊk 'ɑːftə(r)/
lyrics (n) /'lɪrɪks/
male (n) ★★★ /meɪl/
marriage (n) ★★★ /'mærɪdʒ/
meal (n) ★★★ /miːl/
message (n) ★★★ /'mesɪdʒ/
mistake (n) ★★★ /mɪ'steɪk/
month (n) ★★★ /mʌnθ/
newspaper (n) ★★★ /'njuːzˌpeɪpə(r)/
obey (v) ★★ /ə'beɪ/
on time (adj) /ɒn 'taɪm/
online (adj & adv) ★★ /ɒn'laɪn/
opportunity (n) ★★★ /ˌɒpə(r)'tjuːnəti/
opposite (n) ★★★ /'ɒpəzɪt/
(= true, the opposite of false)
option (n) ★★★ /'ɒpʃ(ə)n/
particular (adj) ★★★ /pə(r)'tɪkjʊlə(r)/
permanent (adj) ★★★ /'pɜː(r)mənənt/
place (n) ★★★ /pleɪs/
recent (adj) ★★★ /'riːs(ə)nt/
regularly (adv) ★★★ /'regjʊlə(r)li/
responsible (adj) ★★★ /rɪ'spɒnsəb(ə)l/
result (n) ★★★ /rɪ'zʌlt/
rule (n) ★★★ /ruːl/
service (n) ★★★ /'sɜː(r)vɪs/
shout (v) ★★★ /ʃaʊt/
specialist (noun) ★★ /'speʃəlɪst/
spy (v) ★ /spaɪ/
stress (n) ★★★ /stres/
strict (adj) /strɪkt/
technology (n) ★★★ /tek'nɒlədʒi/
yell (v) ★ /jel/
zone (n) ★★ /zəʊn/

Unit 2

Crimes

burglary (n) ★ /'bɜː(r)gləri/
burgle (v) /'bɜː(r)g(ə)l/
kill (v) ★★★ /kɪl/
mug (v) ★ /mʌg/
mugging (n) /'mʌgɪŋ/
murder (n) ★★★ /'mɜː(r)də(r)/
piracy (n) /'paɪrəsi/
pirate (n & v) /'paɪrət/
rob (v) ★★ /rɒb/
robbery (n) ★ /'rɒbəri/
shoplifting (n) /'ʃɒpˌlɪftɪŋ/
steal (v) ★★★ /stiːl/
theft (n) ★★ /θeft/
vandalise (v) /'vændəlaɪz/

Criminals

burglar (n) ★ /'bɜː(r)glə(r)/
mugger (n) /'mʌgə(r)/
murderer (n) ★ /'mɜː(r)dərə(r)/
robber (n) ★ /'rɒbə(r)/
shoplifter (n) /'ʃɒpˌlɪftə(r)/
thief (n) ★★ /θiːf/
vandal (n) /'vænd(ə)l/

Phrasal verbs connected with investigating and finding

come across (v) ★★★ /kʌm ə'krɒs/
find out (v) ★★★ /faɪnd 'aʊt/
look into (v) ★★★ /lʊk 'ɪntə/
look for (v) ★★★ /'lʊk fə(r)/
turn up (v) ★★★ /tɜː(r)n 'ʌp/
work out (v) ★★★ /wɜː(r)k 'aʊt/

Other words and phrases

afterwards (adv) ★★★ /'ɑːftə(r)wə(r)dz/
ahead (adv) ★★★ /ə'hed/
army (n) ★★★ /'ɑː(r)mi/
arrest (v) ★★ /ə'rest/
basic (adj) ★★★ /'beɪsɪk/
behind (adv) ★★★ /bɪ'haɪnd/
block (v) ★★★ /blɒk/
box (n) ★★★ /bɒks/
bunker (n) /'bʌŋkə(r)/
by accident /baɪ 'æksɪd(ə)nt/
by post /baɪ 'pəʊst/
camera (n) ★★★ /'kæm(ə)rə/
case (= 'criminal case') (n) ★★★ /keɪs/
catch (v) ★★★ /kætʃ/
cheque (n) ★★ /tʃek/
commit (v) ★★★ /kə'mɪt/
corner (n) ★★★ /'kɔː(r)nə(r)/
crash (v) ★★ /kræʃ/
crossroads (n) /'krɒsˌrəʊdz/
damage (v) ★★★ /'dæmɪdʒ/
destroy (v) ★★★ /dɪ'strɔɪ/
detail (n) ★★★ /'diːteɪl/
disappear (v) ★★★ /ˌdɪsə'pɪə(r)/
driving mirror (n) /'draɪvɪŋ mɪrə(r)/
escape (v) /ɪ'skeɪp/
everywhere (adv) ★★★ /'evriˌweə(r)/
expect (v) /ɪk'spekt/
fight (n & v) ★★★ /faɪt/
franc (n) /fræŋk/
gadget (n) /'gædʒɪt/
gang (n) ★★ /gæŋ/
get ready (v) /get 'redi/
guard (n) ★★★ /gɑː(r)d/
(v) ★★ /gɑː(r)d/
gun (n) ★★★ /gʌn/
handbag (n) ★ /'hæn(d)ˌbæg/
handle (n) ★★★ /'hænd(ə)l/
happen (v) ★★★ /'hæpən/
headlights (n) /'hedˌlaɪts/
headquarters (n) ★★ /hed'kwɔː(r)tə(r)z/
identification (n) ★★ /aɪˌdentɪfɪ'keɪʃ(ə)n/
jump out (v) /ˌdʒʌmp 'aʊt/
kidnap (v) ★ /'kɪdnæp/
logic (n) ★★ /'lɒdʒɪk/
magician (n) /mə'dʒɪʃ(ə)n/
mission (n) ★★ /'mɪʃ(ə)n/
navy (adj) ★★ /'neɪvi/
(n) /'neɪvi/
neck (n) ★★★ /nek/
note (n) ★★★ /nəʊt/
outside (adj, adv & n) ★★★ /ˌaʊt'saɪd/

pair (n) ★★★ /peə(r)/
parcel (n) ★ /ˈpɑː(r)s(ə)l/
petrol station (n) /ˈpetrəl steɪʃ(ə)n/
pocket (n) ★★★ /ˈpɒkɪt/
police force (n) /pəˈliːs fɔː(r)s/
popular (adj) ★★★ /ˈpɒpjʊlə(r)/
prison (n) ★★★ /ˈprɪz(ə)n/
property (n) ★★★ /ˈprɒpə(r)ti/
quickly (adv) ★★★ /ˈkwɪkli/
regular (= common) (adj) ★★★ /ˈregjʊlə(r)/
reply (v) ★★★ /rɪˈplaɪ/
revise (v) ★ /rɪˈvaɪz/
rope (n) ★★ /rəʊp/
sack (n) ★★ /sæk/
scene of the crime /ˌsiːn əv ðə ˈkraɪm/
show (v) ★★★ /ʃəʊ/
side road (n) /ˈsaɪd rəʊd/
software (n) ★★★ /ˈsɒf(t)ˌweə(r)/
soldier (n) ★★★ /ˈsəʊldʒə(r)/
solve (v) ★★★ /sɒlv/
speed (v) ★★★ /spiːd/
successful (adj) ★★★ /səkˈsesf(ə)l/
suddenly (adv) ★★★ /ˈsʌd(ə)nli/
sunglasses (n) /ˈsʌnˌglɑːsɪz/
surprise (n) ★★★ /sə(r)ˈpraɪz/
suspicious (adj) ★★ /səˈspɪʃəs/
thick (adj) ★★★ /θɪk/
try (v) ★★★ /traɪ/
turn off (= lights) (v) ★★★ /ˌtɜː(r)n ˈɒf/
unexpectedly (adv) ★★ /ˌʌnɪkˈspektɪdli/
uniform (adj & n) ★★ /ˈjuːnɪfɔː(r)m/
urgent (adj) ★★ /ˈɜː(r)dʒ(ə)nt/
violence (n) ★★★ /ˈvaɪələns/
walking stick (n) /ˈwɔːkɪŋ stɪk/
worried (adj) ★★★ /ˈwʌrid/

Gateway to exams, Units 1–2

clear (adj) ★★★ /klɪə(r)/
conference (n) ★★★ /ˈkɒnf(ə)rəns/
connection (n) ★★★ /kəˈnekʃ(ə)n/
cover (v) ★★★ /ˈkʌvə(r)/
hood (n) /hʊd/
hoodie (n) /ˈhʊdi/
identify (v) ★★★ /aɪˈdentɪfaɪ/
incident (n) ★★★ /ˈɪnsɪd(ə)nt/
jay-walking (n) /ˈdʒeɪˌwɔːkɪŋ/
necessary (adj) ★★★ /ˈnesəs(ə)ri/
professor (n) ★★ /prəˈfesə(r)/
security (n) ★★★ /sɪˈkjʊərəti/
top (= clothes) (n) ★★★ /tɒp/

Unit 3

Countries, nationalities and languages

Argentina (n) /ˌɑː(r)dʒənˈtiːnə/
Argentinian (n) /ˌɑː(r)dʒənˈtɪniən/
Austria (n) /ˈɒstriə/
Austrian (adj & n) /ˈɒstriən/
Brazil (n) /brəˈzɪl/
Brazilian (adj & n) /brəˈzɪliən/
Dutch (adj & n) /dʌtʃ/
Egypt (n) /ˈiːdʒɪpt/
Egyptian (adj & n) /ɪˈdʒɪpʃ(ə)n/
English (adj & n) /ˈɪŋglɪʃ/
French (adj & n) /frentʃ/
German (adj & n) /ˈdʒɜːmən/
the Netherlands (n) /ðə ˈneðələndz/
Italian (adj & n) /ɪˈtæljən/
Japan (n) /dʒəˈpæn/
Japanese (adj & n) /ˌdʒæpəˈniːz/
Poland (n) /ˈpəʊlənd/
Polish (adj & n) /ˈpəʊlɪʃ/
Portuguese (adj & n) /ˌpɔːtʃəˈgiːz/
Romansh (n) /rəʊˈmænʃ/
Russia (n) /ˈrʌʃə/
Russian (adj & n) /ˈrʌʃ(ə)n/
Spanish (adj & n) /ˈspænɪʃ/
Swiss (adj & n) /swɪs/
Switzerland (n) /ˈswɪtsələnd/
Wales (n) /weɪlz/
Welsh (adj & n) /welʃ/

Learning a language

do an exercise (v) /duː ən ˈeksə(r)saɪz/
do homework (v) /duː ˈhəʊmˌwɜː(r)k/
do/study English (v) /duː/ˌstʌdi ˈɪŋglɪʃ/
do/take an exam (v) /duː/ˌteɪk ən ˈɪgzæm/
make a mistake (v) /ˌmeɪk ə mɪsˈteɪk/
memorization (n) /ˌmeməraɪˈzeɪʃ(ə)n/
memorize (v) ★ /ˈmeməraɪz/
practice (n) ★★★ /ˈpræktɪs/
practise (v) ★★ /ˈpræktɪs/
revision (n) ★★ /rɪˈvɪʒ(ə)n/
student (n) ★★★ /ˈstjuːd(ə)nt/
study (v) ★★★ /ˈstʌdi/
translate (v) ★★ /trænsˈleɪt/
translation (n) ★★ /trænsˈleɪʃ(ə)n/

Negative prefixes

illegal (adj) ★★ /ɪˈliːg(ə)l/
impossible (adj) ★★★ /ɪmˈpɒsəb(ə)l/
incorrect (adj) ★ /ˌɪnkəˈrekt/
informal (adj) ★★ /ɪnˈfɔː(r)m(ə)l/
invisible (adj) ★★ /ɪnˈvɪzəb(ə)l/
irregular (adj) ★ /ɪˈregjʊlə(r)/
unhappy (adj) ★★ /ʌnˈhæpi/
unofficial (adj) /ˌʌnəˈfɪʃ(ə)l/
unusual (adj) ★★★ /ʌnˈjuːʒʊəl/

Other words and phrases

accommodation (n) ★★ /əˌkɒməˈdeɪʃ(ə)n/
advice (n) ★★★ /ədˈvaɪs/
airline (n) ★★ /ˈeə(r)ˌlaɪn/
alien (n) ★★ /ˈeɪliən/
annual (n) ★★★ /ˈænjuəl/
apart from (phrase) /əˈpɑː(r)t frəm/
background (n) ★★★ /ˈbækˌgraʊnd/
belong to (v) ★★★ /bɪˈlɒŋ tə/
biscuit (n) ★★ /ˈbɪskɪt/

break (n & v) ★★★	/breɪk/
building (n) ★★★	/'bɪldɪŋ/
business (= count.) (n) ★★★	/'bɪznəs/
calculate (v) ★★	/'kælkjʊleɪt/
career (n) ★★★	/kə'rɪə(r)/
channel (= TV) (n) ★★★	/'tʃæn(ə)l/
chat (n) ★	/tʃæt/
(v) ★★	/tʃæt/
confusion (n) ★★	/kən'fjuːʒ(ə)n/
consonant (n) ★	/'kɒnsənənt/
contain (v) ★★★	/kən'teɪn/
convention (n) ★★★	/kən'venʃ(ə)n/
count (v) ★★★	/kaʊnt/
credits (end of a film) (n) ★★★	/'kredɪts/
dessert (n) ★	/dɪ'zɜː(r)t/
difficulty (n) ★★★	/'dɪfɪk(ə)lti/
discourse (n) ★	/'dɪskɔː(r)s/
dub (n)	/dʌb/
(v) ★	/dʌb/
experience (n & v) ★★★	/ɪk'spɪəriəns/
expression (n) ★★★	/ɪk'spreʃ(ə)n/
factor (n) ★★★	/'fæktə(r)/
factory (n) ★★★	/'fæktri/
familiar (adj) ★★★	/fə'mɪliə(r)/
flirt (v)	/flɜː(r)t/
fuelling stop (n)	/'fjuːəlɪŋ stɒp/
hamburger (n)	/'hæmˌbɜː(r)gə(r)/
instead of (adv)	/ɪn'sted əv/
interpretation (n) ★★★	/ɪnˌtɜː(r)prɪ'teɪʃ(ə)n/
last (v) ★★★	/lɑːst/
level (n) ★★★	/'lev(ə)l/
linguist (n) ★	/'lɪŋgwɪst/
mad about (adj)	/'mæd əbaʊt/
main (n) ★★★	/meɪn/
monument (n) ★★	/'mɒnjʊmənt/
mother-tongue (n)	/ˌmʌðə(r) 'tʌŋ/
mountain (n) ★★★	/'maʊntɪn/
native speaker (n) ★	/ˌneɪtɪv 'spiːkə(r)/
neighbour (n) ★★★	/'neɪbə(r)/
occasionally (adv) ★★★	/ə'keɪʒ(ə)nəli/
office (n) ★★★	/'ɒfɪs/
original (adj) ★★★	/ə'rɪdʒ(ə)nəl/
(n) ★	/ə'rɪdʒ(ə)nəl/
over (= more than) (adv) ★★★	/'əʊvə(r)/
permission (n)	/pə(r)'mɪʃ(ə)n/
picnic (n) ★	/'pɪknɪk/
politician (n) ★★★	/ˌpɒlə'tɪʃ(ə)n/
possession (n) ★★	/pə'zeʃ(ə)n/
sailing (n)	/'seɪlɪŋ/
sauce (n) ★★	/sɔːs/
set up (= start, establish) (v) ★★★	/ˌset 'ʌp/
sign (n) ★★★	/saɪn/
simple (adj) ★★★	/'sɪmp(ə)l/
simplify (v) ★	/'sɪmplɪfaɪ/
skill (n) ★★★	/skɪl/
snow (n) ★★★	/snəʊ/
sound (n) ★★★	/saʊnd/
summary (n) ★★	/'sʌməri/
surfing (n)	/'sɜː(r)fɪŋ/
theme park (n)	/'θiːm pɑː(r)k/
tomato ketchup (n)	/təˌmɑːtəʊ 'ketʃəp/
translator (n)	/træns'leɪtə(r)/
tribe (n) ★★	/traɪb/
Turkish (adj & n)	/'tɜː(r)kɪʃ/
version (n) ★★★	/'vɜː(r)ʃ(ə)n/
vowel (n) ★	/'vaʊəl/
whole (adj & n) ★★★	/həʊl/
yoghurt (n)	/'jɒgə(r)t/

Unit 4

Parts of the body

arm (n) ★★★	/ɑː(r)m/
back (n) ★★★	/bæk/
chest (n) ★★★	/tʃest/
ear (n) ★★★	/ɪə(r)/
elbow (n) ★★★	/'elbəʊ/
finger (n) ★★★	/'fɪŋgə(r)/
foot (n) ★★★	/fʊt/
hand (n) ★★★	/hænd/
head (n) ★★★	/hed/
knee (n) ★★★	/niː/
leg (n) ★★★	/leg/
nose (n) ★★★	/nəʊz/
stomach (n) ★★	/'stʌmək/
throat (n) ★★★	/θrəʊt/
toe (n) ★★	/təʊ/
tooth (n) ★★★	/tuːθ/

Health problems and illnesses

broken (adj) ★★	/'brəʊkən/
cold (adj & n) ★★★	/kəʊld/
cough (n) ★	/kɒf/
earache (n)	/'ɪəreɪk/
flu (n) ★	/fluː/
headache (n) ★	/'hedeɪk/
hurt (v) ★★★	/hɜː(r)t/
pain (n) ★★★	/peɪn/
sore (adj) ★	/sɔː(r)/
stomach ache (n)	/'stʌmək eɪk/
temperature (n) ★★★	/'temprɪtʃə(r)/
toothache (n)	/'tuːθeɪk/
virus (n) ★★★	/'vaɪrəs/

Compound nouns connected with health and medicine

first aid (n)	/ˌfɜː(r)st 'eɪd/
food poisoning (n)	/'fuːd ˌpɔɪz(ə)nɪŋ/
health centre (n)	/'helθ ˌsentə/
heart attack (n) ★	/'hɑː(r)t əˌtæk/
painkiller (n)	/'peɪnˌkɪlə(r)/
waiting room (n)	/'weɪtɪŋ ˌruːm/

Other words and phrases

accident (n) ★★★	/'æksɪd(ə)nt/
admit (v) ★★★	/əd'mɪt/
bitterness (n)	/'bɪtə(r)nəs/
blame (n) ★	/bleɪm/
blame (v) ★★★	/bleɪm/
boat (n) ★★★	/bəʊt/
bored (adj) ★★	/bɔː(r)d/
borrow (v) ★★	/'bɒrəʊ/
bright (adj) ★★★	/braɪt/

chemical (n) ★★★ /'kemɪk(ə)l/
congratulations (n) ★ /kən,grætʃʊ'leɪʃ(ə)nz/
cruelty (n) ★ /'kruːəlti/
cure (n) ★★ /kjʊə(r)/
desert (n) ★★ /'dezə(r)t/
(v) ★ /dɪ'zɜː(r)t/
drama (n) ★★★ /'drɑːmə/
drug (n) ★★★ /drʌg/
emergency (n) ★★★ /ɪ'mɜː(r)dʒ(ə)nsi/
evil (adj & n) ★★ /'iːv(ə)l/
fall (v) ★★★ /fɔːl/
fault (n) ★★★ /fɔːlt/
fear (n) ★★★ /fɪə(r)/
filled (adj) ★★★ /fɪld/
forest (n) ★★★ /'fɒrɪst/
forgive (v) ★★ /fə(r)'gɪv/
get off (a boat) (v) ★★★ /,get 'ɒf/
get rid of (v) ★★ /,get 'rɪd əv/
get well (v) ★★ /,get 'wel/
ghost (n) ★★ /gəʊst/
grant (v) ★★★ /grɑːnt/
guess (n) ★★ /ges/
(v) ★★★ /ges/
guilty (adj) ★★★ /'gɪlti/
hard (= solid) (adj) ★★★ /hɑː(r)d/
human being (n) ★★★ /,hjuːmən 'biːɪŋ/
hygiene (n) ★ /'haɪdʒiːn/
ice (n) ★★★ /aɪs/
innocence (n) ★ /'ɪnəs(ə)ns/
laboratory (n) ★★ /lə'bɒrət(ə)ri/
laptop (n) /'læp,tɒp/
lie, lay (v) ★★★ /laɪ,leɪ/
lock (v) ★★★ /lɒk/
lower (your voice) (v) ★★ /'ləʊə(r)/
mad (adj) ★★ /mæd/
mime (n & v) /maɪm/
misery (n) ★★ /'mɪzəri/
non--stop (adj) /,nɒn'stɒp/
paracetamol (n) /,pærə'siːtəmɒl/
poison (n) ★ /'pɔɪz(ə)n/
politely (adv) ★ /pə'laɪtli/
pray (v) ★★ /preɪ/
prize (n) ★★★ /praɪz/
project (n) ★★★ /'prɒdʒekt/, /'prəʊdʒekt/
(v) ★★ /prə'dʒekt/
raise (your voice) (v) ★★★ /reɪz/
reach (n) ★★ /riːtʃ/
(v) ★★★ /riːtʃ/
recover (v) ★★★ /rɪ'kʌvə(r)/
reduce (v) ★★★ /rɪ'djuːs/
remedy (n) ★★ /'remədi/
ride (v) ★★★ /raɪd/
rubbish (n) /'rʌbɪʃ/
ruin (n) ★★★ /'ruːɪn/
(v) ★★★ /'ruːɪn/
seasick (adj) /'siː,sɪk/
seasickness (n) /'siː,sɪknəs/
separate (adj) ★★★ /'sep(ə)rət/
(v) ★★★ /'sepəreɪt/
ship (n) ★★★ /ʃɪp/
sick (adj) ★★★ /sɪk/
(n) /sɪk/
slip past (v) /,slɪp 'pɑːst/
solid (adj) ★★★ /'sɒlɪd/
stare (v) ★★★ /steə(r)/
strong (adj) ★★★ /strɒŋ/
succeed (v) ★★★ /sək'siːd/
suffer (v) ★★★ /'sʌfə(r)/
summer (n) /'sʌmə(r)/
take over (v) ★★★ /,teɪk 'əʊvə(r)/
turn (n) ★★★ /tɜː(r)n/
twice (adv) ★★★ /twaɪs/
website (n) ★★ /'web,saɪt/
wicked (adj) ★ /'wɪkɪd/
winter (n) ★★★ /'wɪntə(r)/
wonder (v) ★★★ /'wʌndə(r)/

Gateway to exams, Units 3–4

ability (n) ★★★ /ə'bɪləti/
acupuncture (n) /'ækjʊ,pʌŋktʃə(r)/
board game (n) /'bɔː(r)d ,geɪm/
brain (n) ★★★ /breɪn/
chess (n) ★ /tʃes/
crossword (n) ★ /'krɒs,wɜː(r)d/
discovery (n) ★★★ /dɪ'skʌv(ə)ri/
effective (adj) ★★★ /ɪ'fektɪv/

Unit 5

TV programmes

advert (ad/advertisement) (n) ★ /'ædvɜː(r)t/
cartoon (n) ★ /kɑː(r)'tuːn/
chat show (n) ★ /'tʃæt ,ʃəʊ/
comedy (n) ★★ /'kɒmədi/
documentary (n) ★ /,dɒkjʊ'ment(ə)ri/
film (n) ★★★ /fɪlm/
game show (n) /'geɪm ,ʃəʊ/
programme (n) ★★★ /'prəʊgræm/
reality show (n) /ri'æləti ,ʃəʊ/
remote control (n) ★ /rɪ,məʊt kən'trəʊl/
series (n) ★★★ /'sɪəriːz/
soap (n) ★★ /səʊp/
sports programme (n) /'spɔː(r)ts ,prəʊgræm/
the news (n) ★★★ /,ðə 'njuːz/
turn/switch on/off (v) ★★★ /,tɜː(r)n/,swɪtʃ 'ɒn/'ɒf/

Adjectives describing TV programmes

awful (adj) ★★ /'ɔːf(ə)l/
boring (adj) ★★ /'bɔːrɪŋ/
cool (adj) ★★★ /kuːl/
funny (adj) ★★★ /'fʌni/
informative (adj) ★ /ɪn'fɔː(r)mətɪv/
scary (adj) ★ /'skeəri/

Adjectives ending in *-ing* and *-ed*

confusing/ed (adj) ★★/★ /kən'fjuːzɪŋ/kən'fjuːzd/
disappointing/ed (adj) ★/★ /,dɪsə'pɔɪntɪŋ/,dɪsə'pɔɪntɪd/
embarrassing/ed (adj) ★/★ /,ɪm'bærəsɪŋ/,ɪm'bærəst/
frightening/ed (adj) ★/★ /'fraɪt(ə)nɪŋ/'fraɪt(ə)nd/

interesting/ed (adj) ★★★/★★★	/'ɪntrəstɪŋ/'ɪntrəstɪd/
moving/ed (adj) ★★/★★	/'muːvɪŋ/muːvd/
relaxing/ed (adj) ~/★	/rɪ'læksɪŋ/rɪ'lækst/
surprising/ed (adj) ★★★/★★★	/sə(r)'praɪzɪŋ/sə(r)'praɪzd/
tiring/ed (adj) ~/★★★	/'taɪərɪŋ/'taɪə(r)d/

Other words and phrases

a bit (adv)	/ˌə 'bɪt/
addict (n) ★	/'ædɪkt/
agree (v) ★★★	/ə'griː/
anatomy (n)	/ə'nætəmi/
archer (n)	/'ɑː(r)tʃə(r)/
attractive (adj) ★★★	/ə'træktɪv/
authentic (adj) ★	/ɔː'θentɪk/
baddy (n)	/'bædi/
brave (adj) ★★	/breɪv/
broadcast (n) ★	/'brɔːdˌkɑːst/
(v) ★★	/'brɔːdˌkɑːst/
cable (n)	/'keɪb(ə)l/
capture (v)	/'kæptʃə(r)/
century (n) ★★★	/'sentʃəri/
cheat (v) ★	/tʃiːt/
common (adj) ★★★	/'kɒmən/
critic (n) ★★★	/'krɪtɪk/
demonstration (n) ★★	/ˌdemən'streɪʃ(ə)n/
distant (adj) ★★	/'dɪstənt/
doll (n) ★	/dɒl/
electronic (adj) ★★★	/ˌelek'trɒnɪk/
episode (n) ★★	/'epɪsəʊd/
equally (adj) ★★	/'iːkwəli/
exotic (adj) ★	/ɪg'zɒtɪk/
fall asleep (v)	/ˌfɔːl ə'sliːp/
far (= far better) (adv) ★★★	/fɑː(r)/
fitness (n) ★★	/'fɪtnəs/
flat (n) ★★★	/flæt/
general election (n)	/ˌdʒen(ə)rəl ɪ'lekʃ(ə)n/
goal (= football) (n) ★★★	/gəʊl/
gym (n) ★	/dʒɪm/
hunger (n) ★	/'hʌŋgə(r)/
igloo (n)	/'ɪgluː/
image (= picture) (n) ★★★	/'ɪmɪdʒ/
Inuit (n)	/'ɪnuɪt/
iron (= material) (n) ★★	/'aɪə(r)n/
laugh (n) ★★	/lɑːf/
(v) ★★★	/lɑːf/
lazy (adj) ★★	/'leɪzi/
mechanical (adj) ★★	/mɪ'kænɪk(ə)l/
melodramatic (adj)	/ˌmelədrə'mætɪk/
newsreader (n)	/'njuːzˌriːdə(r)/
nowadays (adv) ★★	/'naʊəˌdeɪz/
organiser (n) ★★	/'ɔ(r)gəˌnaɪzə(r)/
outlaw (n)	/'aʊtˌlɔː/
palm tree (n)	/'pɑːm ˌtriː/
parachuting (n)	/'pærəˌʃuːtɪŋ/
persuade (v) ★★★	/pə(r)'sweɪd/
save (n)	/seɪv/
(v) ★★★	/seɪv/
selective (adj) ★★	/sɪ'lektɪv/
sensation (n) ★★	/sen'seɪʃ(ə)n/
sensationalism (n) ★★	/sen'seɪʃ(ə)nəˌlɪz(ə)m/
serious (adj) ★★★	/'sɪəriəs/
silent (adj) ★★★	/'saɪlənt/
slightly (adv) ★★★	/'slaɪtli/
spend (time) (v) ★★★	/ˌspend 'taɪm/
sure (adj) ★★★	/ʃɔː(r)/
team (n) ★★★	/tiːm/
tower (n) ★★	/'taʊə(r)/
transmission (n) ★★	/trænz'mɪʃ(ə)n/
transmit (v) ★★	/trænz'mɪt/
TV guide (n)	/ˌtiː viː 'gaɪd/
TV station (n)	/ˌtiː viː 'steɪʃ(ə)n/
without (adv & conj) ★★★	/wɪð'aʊt/

Unit 6

Geographical features

beach (n) ★★★	/biːtʃ/
desert (n) ★★	/'dezə(r)t/
forest (n) ★★★	/'fɒrəst/
ice cap (n)	/'aɪs ˌkæp/
jungle (n) ★	/'dʒʌŋg(ə)l/
mountain range (n)	/'maʊntɪn ˌreɪndʒ/
rainforest (n) ★	/'reɪnˌfɒrɪst/

The environment

drought (n)	/draʊt/
environment (n) ★★★	/ɪn'vaɪrənmənt/
flood (n) ★★	/flʌd/
global warming (n) ★	/ˌgləʊb(ə)l 'wɔː(r)mɪŋ/
greenhouse effect (n)	/'griːnhaʊs ɪˌfekt/
nuclear disaster (n)	/ˌnjuːkliə(r) dɪ'zɑːstə(r)/
oil spill (n)	/'ɔɪl ˌspɪl/
ozone layer (n)	/'əʊzəʊn ˌleɪə(r)/
pollution (n)	/pə'luːʃ(ə)n/
recycle (v) ★	/riː'saɪk(ə)l/
save (v) ★★★	/seɪv/
waste (n & v) ★★★	/weɪst/

Different uses of *get*

arrive (v) ★★★	/ə'raɪv/
bring (v) ★★★	/brɪŋ/
become (v) ★★★	/bɪ'kʌm/
(= a process or change of state)	
obtain or buy (v) ★★★	/əb'teɪn/
receive (v) ★★★	/rə'siːv/

Other words and phrases

affect (v) ★★★	/ə'fekt/
anniversary (n) ★★	/ˌænɪ'vɜː(r)s(ə)ri/
arsonist (n)	/'ɑː(r)s(ə)nɪst/
atmosphere (n) ★★	/'ætməsˌfɪə(r)/
attraction (n) ★★	/ə'trækʃ(ə)n/
burn (v) ★★★	/bɜː(r)n/
bushfire (n)	/'bʊʃˌfaɪə(r)/
canteen (n) ★	/kæn'tiːn/
catastrophic (adj)	/ˌkætə'strɒfɪk/
celebrate (v) ★★★	/'seləˌbreɪt/
cheap (adj) ★★★	/tʃiːp/
close to (adj & adv)	/'kləʊs ˌtʊ/
community (n) ★★★	/kə'mjuːnəti/
consequence (n) ★★★	/'kɒnsɪkwəns/
convict (n) ★★	/'kɒnvɪkt/

cut down (v) ★★★	/ˌkʌt ˈdaʊn/
definitely (adv) ★★	/ˈdef(ə)nətli/
deliberately (adv) ★★	/dɪˈlɪb(ə)rətli/
disastrous (adj) ★	/dɪˈzɑːstrəs/
dry (adj) ★★★	/draɪ/
(v) ★★	/draɪ/
east (adj & adv)	/iːst/
(n) ★★★	/iːst/
efficient (adj)	/ɪˈfɪʃ(ə)nt/
energy (n) ★★★	/ˈenə(r)dʒi/
excursion (n)	/ɪkˈskɜː(r)ʃ(ə)n/
fancy (v) ★★	/ˈfænsi/
farmer (n) ★★★	/ˈfɑː(r)mə(r)/
footprint (n)	/ˈfʊtˌprɪnt/
frequent (adj) ★★	/ˈfriːkwənt/
fumes (n) ★	/fjuːmz/
fume (v)	/fjuːm/
generate (v) ★★★	/ˈdʒenəreɪt/
glass (= material) (n) ★★★	/ɡlɑːs/
habit (n) ★★★	/ˈhæbɪt/
heat (n) ★★★	/hiːt/
honest (adj) ★★	/ˈɒnɪst/
increase (n) ★★★	/ˈɪnkriːs/
(v) ★★★	/ɪnˈkriːs/
indigenous (adj)	/ɪnˈdɪdʒənəs/
influence (v) ★★★	/ˈɪnfluəns/
lifestyle (n) ★★	/ˈlaɪfˌstaɪl/
material (n) ★★★	/məˈtɪəriəl/
melt (v) ★★	/melt/
mix (v) ★★★	/mɪks/
packaging (n) ★	/ˈpækɪdʒɪŋ/
perhaps (adv) ★★★	/pə(r)ˈhæps/
petrol (n) ★★	/ˈpetrəl/
population (n) ★★★	/ˌpɒpjʊˈleɪʃ(ə)n/
power (n) ★★★	/ˈpaʊə(r)/
(v)	/ˈpaʊə(r)/
protect (v) ★★★	/prəˈtekt/
reef (n) ★	/riːf/
relatively (adv) ★★★	/ˈrelətɪvli/
restriction (n) ★	/rɪˈstrɪkʃ(ə)n/
scientist (n) ★★★	/ˈsaɪəntɪst/
sea level (n)	/ˈsiː ˌlev(ə)l/
shower (n) ★★	/ˈʃaʊə(r)/
(v)	/ˈʃaʊə(r)/
silly (adj) ★★	/ˈsɪli/
slow down (v) ★★★	/ˌsləʊ ˈdaʊn/
space (outer space) (n) ★★★	/speɪs/
suggestion (n) ★★★	/səˈdʒestʃ(ə)n/
thirsty (adj) ★	/ˈθɜː(r)sti/
tonne (n) ★★	/tʌn/
toothbrush (n)	/ˈtuːθˌbrʌʃ/
water (v) ★★★	/ˈwɔːtə(r)/
wild (adj) ★★★	/waɪld/
(n)	/waɪld/

Gateway to exams, Units 5–6

attention (n) ★★★	/əˈtenʃ(ə)n/
environmental (adj) ★★★	/ɪnˌvaɪrənˈment(ə)l/
exploration (n) ★★	/ˌekspləˈreɪʃ(ə)n/
situation (n) ★★★	/ˌsɪtʃuˈeɪʃ(ə)n/

Unit 7

Jobs

builder (n) ★★	/ˈbɪldə(r)/
computer programmer (n)	/kəmˌpjuːtə(r) ˈprəʊɡræmə(r) /
fashion designer (n)	/ˈfæʃ(ə)n dɪˌzaɪnə/
journalist (n) ★★	/ˈdʒɜː(r)nəlɪst/
mechanic (n) ★	/mɪˈkænɪk/
police officer (n) ★	/pəˈliːs ˌɒfɪsə(r)/
receptionist (n) ★	/rɪˈsepʃ(ə)nɪst/
shop assistant (n)	/ˈʃɒp əˌsɪst(ə)nt/

Personal qualities

ambitious (adj) ★★	/æmˈbɪʃəs/
calm (adj) ★★	/kɑːm/
caring (adj)	/ˈkeərɪŋ/
clever (adj) ★★	/ˈklevə(r)/
creative (adj) ★★	/kriˈeɪtɪv/
fit (adj) ★★★	/fɪt/
hard-working (adj) ★	/ˌhɑː(r)d ˈwɜː(r)kɪŋ/
reliable (adj) ★★	/rɪˈlaɪəb(ə)l/
sociable (adj)	/ˈsəʊʃəb(ə)l/
well-organised (adj)	/ˌwel ˈɔː(r)ɡənaɪzd/

Compound adjectives describing people or jobs

badly-paid (adj)	/ˌbædli ˈpeɪd/
blue/brown/green-eyed (adj)	/ˈbluː/ˈbraʊn/ˈɡriːnˌaɪd/
easy-going (adj)	/ˌiːziˈɡəʊɪŋ/
full-time (adj) ★★	/ˈfʊlˌtaɪm/
good-looking (adj) ★★	/ˌɡʊdˈlʊkɪŋ/
part-time (adj) ★★	/ˌpɑːtˈtaɪm/
right/left-handed (adj)	/ˌraɪt/ˌleft ˈhændɪd/
well-paid (adj)	/ˌwel ˈpeɪd/

Other words and phrases

accept (v) ★★★	/əkˈsept/
application form (n) ★★	/æplɪˈkeɪʃ(ə)n ˌfɔː(r)m/
apply (for) (v) ★★★	/əˈplaɪ ˌfɔː(r)/
architect (n) ★★	/ˈɑː(r)kɪˌtekt/
assistant (n) ★★	/əˈsɪst(ə)nt/
au pair (n)	/ˌəʊ ˈpeə(r)/
autograph (n & v)	/ˈɔːtəˌɡrɑːf/
average (n) ★★★	/ˈæv(ə)rɪdʒ/
(v) ★	/ˈæv(ə)rɪdʒ/
cheer up (v)	/ˌtʃɪə(r) ˈʌp/
chewing gum (n)	/ˈtʃuːɪŋ ˌɡʌm/
complicated (adj) ★★	/ˈkɒmplɪˌkeɪtɪd/
condition (n) ★★★	/kənˈdɪʃ(ə)n/
cookery (n) ★	/ˈkʊk(ə)ri/
CV (n) ★	/ˌsiː ˈviː/
delivery boy/girl (n)	/dɪˈlɪv(ə)ri ˌbɔɪ, ˌɡɜː(r)l/
depend on (v) ★★★	/dɪˈpend ˌɒn/
design (v) ★★★	/dɪˈzaɪn/
drag (v) ★★	/dræɡ/
dress up (v) ★★★	/ˌdres ˈʌp/
dynamic (adj) ★★	/daɪˈnæmɪk/
effort (n) ★★★	/ˈefə(r)t/
enclose (v) ★	/ɪnˈkləʊz/
essential (adj) ★★★	/ɪˈsenʃ(ə)l/
exactly (adv) ★★★	/ɪɡˈzæk(t)li/
except (conj) ★★★	/ɪkˈsept/

exotic (adj) ★ /ɪg'zɒtɪk/
extra (n) ★★★ /'ekstrə/
factory worker (n) /'fæktrɪ ˌwɜː(r)kə(r)/
firefighter (n) /'faɪə(r)ˌfaɪtə(r)/
force (n) ★★★ /fɔː(r)s/
gardener (n) ★★ /'gɑː(r)d(ə)nə(r)/
giant (adj) ★★ /'dʒaɪənt/
hang out (v) /ˌhæŋ 'aʊt/
hard hat (n) /'hɑː(r)d ˌhæt/
hit (n) ★★ /hɪt/
(v) ★★★ /hɪt/
home-time (n) /'həʊm ˌtaɪm/
in response to /ˌɪn rə'spɒns tʊ/
inquiries (n) ★★★ /ɪn'kwaɪəriːz/
interpreter (n) ★ /ɪn'tɜː(r)prɪtə(r)/
issue (= question) (n) ★★★ /'ɪʃuː/
knowledge (n) ★★★ /'nɒlɪdʒ/
look forward to ★★★ /ˌlʊk 'fɔː(r)wə(r)d tʊ/
lottery (n) ★ /'lɒtəri/
lucky (adj) ★★★ /'lʌki/
manual (n) ★★ /'mænjʊəl/
mate (= friend) (n) ★★ /meɪt/
miner (n) ★ /'maɪnə(r)/
offer (v) ★★★ /'ɒfə(r)/
outdoors (adv & n) /ˌaʊt'dɔː(r)z/
paperwork (n) ★ /'peɪpə(r)ˌwɜː(r)k/
parrot (n) ★ /'pærət/
peace (n) ★★★ /piːs/
rely on (v) ★★★ /rɪ'laɪ ɒn/
report (n) ★★★ /rɪ'pɔː(r)t/
ride operator (n) /'raɪd ˌɒpəreɪtə(r)/
screen (n) ★★★ /skriːn/
(v) ★ /skriːn/
sign (v) ★★★ /saɪn/
smoke (v) ★★ /sməʊk/
stuck (adj) /stʌk/
suit (n) ★★★ /suːt/
suppose (v) ★★★ /sə'pəʊz/
take a long time /ˌteɪk ə lɒŋ 'taɪm/
toothpaste (n) /'tuːθˌpeɪst/
turn round (v) ★★ /ˌtɜːn 'raʊnd/
variety (n) ★★★ /və'raɪəti/
vegetarian (n) /ˌvedʒə'teəriən/
wages (n) ★★★ /'weɪdʒɪz/
wing (n) ★★★ /wɪŋ/

Unit 8

Relationships

(to) ask (somebody) out (v) /ˌɑːsk 'aʊt/
(to) chat (to somebody) (v) ★★ /'tʃæt tʊ/
(to) fall in love (with somebody) (v) /ˌfɔːl ɪn 'lʌv/
(to) get back together (with somebody) (v) /ˌget ˌbæk tə'geðə(r)/
(to) get married (to somebody) (v) /ˌget 'mærid/
(to) get on well (with somebody) (v) /ˌget ˌɒn 'wel/
(to) go out (with somebody) (v) /ˌgəʊ 'aʊt/
(to) have an argument (with somebody) (v) /ˌhæv ən 'ɑː(r)gjʊmənt/
(to) meet (somebody) (v) ★★★ /miːt/
(to) split up (with somebody) (v) /ˌsplɪt 'ʌp/

Feelings

anger (n) ★★ /'æŋgə(r)/
boredom (n) ★ /'bɔː(r)dəm/
excitement (n) ★★ /ɪk'saɪtmənt/
happiness (n) ★★ /'hæpinəs/
loneliness (n) /'ləʊnlinəs/
sadness (n) ★ /'sædnəs/

Adjectives

afraid (adj) ★★★ /ə'freɪd/
angry (adj) ★★★ /'æŋgri/
excited (adj) ★★ /ɪk'saɪtɪd/
happy (adj) ★★★ /'hæpi/
lonely (adj) ★★ /'ləʊnli/
sad (adj) ★★★ /sæd/

Noun suffixes

freedom (n) ★★★ /'friːdəm/
friendship (n) ★★ /'fren(d)ʃɪp/
illness (n) ★★★ /'ɪlnəs/
madness (n) ★ /'mædnəs/
relationship (n) ★★★ /rɪ'leɪʃ(ə)nʃɪp/
sadness (n) ★ /'sædnəs/
weakness (n) ★★ /'wiːknəs/

Other words and phrases

abdicate (v) /'æbdɪkeɪt/
abdication (n) /ˌæbdɪ'keɪʃ(ə)n/
ancient (adj) ★★★ /'eɪnʃ(ə)nt
apologise (v) /ə'pɒlədʒaɪz/
argument (n) ★★★ /'ɑː(r)gjʊmənt/
balcony (n) ★ /'bælkəni/
be like somebody /biː 'laɪk ˌsʌmbədi/
bowling (n) ★ /'bəʊlɪŋ/
broken-hearted (adj) /ˌbrəʊkən 'hɑː(r)tɪd/
camp (n) ★★★ /kæmp/
couple (two people) (n) ★★★ /'kʌp(ə)l/
criticise (v) /'krɪtɪsaɪz/
dry oneself (v) /'draɪ wʌnˌself/
enemy (n) ★★★ /'enəmi/
fair (= beautiful) (adj) /feə(r)/
flower (n) ★★★ /'flaʊə(r)/
(v) /'flaʊə(r)/
give up (= relinquish) (v) ★★★ /ˌgɪv 'ʌp/
grave (n) ★★ /greɪv/
happy ending (n) /ˌhæpi 'endɪŋ/
hold (v) ★★★ /həʊld/
ideal (adj) ★★★ /aɪ'dɪəl/
(n) ★★ /aɪ'dɪəl/
journey (n) ★★★ /'dʒɜːni/
knife (n) ★★★ /naɪf/
light (opposite of heavy) (adj) ★★★ /laɪt/
mainly (adv) ★★★ /'meɪnli/
matter (v) ★★★ /'mætə(r)/
moral (adj) ★★★ /'mɒrəl/
neither (conj & pron) ★★★ /'naɪðə(r)/, /'niːðə(r)/
pacifist (n) /'pæsɪfɪst/
perfectionist (n) /pə(r)'fekʃənɪst/
play (n & v) ★★★ /pleɪ/
potion (n) /'pəʊʃ(ə)n/
press (n, = newspapers) (n) ★★★ /pres/
priest (n) ★★ /priːst/

Prime Minister (n) ★★★ /ˌpraɪm ˈmɪnɪstə(r)/
promise (n & v) ★★★ /ˈprɒmɪs/
questionnaire (n) ★★ /ˌkwestʃəˈneə(r)/
respect (n) ★★★ /rɪˈspekt/
(v) ★★ /rɪˈspekt/
scandal (n) ★★ /ˈskænd(ə)l/
ski (v) ★ /skiː/
something else (pron & adv) /ˌsʌmθɪŋ ˈels/
soon (adv) ★★★ /suːn/
stay in (v) ★★★ /ˌsteɪ ˈɪn/
still (= time) (adv) ★★★ /stɪl/
stone (n) ★★★ /stəʊn/
storm (n) /stɔːm/
studies (n) /stʌdiz/
tolerant (adj) /ˈtɒlərənt/
tradition (n) ★★★ /trədɪʃ(ə)n/
wealthy (adj) ★★ /ˈwelθi/

Gateway to exams, Units 7–8

au pair (n) /ˌəʊ ˈpeə(r)/
alternative (adj & n) ★★★ /ɔːlˈtɜː(r)nətɪv/
dimension (n) ★★ /daɪˈmenʃ(ə)n/
grape (n) ★ /greɪp/
ingredient (n) ★★ /ɪnˈgriːdiənt/
jam (n) ★ /dʒæm/
jar (n) ★ /dʒɑː(r)/
kiwi (n) /ˈkiːwiː/
lime (n) ★ /laɪm/
mixture (n) ★★★ /ˈmɪkstʃə(r)/
obviously (adv) ★★★ /ˈɒbviəsli/
positive (adj) ★★★ /ˈpɒzətɪv/
(n) /ˈpɒzətɪv/
product (n) /ˈprɒdʌkt/
recipe (n) ★★ /ˈresəpi/
sell (v) ★★★ /sel/
traditional (adj) ★★★ /trəˈdɪʃ(ə)nəl/

Unit 9

Fiction

comic (n) /ˌkɒmɪk/
crime novel (n) /ˈkraɪm ˌnɒv(ə)l/
fairy tale (n) /ˈfeəri ˌteɪl/
fantasy (n) ★★ /ˈfæntəsi/
graphic novel (n) /ˌgræfɪk ˈnɒv(ə)l/
historical fiction (n) /hɪˌstɒrɪk(ə)l ˈfɪkʃ(ə)n/
horror (n) ★★ /ˈhɒrə(r)/
play (n) ★★★ /pleɪ/
romance (n) ★ /rəʊˈmæns/
science fiction (n) ★ /ˌsaɪəns ˈfɪkʃ(ə)n/
thriller (n) ★ /ˈθrɪlə(r)/

Non-fiction

atlas (n) /ˈætləs/
autobiography (n) /ˌɔːtəʊbaɪˈɒgrəfi/
biography (n) ★ /baɪˈɒgrəfi/
cookbook (n) /ˈkʊkˌbʊk/
dictionary (n) ★★ /ˈdɪkʃən(ə)ri/
encyclopedia (n) ★ /ɪnˌsaɪkləˈpiːdiə/
guidebook (n) ★ /ˈgaɪdˌbʊk/
magazine (n) ★★★ /ˌmægəˈziːn/
manual (n) ★★ /ˈmænjʊəl/
newspaper (n) ★★★ /ˈnjuːzˌpeɪpə(r)/
textbook (n) /ˈteks(t)ˌbʊk/

Phrasal verbs connected with reading and writing

cross out (v) ★★ /ˌkrɒs ˈaʊt/
fill in (v) ★★★ /ˌfɪl ˈɪn/
flick through (v) ★ /ˌflɪk ˈθruː/
look up (v) ★★ /ˌlʊk ˈʌp/
read on (v) ★★★ /ˌriːd ˈɒn/
read out (v) ★★★ /ˌriːd ˈaʊt/
turn over (v) ★★★ /ˌtɜː(r)n ˈəʊvə(r)/

Other words and phrases

adaptation (n) ★ /ˌædæpˈteɪʃ(ə)n/
almost (adv) ★★★ /ˈɔːlməʊst/
apparent (adj) ★★★ /əˈpærənt/
assassination (n) ★ /əˌsæsɪˈneɪʃ(ə)n/
author (n) ★★★ /ˈɔːθə(r)/
best-selling (adj) /ˌbestˈselɪŋ/
blood (n) ★★★ /blʌd/
boarding school (n) /ˈbɔː(r)dɪŋ ˌskuːl/
carefully (adv) /ˈkeə(r)ˌf(ə)li/
certainly (adv) ★★★ /ˈsɜː(r)t(ə)nli/
climb (n & v) ★★★ /klaɪm/
combine (v) ★★★ /kəmˈbaɪn/
cover (= for a book) (n) ★★★ /ˈkʌvə(r)/
cowboy (n) /ˈkaʊˌbɔɪ/
credit card (n) ★★ /ˈkredɪt ˌkɑː(r)d/
customer (n) ★★★ /ˈkʌstəmə(r)/
dragon (n) /ˈdrægən/
elf (n) /elf/
end up (v) ★★★ /ˌend ˈʌp/
floor (= storey) (n) ★★★ /flɔː(r)/
following (adj) ★★★ /ˈfɒləʊɪŋ/
handsome (adj) ★★ /ˈhæns(ə)m/
happily ever after /ˈhæpɪli ˌevə(r) ˈɑːftə(r)/
have an impact (v) /ˌhæv ən ˈɪmpækt/
how long /ˌhaʊ ˈlɒŋ/
how often /ˌhaʊ ˈɒf(ə)n/
in stock /ˌɪn ˈstɒk/
inspiration (n) ★★ /ˌɪnspəˈreɪʃ(ə)n/
intrigue (n) /ˈɪntriːg/
jump in (v) /ˌdʒʌmp ˈɪn/
keep up (v) ★★★ /ˌkiːp ˈʌp/
make up (= invent) (v) ★★★ /ˌmeɪk ˈʌp/
mysterious (adj) ★★ /mɪˈstɪəriəs/
order (v) ★★★ /ˈɔː(r)də(r)/
(= ask for something in a shop/restaurant)
passion (n) ★★ /ˈpæʃ(ə)n/
path (n) ★★★ /pɑːθ/
predator (n) ★★ /ˈpredətə(r)/
previous (adj) ★★★ /ˈpriːviəs/
publication (n) ★★★ /ˌpʌblɪˈkeɪʃ(ə)n/
reach (v) ★★★ /riːtʃ/
related (adj) ★★ /rɪˈleɪtɪd/
reunion (n) /riːˈjuːniən/
ring (= wedding ring) (n) ★★★ /rɪŋ/

risk (v) ★★★	/rɪsk/
scuba-diving (n)	/'skuːbə ˌdaɪvɪŋ/
section (n) ★★★	/'sekʃ(ə)n/
shock (n) ★★★	/ʃɒk/
sinister (adj)	/'sɪnɪstə(r)/
spend (= money) (v) ★★★	/spend/
sufficient (adj) ★★★	/sə'fɪʃ(ə)nt/
survive (v) ★★★	/sə(r)'vaɪv/
survivor (n) ★	/sə(r)'vaɪvə(r)/
though (adv & conj) ★★★	/ðəʊ/
together (adv) ★★★	/tə'geðə(r)/
troll (n)	/trɒl/
unnecessary (adj) ★★	/ʌn'nesəs(ə)ri/
whisper (v) ★★	/'wɪspə(r)/
witch (n) ★	/wɪtʃ/
wolf (n) ★	/wʊlf/

Unit 10

Computers and computing

hard drive (n)	/ˌhɑː(r)d 'draɪv/
keyboard (n) ★	/'kiːˌbɔː(r)d/
mouse (n) ★★	/maʊs/
mouse pad (n)	/'maʊs ˌpæd/
printer (n) ★★	/'prɪntə(r)/
speaker (n) ★★★	/'spiːkə(r)/
USB port (n)	/ˌjuː es 'biː ˌpɔː(r)t/
webcam (n)	/'webˌkæm/

The Internet

blog (n & v)	/blɒg/
broadband (n)	/'brɔːdˌbænd/
chat online (v)	/ˌtʃæt ɒn'laɪn/
download (v)	/ˌdaʊn'ləʊd/
search engine (n) ★	/'sɜː(r)tʃ ˌendʒɪn/
surf the Net (v)	/ˌsɜː(r)f ðə 'net/
website (n) ★★	/'webˌsaɪt/

Collocations with *email*

bounce back (v) ★★	/ˌbaʊns 'bæk/
check email (v)	/ˌtʃek 'iːmeɪl/
delete an email (v)	/də'liːt ən ˌiːmeɪl/
email account (n)	/'iːmeɪl əˌkaʊnt/
email address (n)	/'iːmeɪl əˌdres/
forward an email (v)	/'fɔː(r)wə(r)d ən 'iːmeɪl /
reply to an email (v)	/rɪˌplaɪ tʊ ən 'iːmeɪl /
send an email (v)	/ˌsend ən 'iːmeɪl/

Other words and phrases

academic (adj) ★★★	/ˌækə'demɪk/
(n)	/ˌækə'demɪk/
accidentally (adv) ★	/ˌæksɪ'dent(ə)li/
analyse (v) ★★	/'ænəlaɪz/
assess (v) ★★	/ə'ses/
assessment (n)	/ə'sesmənt/
block (n) ★★★	/blɒk/
(v) ★★	/blɒk/
butcher's (n) ★	/'bʊtʃə(r)z/
button (n) ★★	/'bʌt(ə)n/
chip (= silicon) (n) ★★	/tʃɪp/
component (n) ★★	/kəm'pəʊnənt/
data (n) ★★★	/'deɪtə/
designer clothes (n)	/dɪ'zaɪnə(r) ˌkləʊðz/
diameter (n) ★	/daɪ'æmɪtə(r)/
dishonest (adj) ★	/dɪs'ɒnɪst/
document (n) ★★★	/'dɒkjʊmənt/
eclipse (n & v)	/ɪ'klɪps/
enormous (adj) ★★★	/ɪ'nɔː(r)məs/
entertainment (n) ★★	/ˌentə(r)'teɪnmənt/
export (n) ★★★	/'ekspɔː(r)t/
(v) ★★	/ɪk'spɔː(r)t/
frustrating (adj) ★	/frʌ'streɪtɪŋ/
hard copy (n)	/'hɑː(r)d ˌkɒpi/
import (n) ★★	/'ɪmpɔː(r)t/
(v) ★★	/ɪm'pɔː(r)t/
ingot (n)	/'ɪŋgət/
invest (v) ★★★	/ɪn'vest/
military (adj) ★★	/'mɪlɪt(ə)ri/
(n)	/'mɪlɪt(ə)ri/
model train (n)	/ˌmɒd(ə)l 'treɪn/
mosque (n) ★	/mɒsk/
objective (n) ★★★	/əb'dʒektɪv/
owner (n) ★★★	/'əʊnə(r)/
particle (n) ★★	/'pɑː(r)tɪk(ə)l/
password (n) ★	/'pɑːsˌwɜː(r)d/
per (prep) ★★★	/pɜː(r)/
physics (n)	/'fɪzɪks/
practical (adj) ★★★	/'præktɪk(ə)l/
(n)	/'præktɪk(ə)l/
product (n) ★★★	/'prɒdʌkt/
protest (n) ★★★	/'prəʊtest/
(v) ★★	/prə'test/
punish (v) ★★	/'pʌnɪʃ/
record (n) ★★★	/'rekɔː(r)d/
(v) ★★★	/rɪ'kɔː(r)d/
refine (n)	/rɪ'faɪn/
reputation (n) ★★★	/ˌrepjʊ'teɪʃ(ə)n/
research (n) ★★★	/'riːsɜː(r)tʃ/
resident (n) ★★★	/'rezɪd(ə)nt/
sand (n) ★★★	/sænd/
(v)	/sænd/
tiny (adj) ★★★	/'taɪni/
transistor (n)	/træn'zɪstə(r)/
valley (n) ★★★	/'væli/
various (adj) ★★★	/'veəriəs/

Gateway to exams, Units 9–10

interaction (n) ★★	/ˌɪntər'ækʃ(ə)n/
member (n) ★★★	/'membə(r)/
print (v) ★★★	/prɪnt/
publisher (n) ★★	/'pʌblɪʃə(r)/
spectacular (adj) ★★	/spek'tækjʊlə(r)/
(n)	/spek'tækjʊlə(r)/
turn into (v) ★★★ (= turn a book into a film)	/ˌtɜː(r)n 'ɪntə/

Study skills

Unit 1

GRAMMAR: Using reference material

- When you have problems with grammar, use reference material to find help.
- In this book there are grammar explanations on the Language Reference page at the end of each unit. These explanations help you to understand the correct ***use*** of the grammar (when and why to use the grammatical structure) and also the ***form*** (the correct parts of the structure).
- After reading about the grammar you can check that you understand it by doing the practice exercises on the revision page opposite.
- You can also use grammar books, either in English or in your own language.
- Look at the grammar help on www.macmillanenglish.com/gateway. Other Internet websites can also provide help with typical grammar problems.

WRITING: Keeping a mistakes checklist

It is normal to make mistakes when you write. That is why it is important to read your work carefully when you finish. Check for mistakes with:

- punctuation
- capital letters
- word order
- spelling
- tenses
- vocabulary
- missing words
- agreement between the subject and verb.

You can learn from your mistakes. Make a list of mistakes that you make with the correction next to it. Use it as a checklist when you are checking your writing. Look at this example:

Mistake	Correction	Explanation
In general, I think the money is important.	In general, I think money is important.	When we talk about things in general we do not use the definite article.

Unit 2

VOCABULARY: Using a dictionary

Dictionaries are very useful. Here are some ideas for using them well:

- You can't always have a dictionary with you, for example, in exams. Don't depend on the dictionary too much. First, guess the word and then use your dictionary to check.
- When you are reading, don't use the dictionary to look up every word you don't know. You don't need to understand every word in a text to do the exercises or to understand the general meaning. Only look for words which appear important or appear frequently.
- Don't just look at the first definition for a word. Many English words have very different meanings. Look at them all and choose the right one for your context.
- Don't just think about the meaning of the word that you look up. Think also about the type of word, the form and spelling of the word, and the other words it often goes with.

READING: Prediction

Before you read a text, look at the pictures or photos that go with it. Read the title of the text too. This can help you to think about the topic of the text and to predict some of the ideas and words in it. This can help you to understand more when you read the text for the first time.

Unit 3

Knowing what type of learner you are

It is useful to know what type of learner you are because it can help you to improve. Here are some things to think about:

- Some people like working alone. But remember that language is usually a question of communication and working with a partner can be a great way to start communicating in English.
- Writing usually gives you time to think and prepare your message. But writing also needs to be very precise and correct.
- Speaking is quick and spontaneous. So when you speak, mistakes are normal. The important thing is that other people understand you.
- Mistakes are an essential part of learning a language. We can learn a lot from our mistakes.
- Some people don't like learning grammar, but grammar and vocabulary are the basic ingredients of any language. They help you to communicate.
- Some people like studying with a dictionary, others with a grammar book or a computer. They can all help you to learn more outside the classroom. Find out what is good for you. When you spend a lot of time doing English, you are always improving.
- You can improve your memory. In general, we learn more with short, frequent revision.

LISTENING: Keeping calm

The worst thing that you can do when listening to English is panic because you don't understand something. It isn't usually necessary to understand every word. There is often repetition, and there are words that you don't need to understand to be able to do the activity. Concentrate on the information you need to answer the questions.

Unit 4

VOCABULARY: Keeping vocabulary records

To learn vocabulary, it is essential to keep a record of new words.

- Write down the meaning of new words. You can write a synonym, a definition, an example sentence, a translation, or you can draw a picture.
- It is also important to write down the type of word (e.g. noun, verb, adjective, adverb, preposition, pronoun) and any other special information (e.g. pronunciation, irregular forms).
- It is a good idea to learn words in groups. Write down vocabulary in the groups that appear in this book e.g. parts of the body, health problems, crimes, etc.
- Some people write down new vocabulary using diagrams like this:

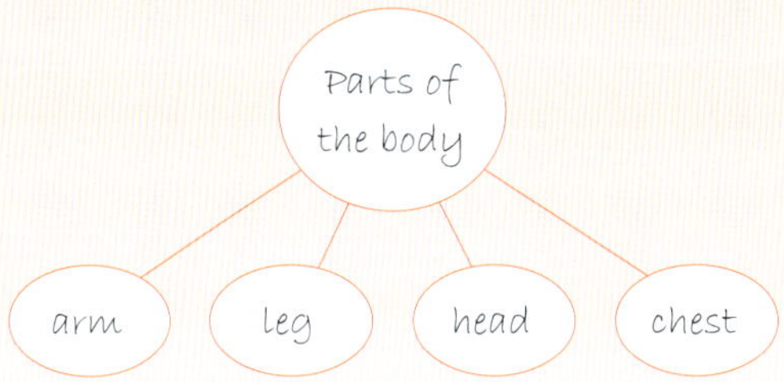

SPEAKING: Words you don't know

When you don't know a word, don't stop and don't use a word in your own language. Here are some things you *can* do, using the word ***freedom*** as an example:

- use a synonym or similar word like ***liberty*** or ***independence***
- use a more basic or general word or expression, ***being free***
- say ***It's the opposite of*** ....
  e.g. ***It's the opposite of captivity***.
- explain the word using different words, ***It's when you can do what you want***.

Unit 5

READING: Reading for general information

The first time you read a text, read it quickly. Do not stop if there are words you do not understand. Just try to understand the general meaning. Look for specific information the second time you read. Give yourself a time limit. It can help you to get a general understanding and not look at details.

GRAMMAR: Use and form

When we study grammar we need to think about two basic things:

- we need to know the meaning and when to *use* the structure. For example, with ***too*** we need to know that we use it to talk about people, things or actions that are *excessive*.
- we need to know the *form* (including spelling). For example, we need to know that the word ***too*** comes *before* adjectives.

Remember to think about both use and form when you do grammar activities.

Unit 6

LISTENING: First listening, second listening

- The first time you listen to a new text, the idea is to understand the general meaning, not to understand all the details. The first listening activity will usually help you to do this by asking general questions.
- The second time you listen you will need to listen for more specific information.

WRITING: Organising ideas into paragraphs

- A paragraph is a number of sentences which talk about one or two main ideas. When you want to start to talk about a new main idea, you start a new paragraph. Paragraphs make your writing clear, organised and easy to understand.
- Before you start a piece of writing, make a note of the ideas that you want to include. Then put your ideas in a logical order and organise them into paragraphs.

Unit 7

VOCABULARY: Efficient vocabulary revision

- Frequent revision is the best way to learn new words. Look at your vocabulary notebook or list every week and test yourself to see how much you remember. It is very difficult to learn vocabulary by revising just once before an exam or test.
- There will be some words from your vocabulary list that become very easy for you to remember. Stop testing yourself on them so that your revision list isn't too long.
- It is easier to learn vocabulary in groups, e.g. parts of the body, crimes, or adjectives ending in *-ing* and *-ed*. One word in a group can help you remember others in the same group.

SPEAKING: Making mistakes

- When you speak in a different language it is normal to make mistakes. The most important thing is to communicate with your partner.
- If you make small mistakes, either correct them when you make them or remember to work on them later.
- If your partner doesn't understand you, you need to change what you say so that your partner *does* understand.
- Remember: mistakes are a natural part of learning. If you don't say anything, you will never get better.

Unit 8

READING: Reading for specific information

The first reading activity usually checks that you understand the general meaning of the text. The next activities check that you understand specific information. When you read for specific information, read the question carefully and then find the exact place where you think the answer comes. Then read this section carefully, looking for details.

LISTENING: Listening outside the classroom

The best way to improve your listening is by listening to as much English as possible. Apart from listening in class, try to listen to:

- CDs or audio files that come with books or readers
- original version films
- DVDs in English (with or without subtitles)
- songs
- the radio or Internet radio.

Unit 9

READING: Reading for pleasure

Usually reading for pleasure means reading a whole book, magazine or website because you want to read it. There will probably be many words that you do not understand. It is not a good idea to stop every time you see a new word because you will never finish the story/article and you probably won't enjoy reading it. Only look up words that appear to be essential to understand the text, and that appear again and again. The main idea is to understand the general meaning … and to enjoy reading!

WRITING: Brainstorming

- Brainstorming is a good idea before writing because it helps you to have lots of ideas to write about. A common problem for writers is not knowing what to write about. Brainstorming helps you to think of original and interesting ideas.
- We can use diagrams called mind maps to help us to brainstorm ideas. Look at this example:

- When you finish brainstorming, choose the best ideas and decide how to organise them in a logical order.

Unit 10

READING: Guessing from context

You cannot usually use dictionaries in reading exams so when there are words that you do not understand, look carefully at the context to help you to guess the meaning. Look at the sentences and words just before and after the word. This can help you to find out the type of word (noun, verb, adjective, etc) and the meaning.

SPEAKING: Practice makes perfect

Speaking English is like riding a bike or playing tennis. You can only get better if you actually do it. The more you speak, the better you get. Speak as much English as possible in class, and outside the class.

Spelling rules

The third person singular

We usually add ***s*** to the verb.

like – likes
walk – walks

We add ***es*** to verbs that end in ***-s***, ***-sh***, ***-ch*** or ***-x***.

watch – watches
wash – washes
kiss – kisses

We add ***es*** to the verbs *go* and *do*.

go – goes
do – does

With verbs that end in a consonant + **y**, we omit the **y** and add ***ies***.

go – goes
do – does

With verbs that end in a vowel + **y**, we add ***s***.

play – plays
say – says

Verb + *-ing*

We usually add ***-ing*** to the verb to form the present participle.

jump – jumping
study – studying
sleep – sleeping

When verbs end in one or more consonants + ***e***, we omit the ***e*** and add ***-ing***.

have – having
make – making
dance – dancing

When a verb has only one syllable and finishes with one vowel and one consonant (except ***w***, ***x*** or ***y***), we double the consonant and add ***-ing***.

put – putting
swim – swimming
sit – sitting

When verbs end in ***-ie***, we change the ***-ie*** to ***-y*** and add ***-ing***.

lie – lying
die – dying

Pronunciation guide

Vowels

/ɑː/	arm, large
/æ/	cap, bad
/aɪ/	ride, fly
/aɪə/	diary, science
/aʊ/	how, mouth
/aʊə/	our, shower
/e/	bed, head
/eɪ/	day, grey
/eə/	hair, there
/ɪ/	give, did
/i/	happy, honeymoon
/iː/	we, heat
/ɪə/	ear, here
/ɒ/	not, watch
/əʊ/	cold, boat
/ɔː/	door, talk
/ɔɪ/	point, boy
/ʊ/	foot, could
/u/	annual
/uː/	two, food
/ʊə/	sure, tourist
/ɜː/	bird, heard
/ʌ/	fun, come
/ə/	mother, actor

Consonants

/b/	bag, rubbish
/d/	desk, cold
/f/	fill, laugh
/g/	girl, big
/h/	hand, home
/j/	yes, young
/k/	cook, back
/l/	like, fill
/m/	mean, climb
/n/	new, want
/p/	park, happy
/r/	ring, borrow
/s/	say, this
/t/	town, city
/v/	very, live
/w/	water, away
/z/	zoo, his
/ʃ/	shop, machine
/ʒ/	usually, television
/ŋ/	thank, doing
/tʃ/	cheese, picture
/θ/	thing, north
/ð/	that, clothes
/dʒ/	jeans, bridge

Exam success

Unit 1

READING: Multiple-choice activities

In this type of activity you choose the best answer from three or four different answers.

Step 1: Read the text quickly to get a general understanding.

Step 2: Read all the answers carefully. Sometimes the difference between two answers is just one word.

Step 3: Find the section of the text where you think each answer comes and read it again slowly, in more detail.

Step 4: If you aren't 100% sure which answer is best, take away any answers which you know are not correct.

Step 5: When you finish, check that you have an answer for each question. Never leave answers blank in an exam.

SPEAKING: Information role-plays

- Find out the situation and the information that you need to ask for and give.
- If you don't understand what the examiner or your partner is saying, ask them in English to repeat or to speak more slowly. Use expressions like: ***Sorry, can you say that again?*** or, ***Sorry, could you speak more slowly?***
- Listen to your partner and the examiner. In a conversation we speak ***and*** listen.
- Show that you're interested in what the other person is saying. Use expressions like: ***Really? That's interesting. Do you? Me too.***
- Use ***Well***, ***Hmm*** or ***Let me think*** to give you time to think of what you want to say next.
- Use basic question words like ***Who? What? When? Where? How? Why?*** to help you think of more questions to keep the conversation going.

Unit 2

LISTENING: True/false activities

In this type of activity you have to listen and decide if answers are true or false. You usually hear the text twice. The questions are usually in the same order as you hear them in the recording.

Step 1: Read the questions before you listen. They can give you ideas about the topic of the text and the vocabulary you are going to hear.

Step 2: You can usually hear the recording twice. Try not to panic if you do not understand information the first time. If you don't hear the answer to one question, start listening immediately for the answer to the next question.

Step 3: Use the second listening to find the answers you didn't hear the first time and to check the answers you already have.

Step 4: When you finish, check that you have an answer for each question. Never leave answers blank in an exam.

WRITING: Knowing about evaluation

In exams it is important to know how many marks there are for different sections and to know what the examiners want. Usually examiners in writing exams want to see if you can:

- answer the question and include the information they ask for
- write clearly
- organise your ideas logically
- use accurate and varied grammar
- use accurate and varied vocabulary
- use punctuation and capital letters correctly.

Unit 3

USE OF ENGLISH: Multiple-choice cloze activities

In this type of activity, you have a text with gaps. You must fill in each gap with one of three or four answers given.

Step 1: Read the complete text without thinking about the gaps. This helps you to get a general understanding of the text.

Step 2: Before you look at the answers, think about the *type* of word you need (noun, verb, pronoun, article, etc) and the general *meaning*.

Step 3: Read the answers. Choose the one which you think is best. Look very carefully at the words which come just before and just after the gap. Do they help you to find the best answer?

Step 4: If you aren't sure which answer is right, take away any answers which you know are not correct.

Step 5: Read the sentence again with your answer in the gap to check it.

Step 6: When you finish, check that you have an answer for each question. Never leave answers blank in an exam.

SPEAKING: Evaluation

In exams it is important to know how many marks there are for different sections and to know what the examiners want. Usually examiners in speaking exams want to see if you can:

- communicate successfully
- speak fluently
- use accurate and varied grammar
- use accurate and varied vocabulary
- pronounce words clearly.

Unit 4

READING: Matching activities

In this type of activity, you have to say which text or part of a text contains a specific piece of information.

Step 1: Read all the texts or parts of the text quickly to get a general understanding.

Step 2: Read the piece(s) of information that you need to find. Look for key words that help you to find the text or part of the text which contains the information.

Step 3: Read that specific text or part of the text again in more detail.

Step 4: If you are not sure that you have found the correct answer, read other sections again in more detail.

Step 5: When you finish, check that you have an answer for each question. Never leave answers blank in an exam.

WRITING: Content and style

- When a question tells you to put information in your text, you lose marks if you do not include the information. You can use your imagination but you must remember to include all the information in the instructions.
- When you write letters, messages and notes it is essential to write in the correct style. When you write to a friend, use contractions and informal expressions. When you write a formal or semi-formal letter, message or note, do not use contractions or informal language. If your letter is grammatically correct but not in the correct style, you lose marks.

Unit 5

LISTENING: Identifying the speaker activities

In this type of activity you match different speakers with the things they say.

Step 1: Before you listen, think about the topic of the listening. This will help you to predict ideas and words that could appear in the recording.

Step 2: Read the questions to know how many speakers there are and what they may say.

Step 3: When you listen, remember that in the recording the speakers will probably express the same ideas using different words and expressions. Thinking of synonyms for the words in the statements can help you to identify the answers.

Step 4: Don't worry if you don't understand everything the first time you listen. Usually you listen twice. Use the second listening to find the answers you didn't hear the first time and to check the answers you already have.

SPEAKING: Negotiating

In negotiating activities, you usually work with another person. The examiner explains a situation where you and the other speaker need to come to a decision. In this type of exercise, remember that there isn't usually a right or wrong answer. The examiner wants to hear you speaking English.

If you can't think of something to say:

- Ask your partner a question like ***What do you think?*** This gives you time to think of what you can say next.
- Use fillers like ***Well***, ***Hmm*** or ***Let me think*** to give you time to think of what you want to say next.
- Don't be afraid to say something that you think is obvious.
- Remember to give full explanations for your opinions and ideas.
- Listen to what your partner or the examiner is saying. In a conversation we speak ***and*** listen.
- If you don't understand what the examiner or your partner is saying, ask them in English to repeat or to speak more slowly. Use expressions like: ***Sorry, can you say that again?*** or, ***Sorry, could you speak more slowly?***

Unit 6

USE OF ENGLISH: Sentence transformation activities

In this type of activity you have a sentence and you must complete a second sentence so that it means the same as the original sentence. In some exercises you must use a word that they give. In this case, you cannot change the form of this word. Generally you can only use between two and five words, including the word they give you.

Step 1: Read the original sentence carefully. Think about the meaning of the sentence, the type of structure(s) used, the tense(s) used, etc.

Step 2: If they give you a word, think about its meaning. Think also about the grammatical function of the word. Does it always or usually go with another word or tense?

Step 3: Write your sentence.

Step 4: When you finish, check that you:
a) have not changed the meaning from the original sentence.
b) have not changed the form of the word they gave you.
c) have not written more than the maximum number of words permitted.

WRITING: Writing in exam conditions

- When you write in exam conditions, you cannot usually use a dictionary or grammar book. If you do not know a word, think of a similar word or a more basic or general word. Do not leave a gap or write the word in your own language. If necessary, change what you were going to say.
- If you are not sure how to use a grammatical structure, think of a different way to say the same thing.
- Answer the question. Sometimes you can get 0 points if you don't answer the question.
- Pay attention to the maximum and minimum number of words in the instructions.
- Plan and organise your writing and check it carefully for mistakes when you have finished.

Unit 7

READING: True/false activities

In this type of activity you decide if statements are true or false depending on the information in the text.

Step 1: Read the text quickly to get a general understanding.

Step 2: Read the sentences that you need to say are true or false.

Step 3: Find the parts of the text where the information comes. Read them again in more detail.

Step 4: If there is no information to say if a sentence is true, mark the statement false.

Step 5: When you finish, check that you have an answer for each question. Never leave answers blank in an exam.

LISTENING: Multiple-choice activities

In this type of activity you choose the best answer from three or four different answers.

You usually hear the text twice. The questions are usually in the same order as you hear them in the recording.

Step 1: Read the different answers before you listen. They can give you ideas about the topic of the text and the vocabulary you are going to hear in it. Remember that sometimes the difference between two answers is just one word.

Step 2: You usually hear the recording twice. Try not to panic if you do not understand information the first time. If you don't hear the answer to one question, start listening immediately for the answer to the next question.

Step 3: Use the second listening to find the answers you didn't hear the first time and to check the answers you already have.

Step 4: When you finish, check that you have an answer for each question. Never leave answers blank in an exam.

Unit 8

SPEAKING: Reporting past events

In this type of activity you have to talk about something (real or imaginary) that happened in the past. You may need to speak alone or have a conversation with the examiner or another student.

- Remember to use past tenses correctly. We use the past simple for completed activities in the past. The past continuous is for activities in progress at a moment in the past. We can use it to describe scenes in the past. The past perfect is for activities that happened before other activities in the past.
- Use expressions of time and sequence (***first***, ***next***, ***then***, ***later***, etc.) to make the order of events clear.
- Use basic question words like ***Who? What? When? Where? How? Why?*** to help you think of more things to say.
- Use fillers like ***Well***, ***Hmm*** or ***Let me think*** to give you time to think of what you want to say next.
- If you don't understand what the examiner or your partner is saying, ask them in English to repeat or to speak more slowly. Use expressions like: ***Sorry, can you say that again?*** or, ***Sorry, could you speak more slowly?***

WRITING: Answering the question

- Remember that in writing exams you lose marks if you do not answer the question. It is not enough to write no grammatical mistakes and with a wide variety of vocabulary. You must also include all the information that appears in the question.
- Reading the question carefully can also help you to decide which tenses and vocabulary you need to use in your writing.

Unit 9

READING: Missing sentence activities

In this type of activity you have to fill gaps in a text with sentences taken out of the text. The sentences are often the first in each paragraph. There are sometimes more sentences than gaps.

Step 1: Read the text quickly to get a general idea of what it is about. To do this type of exercise you do not usually have to understand every word, so don't panic if you don't understand everything.

Step 2: Read the sentences which go in the text. What does each sentence talk about?

Step 3: Find the sections of the text which correspond to the information in the sentences and read them again slowly, in more detail. Put each sentence in the most probable gap.

Step 4: Check by reading the text with your answers in the correct place. Do the sentences go together logically? Do words like ***this*** or ***it*** make sense? Check also that you have one answer for each question. Never leave answers blank in an exam.

LISTENING: Completing notes

- Always read the incomplete notes *before* you listen. This helps you to know what to listen for. Look carefully at the words that come just before or after each space and think about what *type* of word is missing (noun, verb, adjective, adverb, etc).
- It is not usually necessary to understand every word that you hear. Listen out for the sections which correspond to the information in the notes. Then pay special attention to these sections.
- Usually you only need to write one or two words in each space. Be careful with spelling and your handwriting.
- Don't worry if you don't understand everything the first time you listen. Usually you listen twice. Use the second listening to find the answers you didn't hear the first time and to check the answers you already have.

Unit 10

USE OF ENGLISH: Cloze activities

In this type of activity, you have a text with gaps. You must fill in each gap by thinking of a word which is grammatically correct and is logical.

Step 1: Read the complete text without thinking about the gaps. This is to get a general understanding of the text.

Step 2: Look again at the gaps and especially the words which come just before and after the gap. Do those words need a special preposition? Is an article or auxiliary verb missing? Think about the type of word you need (noun, verb, pronoun, article, etc.) and the general meaning.

Step 3: Fill in the gap with the word that you think is best. Read the sentence again with your answer in the gap to check it. Check that the meaning is logical, but check also that the words fit in grammatically. Sometimes there may be more than one possible answer but you only need to put one.

Step 4: When you finish, check that you have one answer for each question. Never leave answers blank in an exam.

SPEAKING: A conversation based on a photo

In this type of activity you have to talk about one or possibly two photos. If there are two photos, sometimes you must say things that are similar and/or different in the photos. You usually have some time to look at the photo(s) and prepare what you are going to say. Do not write out a complete description to read out aloud.

- If you cannot think of things to say, remember to use the questions ***What? Who? Where? Why? When?*** etc to give you ideas.
- Think of possible questions that the examiner will ask you about the photo. If you don't know a word, don't worry. Think of similar words, more basic or general words, or explain the word. The examiners want to hear you speaking English.
- Use fillers like ***Well***, ***Hmm*** or ***Let me think*** to give yourself time to think of what you are going to say next.
- If you aren't 100% sure of what you can see, speculate using expressions like ***It might be***, ***I'm not sure but I think***, ***It looks like***, etc. Don't be afraid of saying simple, obvious things. The important thing is to say something.

Speaking bank

General

When you don't understand

Sorry, can you say that again?
Sorry, could you speak more slowly?

Checking understanding

Sorry, did you say … ?
Do you mean?
Could you repeat that?
Pardon?
I'm not sure I understood.

Showing interest

Really?
That's interesting.
That's incredible!
I see.
Do you?
Me too.

Filling the conversation

Errr …
Well …
The thing is …
I'm not (really/totally/completely) sure but …
Maybe …
You know …
I think …
I imagine …
It looks like …
I imagine that …
Let me think.
What do you think?

When you don't know a word

It's like/similar to …
It's the opposite of …
It's when you …

Talking about the past

Expressions of sequence and time

At first	*In the end*
First of all	*Finally*
Then	*Suddenly*
Next	*A few minutes/hours/days later*
After that	*The next day*

Using different past tenses

1 *Past simple = A completed action in the past.*
2 *Past continuous = An activity in progress at a moment in the past. We often use it to describe scenes in the past.*
3 *Past perfect = An activity that happened before another action in the past.*

Describing a photo

Starting

This is a picture of …
I can see …

Position

On the right/left
In the middle
At the top
At the bottom
In the background
In the foreground

Speculation

I think …
I'm not sure but I think that …
It looks as if …
It looks like …
I imagine that …
It may/might/could be …
It's not clear if …
They're probably …
It might be …

Common situations

Asking for personal information

How old are you?
Have you got any brothers or sisters?
What do you do at the weekend/in the evenings/on Wednesdays?
Do you like . . . ?
What do you think of . . . ?
How often do you . . . ?

Asking for opinions

What do you think?
What's your opinion/view?
Do you agree?
What about you?

Giving opinions

Personally,
I think (that) . . .
I don't think (that) . . .
I don't really know if . . .
In my view,
In my opinion,
As I see it,

Agreeing

I agree (with you) that . . .
That's true.
You're right.
I see what you mean.

Disagreeing

I disagree (with you) that . . .
I see what you mean, but . . .
I'm not sure that's true.

Making suggestions

Shall we (do something)?
Why don't we (do something)?
Let's (do something).
How about (doing something)?

Responding to suggestions

Great!
Yes, but . . .
OK.
I'm not sure.
Fine.
I know what you mean, but . . .
Yes, let's (do something).
No, I prefer . . .
Good idea.
Why don't we . . . ?
You're right.
No, I prefer (to do something).
Me too/Me neither.
But what about . . .?

Asking about somebody's plans

What are you up to at the weekend?
Are you up to anything at the weekend?
Do you fancy (verb + -ing)?

Arranging to meet

What time shall we meet?
Where shall we meet?
Why don't we meet at . . . ?

Responding to plans and arrangements

Sure./Fine./OK./Great./Good idea.
Not really./Sorry, I can't./Sorry, I'm busy./I prefer . . . .

Making polite requests

Can you tell me what the wages are?
Could I ask for some information first?
Could you tell me if the job is full-time or part-time?
Would you mind . . . ?
Would you be able to . . . ?

Making offers

Can I help you?
Do you want me to . . . ?
Would you like me to . . . ?
Shall I . . . for you?
How about if I . . . for you?

Writing bank

Informal emails

page 15 (Unit 1)
page 67 (unit 5)
page 105 (Unit 8)

Start: *Hi*

Style: Informal. Use contractions. We can also use emoticons (e.g. ☺).

Useful expressions:

- To begin, ask questions like *How are you?, How are things?, Are you doing exams/on holiday at the moment?*
- Use *By the way* to change the subject.

End:

- *That's all for now.*
- *Write back soon.*
- *All the best, love....*

Notes and messages

page 53 (Unit 4)

Start: Simply write the name of the person you are writing to.

Style: Write short, direct sentences. Use imperatives like *Call me*, rather than *Could you call me?* Use abbreviations.

Useful abbreviations:

PS, e.g., NB, asap, i.e., etc, Tel., St., Rd.

Useful expressions:

- *Congratulations!* (good news)
- *I was really sorry to hear that...* (bad news)
- *Get well soon.* (for sickness and accidents)

Informal letters

page 27 (Unit 2)

Start: Write your address and the date in the top right corner. Then we write *Dear* or *Hi* and the name of the person you are writing to.

Style: Informal. Use contractions.

Useful expressions:

- Begin *Thanks for your letter* or *I'm writing to tell you about...*
- Ask questions like *How are you?, How are things?, Are you doing exams/on holiday at the moment?*
- Use *By the way* to change the subject.

End:

- *Write back soon.*
- *That's all for now.*
- *All the best.*

Giving opinions/ discursive essays

page 67 (unit 5)
page 79 (Unit 6)

Start: Make a general statement to introduce the topic.

Useful expressions:

- To give your opinions, use *Personally, I think, As far as I'm concerned, In my opinion, I agree/disagree with...*
- To explain and justify your opinions, use *This is because, For example.*
- To give a conclusion, use *To sum up, In conclusion.*

Useful linkers:

- To put opinions and ideas in sequence, use *Firstly, Next, Finally.*
- To add opinions and ideas, use *Furthermore, What's more.*
- To contrast ideas and opinions, use *However, Nevertheless.*

End: Write a conclusion, restating the most important point(s).

Formal letters

page 79 (Unit 6), page 93 (unit 7)

Start: Write your address and the date in the top right corner. Write the address of the person you are writing to a little lower, on the left. Then write *Dear Mr (Smith)* (for a man), *Dear Mrs (Smith)* (for a married woman), or *Dear Ms (Smith)* (when we make no distinction if a woman is married or not). When we do not know the name of the person we are writing to, we write *Dear Sir or Madam.*

Style: Formal. Do not use contractions.

Useful expressions in job applications:

- Begin *I am writing in response to the advertisement in …*
- Use *I would like to apply for the job of … , I enclose a CV with information about myself, I have experience of …*
- End *I look forward to hearing from you.*

Useful expressions in letters to a newspaper:

- Begin *I am writing in response to the article …*
- Use *Personally, I agree/disagree with …*
- End *I will be interested in hearing other readers' opinions on this question.*

Useful linkers:

- To put opinions and ideas in sequence, use *Firstly, Next, Finally.*
- To add opinions and ideas, use *Furthermore, What is more.*
- To contrast ideas and opinions, use *However, Nevertheless.*

End: When we know the name of the person we are writing to, use *Yours sincerely.* When we don't know the name of the person we are writing to, use *Yours faithfully.*

Informal letters

page 119 (Unit 9)

Start: Give your questionnaire a title.

Useful words:

Who, Which, When, Where, Why, How, How much, How many, How often …

Be careful with different types of question.

1. In subject questions, the question word (*who, what*, etc) is the subject of the verb. The auxiliary verb (*do, does, did*) is not necessary, e.g. *Who likes reading magazines?*
2. In object questions, the question word (*who, what*, etc) is the object of the verb. The auxiliary verb (*do, does, did*) is necessary, e.g. *What do you like reading?*
3. When we have *to be* or a modal verb (*can, will, should*), we do not need the auxiliary verb *do* to make questions, e.g. *Should children read newspapers?*

End: The last question(s) can ask for a general conclusion.

Stories, narratives and anecdotes

page 105 (unit 8)

Start: Explain and describe where and when the story began and who was in the story.

Useful expressions:

- To explain the sequence of events, use *At first, First of all, Next, Then, After that, Finally, In the end.*
- To say when things happened, use, for example, *Last weekend, Two weeks ago, On Friday, On Saturday night.*

Use different past tenses.

1. Past simple = A completed action in the past.
2. Past continuous = An activity in progress at a moment in the past. We often use it to describe scenes in the past.
3. Past perfect = An activity that happened before another action in the past.

Text messages

page 131 (Unit 10)

Useful abbreviations:

PLS	@	L8R	B	BCZ	L8
MSG	SPK	THX	2DAY	2MORO	WKND
XLNT	2nite	2	YR	C	U
WOT	R	B4	GR8		

Infinitive	Past simple	Past participle
be	was/were	been
beat	beat	beaten
become	became	become
begin	began	begun
break	broke	broken
bring	brought	brought
build	built	built
burn	burnt	burnt
buy	bought	bought
catch	caught	caught
choose	chose	chosen
come	came	come
cost	cost	cost
cut	cut	cut
do	did	done
draw	drew	drawn
drink	drank	drunk
drive	drove	driven
eat	ate	eaten
fall	fell	fallen
feel	felt	felt
find	found	found
fly	flew	flown
forget	forgot	forgotten
forgive	forgave	forgiven
get	got	got
give	gave	given
go	went	gone
grow	grew	grown
hang out	hung out	hung out
have	had	had
hear	heard	heard
hide	hid	hidden
hit	hit	hit
hurt	hurt	hurt
keep	kept	kept
know	knew	known
lay	laid	laid
leave	left	left
learn	learned/learnt	learned/learnt

Infinitive	Past simple	Past participle
let	let	let
lie	lay	lain
lose	lost	lost
make	made	made
mean	meant	meant
meet	met	met
pay	paid	paid
put	put	put
read	read	read
ride	rode	ridden
ring	rang	rung
run	ran	run
say	said	said
see	saw	seen
sell	sold	sold
send	sent	sent
set up	set up	set up
shine	shone	shone
shoot	shot	shot
show	showed	shown
sing	sang	sung
sit	sat	sat
sleep	slept	slept
speak	spoke	spoken
speed	sped	sped
spell	spelt	spelt
spend	spent	spent
split up	split up	split up
stand up	stood up	stood up
steal	stole	stolen
swim	swam	swum
take	took	taken
teach	taught	taught
tell	told	told
think	thought	thought
understand	understood	understood
wake up	woke up	woken up
wear	wore	worn
win	won	won
write	wrote	written

Unit 2

Student B: Prepare questions to ask your partner to find the missing information.

1 Was Bonnie Parker very intelligent?

Then interview your partner.

Student B

Bonnie and Clyde were a pair of notorious criminals. Bonnie Parker was born in 1910 in Rowena, Texas. She (a) .... very intelligent. Clyde's full name was Clyde Barrow. He was born in 1909 in (b) .... Bonnie met Clyde in 1930. They (c) .... in the next four years. They robbed 15 banks, although generally they preferred small shops and petrol stations. They often stole cars too. Once Clyde sent a letter to (d) ...., to thank him. He told him that his cars were his favourite cars to steal! But Clyde also had a violent side. He (e) .... ten or eleven people. In January 1934 Clyde helped some friends to escape from a Texas prison. But the Texas police decided (f) .... Six police officers killed the pair of criminals when they were in their car. Bonnie and Clyde were so famous that many people went to see the car and tried to (g) .... !

Unit 3

The Sydney English Centre, Australia

Course begins: 16th August
Course lasts: 12 days
Accommodation organised
Price: 930 Australian dollars

Other activities include: swimming, surfing, excursion to the Blue Mountains

The San Francisco English Centre, USA

Course begins: 21st July
Course lasts: One month
Accommodation organised
Price: 4,325 US dollars

Other activities include: mountain biking, excursion to a theme park, karaoke evenings

Unit 6

1 desert
2 Canberra
3 Captain James Cook in 1770
4 prison convicts, beginning in 1788 and ending in 1848
5 A 2,600 km long structure made of living coral off the north-east coast of Australia. The big rock in the middle of Australia is called Uluru (or Ayers Rock). The most famous beach near Sydney is Bondi Beach, but there are no sharks.
6 A common myth says that Captain Cook asked an indigenous Australian 'What's that animal?', pointing to a kangaroo. The man replied 'I don't understand you', or 'kangaroo' in his language.
7 an indigenous Australian musical instrument
8 Russell Crowe, 'Best Actor' for *Gladiator* and Mel Gibson, 'Best Director' for *Braveheart*. Crowe was born in New Zealand but went to live in Australia as a child and lives there now. Gibson was born in the USA but lived in Australia when he was young. Later he moved back to the USA and lives there now.

Unit 7

Grantham Gardens

No experience necessary.
Job is from 20th June to 20th September
Full-time work only: 38 hours a week
Don't work weekends
Wages: £6.80 an hour
Need to be reliable, hard-working
Don't need to be particularly strong
Send letter and CV to: *Janet Doors, Grantham Gardens, PO Box 372, Lincoln*

Champions Camp

Good to have experience of sports camps, but not essential
Job is for July and September
Full-time work only: residential, living with the children doing the camp
Wages: £7.90 an hour
Need to be fit, interested in sport, caring, self-reliant
Don't need to speak foreign languages
Send letter and CV to: *Mr Christopher Jones, Champions Camp, PO Box 730, Chester*

Unit 8

1 Mostly Section 1: You are a perfectionist.

Personality: You're very hard-working and always want to do your best, but sometimes you're too serious.
Romance: Your relationships are intense but short. If your partner isn't perfect you always have arguments.
Ideal jobs: Fashion designer, TV producer, journalist
Advice: You should be more relaxed. Not everybody is as perfect as you.

2 Mostly Section 2: You are a romantic.

Personality: You're very caring and get on well with others, but you can get very sad when people don't think about you.
Romance: You're a total romantic and believe in true love. You need your partner to be 100% in love with you.
Ideal jobs: Artist, novelist, actor.
Advice: You shouldn't get too unhappy if things go wrong.

3 Mostly Section 3: You're a thinker.

Personality: You're a reliable friend because you're good at listening to people and helping them with problems. But sometimes you spend too much time alone, thinking about things.
Romance: You're very practical about relationships but you need to relax and enjoy yourself more.
Ideal jobs: Politician, teacher, computer programmer
Advice: You have to do more and think less. Don't worry about the consequences of your actions – just do it!

4 Mostly Section 4: You're a leader.

Personality: You have to be in control. You're strong and ambitious but that can be a weakness too because some people will think you are too interested in being the boss.
Romance: You think it's easy to make somebody fall in love with you. But some people may think you are frightening!
Ideal jobs: Company director, police officer, bank manager
Advice: You should think of others. Be more tolerant of people who aren't as direct as you.

Macmillan Education
Between Towns Road, Oxford OX4 3PP
A division of Macmillan Publishers Limited
Companies and representatives throughout the world

ISBN 978-0-230-72344-3
ISBN 978-0-230-41760-1 (plus Gateway Online)

Page make-up by Laila Meachin, Giles Davies and Right-on-the-Line Ltd
Illustrated by Jamel Akib (p97), Fred Blunt (pp50r, 51l), Jim Hansen (pp18, 26, 27, 28, 86), Joanna Kerr (p77), Peter Lubach (p51r), Gillian Martin (p23), Ed McLachlan (pp13, 19, 21, 25, 91), Julian Mosedale (pp11, 101), MPS India (p133), ODI (p70), Mark Ruffle (pp44, 99), Martin Saunders (pp34, 36, 37, 125l), Pablo Velarde (p46) and Simon Williams (pp8, 24, 50l, 55, 96, 117)
Cover design by Andrew Oliver
Cover photos by **CERN/** Maximilien Brice; **Getty/** Bread and Butter, Getty/ Charles Gullung, Getty/ Kim Heacox; **Science Photo Library/** Mehau Kulyk.

Author's acknowledgements:
I would like to thank the whole Macmillan team in Oxford for their dedication and hard work during the creation of this book. A big thanks also to all the students that I have had the pleasure of teaching at Colegio Europeo Aristos, Getafe and to my colleagues there. Finally, writing this book would not have been possible without the support of my wonderful family. All my love and thanks to Gemma, Jamie and Becky.

The publishers would like to thank all of those who reviewed or piloted Gateway: Benjamin Affolter, Evelyn Andorfer, Anna Ciereszynska, Regina Culver, Anna Dabrowska, Ondrej Dosedel, Lisa Durham, Dagmar Eder, Eva Ellederovan, H Fouad, Sabrina Funes, Luiza Gervescu, Isabel González Bueno, Jutta Habringer, Stela Halmageanu, Andrea Hutterer, Nicole Ioakimidis, Mag. Annemarie Kammerhofer, Sonja Lengauer, Gabriela Liptakova, María Cristina Maggi, Silvia Miranda Barbara Nowak, Agnieska Orlińska, Anna Orlowska, María Paula Palou Marta Piotrowska, N Reda, Katharina Schatz, Roswitha Schwarz, Barbara Ścibor, Katarzyna Sochacka, Joanna Spoz, Marisol Suppan, Stephanie Sutter, Halina Tyliba, Prilipko, Vladyko, Pia Wimmer, Katarzyna Zadrożna-Attia, and Katarzyna Zaremba-Jaworska.

The author and publishers would like to thank the following for permission to reproduce their photographs:
AKG Images/ TOUCHSTONE TELEVISION/ Album p49(b); **Alamy/** Brent Waltermire p7(l), Oleksiy Maksymenko p7(br), Kevin Browne p22(m), Ted Pink p26(a), Adrian Sherratt p26(c), Eye-Stock p26(e), Lenscap p26(d), Stuart Abraham p45(t), foodfolio p45(br), Jeff Greenberg p52(a), dacology p58(b), Jiri Rezac p63(a), Eddie Gerald p64(b), FRANCIS DEAN p64(c), Helene Rogers p64(e), Alex Segre p64(d), David White p70(ba), Caro p74(t), Photofusion Picture Library p76(d), Lourens Smak p77, Sally and Richard Greenhill p78(a), Jim Nicholson p85(l), Stock Connection Blue p88(mr), Jim West p88(ml), Jeff Greenberg p88(tl), Picture Partners p89(tr), Emilio Ereza p98, Alan Roberts p111(tr), uk retail Alan King p118; **Andrew Weldon** p128; **Ardea/** Mark Boulton p70(bd); **BANANASTOCK** pp6(d), 12(b), 78(d and e), 84(d and f); **BRAND X** p111(tml); **CERN/** Maximilien Brice p126(t); **ComStock** p71(l); **Corbis/** Sagel & Kranefeld p7(tr), Tony Costa p11, Tim Pannell p12(t); Rick Barrentine p14(tl), MedioImages p14(tr), moodboard p15(br), Columbia Pictures/ZUMA p23, Goodshoot p25, Envision p34(tl), PATRICK SEEGER/ POOL/epa p38(c), Frank Trapper p38(b), Kurt Krieger p38(d), Visuals Unlimited p45(bl), Tom Stewart p52(b), TRAPPER FRANK/CORBIS SYGMA p61(r), Hulton-Deutsch Collection p62(b), Atlantide Phototravel p64(a), John Springer Collection p65, Holger Winkler/A.B. p66(a), LWA-Sharie Kennedy p66(b), Theo Allofs p70(bc), Tom Van Sant p74(tm), Atlantide Phototravel p75(1), Paul Thompson p79(b), Atsuko Tanaka p84(a), Granger Wootz/Blend Images p84(h), FORESTIER YVES/CORBIS SYGMA p85(r), Richard Morrell p87(c), Christophe karaba/epa p87(r), Paul Barton p88(tr), Comstock Select p88(c), James Collins p104(b), Michelle Pedone p105(a), Colin McPherson p111(b), Kevin Dodge p123, Andrew Brusso p126(b), Gerald French p127(t), Bettmann p129(m), moodboard p130(a); **CORBIS** pp6(e), 15(bl), 66(c), 70(ta), 84(c); **DIGITAL VISION** p87(d); **Getty/** Charles Gullung p6(c), Peter Nicholson p14(bl), Phillip Graybill p14(br), Plustwentyseven p15(tl), Lars Borges p20, Hulton Archive p21, Steve Gorton p22(t), Jeremy O'Donnell p22(b), Demetrio Carrasco p26(b), Stephen Studd p40(r), Jose Luis Banus-March p40(t), Max Dannenbaum p40(b), Neil Beckerman p44, Gaye Gerard p49(t), Steve Granitz p61(l), John Giustina p66(d), Laurence Monneret p66(e), White Packert p66(f), Kim Heacox p70(td), John Gurzinski p71(r), Zigy Kaluzny p75(3), Steve Bonini p78(b), Yellow Dog Productions p84(b), Greg Wood p88(bl), Steve McAlister p89(tl), Shirlaine Forrest p89(b), Annie Griffiths Belt p92(l), Jill Gocher p92(r), Chev Wilkinson p104(t), Stockbyte p105(c), Bread and Butter p105(b), Scott Kleinman p111(teacher), Panoramic Images p127(b), Hulton Archive p135; **GETTY** p34(br); **Goodshoot** pp35(bl), 70(tb); **IMAGE SOURCE** pp6(b), 6(f), 26(f), 30, 70(te), 70(tf), 79(t); **Lonely Planet Images/** Rachel Lewis p32(r); **Macmillan Publishers Ltd** pp119 (montage),122, Macmillan Publishers Ltd/David Tolley pp34(bl), 90(l); **Masterfile/** Siephoto p90(r); **Paul Bricknell** p63(b); **PHOTOALTO** pp6(a); **PHOTODISC** p130(b); **Photolibrary.com/** Tim Hall p15(br), Bay Hippisley p24, Foodfolio Foodfolio p34(tr), Pixtal Images p35(br), Jose Fuste Raga p35(tl), Angelo Cavalli p35(ml), Chris Cheadle p39, Michael Weber p40(l), DELOCHE – p52(c), RE. Johnson p73, Tom Till p74t, Claire Leimbach p74(bm), Stefan Kiefer p84(e), NONSTOCK p87(a), Jaume Gual p113(b), Foodfolio Foodfolio p129(b), Thomas Craig p130(ba), Terry Vine p130(bb), Leland Bobbé/Bettmann p134; **Photoshot** p75(4), Sigrid Olsson p78(c), Bilderlounge p84(g); **PIXTAL** p70(tc); **Reuters/** NASA p75(2), Max Rossi p100; **Rex Features/** KPA/Zuma p38(a), NBCUPHOTOBANK p58(d), c.20thC.Fox/Everett p58(a), Channel 4 p58(c), Courtesy Everett Collection p63(m), Universal/Everett/Rex Features p63(b), Humberto Carreno p74(b), RICHARD YOUNG p82, Sipa Press p87(b), Tina Norris p108, c.MGM/Everett p111(tmr), Ray Tang p111(tl), LINDA MATLOW p115(t), Debra L. Rothenberg p129(t); **Robert Harding World Imagery/** Roy Rainford p35(mr); **Science and Society Picture Library/** National Media Museum p62(t); **Science Photo Library/** MEHAU KULYK p56; **STOCKBYTE** p76(c); **The Picture Desk/** PARAMOUNT/ THE KOBAL COLLECTION p37(b), NEW LINE/ SAUL ZAENTZ/ WING NUT/ THE KOBAL COLLECTION p116(r); **Photo** p10 extracted from World's Strictest Parents and reproduced with the kind permission of Twenty Twenty Television.
Photo p32(l) reproduced with the kind permission of Hippocrene Books.
P33(r): *Harry Potter and the Deathly Hallows*, by J.K. Rowling, reproduced with the kind permission of Bloomsbury/ Rosman Russia; **Photo** p37(t) reproduced with the kind permission of Ted Gibson, Massachusetts Institute of Technology. **Photo** p110(b): *Hamlet*, by William Shakespeare, reproduced with the kind permission of Penguin Books. **Photo** p110(c) reproduced with the kind permission of Doubleday/ Random House Ltd. **Photo** p110(f): *Revelation Space* by Alastair Reynolds, published by Victor Gollancz, an imprint of The Orion Publishing Group, London; **Photos** p110(d) and p115(b) reproduced with the kind permission of Pan Macmillan/ Palgrave; **Photo** p110(e): *The Bourne Identity* by Robert Ludlum, published by Orion Books, an imprint of The Orion Publishing Group, London; **Photo** p110(g): *Love in a Cold Climate*, by Nancy Mitford, reproduced with the kind permission of Penguin Books; **Photo** p113(t) reproduced with the kind permission of Emma Urquhart; **Photo** p116(l): *The Fellowship of the Ring*, (c) 2001, JRR Tolkien, reproduced with the kind permission of HarperCollins Publishers; **Photos** p124 reproduced with the kind permission of Intel Corporation.

Macmillan Readers covers images:
Dr Jekyll and Mr Hyde, cover image Corbis p48; *Frankenstein*, cover image Corbis/ Bettmann p48

Commissioned photography by
Paul Bricknell p76(a,b); Dean Ryan pp131 (t,b).

The authors and publishers would like to thank the following for permission to reproduce the following copyright material:
Extracted material from *'Native English' is losing its power'* by Indrajit Basu, first appeared in Asia Times Online 15.09.06, reprinted by permission of the publisher;
Extract from *'Is This Britain's Unluckiest Man?'* copyright © Metro 2006, first published in Metro 23.11.06, reprinted by permission of the publisher;
Material from *'Answers from young people'* by Tim Berners-Lee used by permission of the publisher;
How To Save A Life – Words and Music by Joseph King and Isaac Slade, copyright © 2005 Aaron Edwards Publishing and EMI April Music Inc. EMI Music Publishing Ltd., London W8 5SW Reproduced by permission of International Music Publications Ltd. (a trading name of Faber Music Ltd.) All Rights Reserved;
I Need A Holiday – Words & Music by Roy Stride copyright © 2007. Reproduced by permission of EMI Music Publishing Limited, London W8 5SW;
Extract from *'Q: How do you make £1.6m a year and drive a Ferrari?* A: Sell Essays for £400' by Matthew Taylor and Riazat Butt, copyright© The Guardian 2006, first published in The Guardian 29.07.06, reprinted by permission of the publisher;
Extract from *'To dub you have to be as good an actor. Or better'* first appeared in The Guardian Online 03.05.06, reprinted by permission of the publisher;
Extract from *'Maximum Ride: the Angel Experience'* by James Patterson, copyright James Patterson 2005, reprinted by permission of the publisher;
Material from *'Romeo and Juliet'* retold by Rachel Bladon for Macmillan Readers, copyright © Rachel Bladon 2007, reprinted by permission of the publisher;
Material from *'Dr Jeckyll and Mr Hyde'* retold by Stephen Colbourn for Macmillan Readers, copyright © Stephen Colbourn 2005, first published 2005, reprinted by permission of the publisher;
Material from *'Frankenstein'* retold by Margaret Tarner for Macmillan Readers, copyright © Margaret Tarner 2005, first published 1986, reprinted by permission of the publisher;
Extract from *'Internet date was man I'd loved for 15 years'* by Lisa Ash and Julie McCaffrey, copyright © Lisa Ash and Julie McCaffrey 2005, first appeared The Daily Mirror 10.11.05, reprinted by permission of the publisher;
Extract from *'Mother Tongue'* by Bill Bryson copyright Bill Bryson 1991, reprinted by permission of Penguin Books Limited;
Girls Just Wanna Have Fun – Words and Music by Robert Hazard copyright © Sony/ATV Music Publishing Limited 1979, reprinted by permission of the publishers. All Rights Reserved;
Material from *'Casino Royale'* by Ian Fleming copyright © Ian Fleming Publications Ltd 1953, reprinted with permission from Ian Fleming Publications Ltd.

Dictionary extracts taken from Macmillan Essential Dictionary copyright © Macmillan Publishers Limited 2003 and Macmillan English Dictionary 2nd Edition copyright © Macmillan Publishers Limited 2007

Printed and bound in Thailand

2015 2014 2013 2012 2011
10 9 8 7 6 5 4 3 2 1